THE
HAUNTED
DUSK

THE HAUNTED DUSK

American Supernatural Fiction, 1820–1920

EDITED BY HOWARD KERR,
JOHN W. CROWLEY,
AND CHARLES L. CROW

The University of Georgia Press
Athens

Copyright © 1983 by the University of Georgia Press
Athens, Georgia 30602
All rights reserved

Set in 10 on 12 Trump Medieval
Designed by Francisca Vassy

The paper in this book meets the guidelines for permanence and durability of the Committee on Production Guidelines for Book Longevity of the Council on Library Resources.

Printed in the United States of America

Library of Congress Cataloging in Publication Data

Main entry under title:

The Haunted dusk.

   1. American fiction—History and criticism—Addresses, essays, lectures. 2. Supernatural in literature—Addresses, essays, lectures. 3. Occultism in literature—Addresses, essays, lectures. 4. Ghost stories, American—History and criticism—Addresses, essays, lectures. I. Kerr, Howard. II. Crowley, John William, 1945–   III. Crow, Charles L.

PS374.S83H3   813'.0872'09   82-7011
ISBN 0-8203-0630-4   AACR2

Contents

Introduction

Howard Kerr, John W. Crowley, and Charles L. Crow

I

Washington Irving and the American Ghost Story

G. R. Thompson

I I

Phantasms of Death in Poe's Fiction

J. Gerald Kennedy

37

Philanthropy and the Occult in the Fiction of Hawthorne,
Brownson, and Melville

Carolyn L. Karcher

67

"I Must Have Died at Ten Minutes Past One": Posthumous Reverie
in Harriet Prescott Spofford's "The Amber Gods"

Barton Levi St. Armand

99

Ghostly Rentals, Ghostly Purchases: Haunted Imaginations
in James, Twain, and Bellamy

Jay Martin

I2I

James's Last Early Supernatural Tales: Hawthorne
Demagnetized, Poe Depoetized

Howard Kerr

133

Psychology and the Psychic in W. D. Howells's "A Sleep
and a Forgetting"

John W. Crowley and Charles L. Crow

149

"When Other Amusements Fail": Mark Twain and the Occult

Alan Gribben

169

Jack London: Up from Spiritualism

Charles N. Watson, Jr.

191

The Color of "the Damned Thing": The Occult
as the Suprasensational

Cruce Stark

209

The Contributors

229

Index

231

THE
HAUNTED
DUSK

Introduction

Howard Kerr, John W. Crowley, and Charles L. Crow

Between 1820 and 1920, the great age of the American ghost story, most major and countless minor writers tried their hands at supernatural fiction. Not ghosts alone, but vampires, ghouls, and other marvelous beings, inexplicable disruptions of natural process, and psychical phenomena such as clairvoyance, veridical phantasms, and out-of-body projection attracted romancers and realists alike. Often such tales confronted important issues: the crisis of religious faith and the question of personal immortality, the eruption of socially forbidden impulses, and the nature and condition of women. At the same time, as part of the development of modern psychological fiction, these works explored the mysteries of consciousness and the unconscious. Developed to a high art by writers from Washington Irving to Jack London, American supernatural fiction was a distinctive and significant type.

This chapter of our literary history is the subject of *The Haunted Dusk*. The essays gathered here (all but two published for the first time)[1] examine supernatural fiction by well-known figures—Washington Irving, Edgar Allan Poe, Nathaniel Hawthorne, Herman Melville, Henry James, Mark Twain, W. D. Howells, Edward Bellamy, Ambrose Bierce, and Jack London—and by less familiar writers such as Orestes Brownson, Harriet Prescott Spofford, and Elizabeth Stuart Phelps. Taken together, these studies chart the course of the genre from its emergence out of Gothicism to its merger with psychologism early in this century.

They also confirm, we hope, Howells's belief that American writers seem to have a special aptitude for handling the "filmy textures" and "vague shapes" of the occult. Introducing *Shapes that Haunt the Dusk* (1907), an anthology of psychical tales from which our title is adapted, Howells asserted that the Americans' "love of the supernatural is their common inheritance from no particular ancestry." Their fiction, he added, often gathers in the gray "twilight of the reason," on "the borderland between experience and illusion."[2] Howells's geographical metaphor was derived, of course, from Hawthorne's idea of a moonlit "neutral territory, somewhere between the real world and fairy-land, where the Actual and the Imaginary may meet, and each imbue itself with the nature of the other."[3] Whether literally, as in Cooper's *The Spy*, or metaphorically, as in Hawthorne's works, the neutral territory/borderland was the familiar setting of the American romance. As American writers came to realize, not only was there a borderland between East and West, civilization and wilderness, but also between the here and the hereafter, between conscious and unconscious, "experience and illusion"—psychic frontiers on the edge of territories both enticing and terrifying.

Supernatural fiction contains its own generic borderland: a neutral territory, which Tzvetan Todorov calls "the fantastic," between "the marvelous" and "the uncanny." According to Todorov, "The fantastic is that hesitation experienced by a person who knows only the laws of nature, confronting an apparently supernatural event." Once the event is satisfactorily explained (and sometimes it is never explained), we have left the fantastic for an adjacent genre—either "the uncanny," where the apparently supernatural is revealed as illusory, or "the marvelous," where the laws of ordinary reality must be revised to incorporate the supernatural. As long as uncertainty reigns, however, we are in the ambiguous realm of the fantastic.[4]

The reader's hesitation in the fantastic borderland, often echoed by the hesitation of a character within the story, is one hallmark of supernatural fiction. Not surprisingly, since readers will experience different kinds and degrees of hesitation and disagree about the nature of a problematical occurrence, criticism of supernatural fiction is frequently marked by dissension—consider, for example, the number of contradictory "solutions" explaining the "real," "psychological," or "ambiguous" apparitions of Henry James's *Turn of the Screw*. In any event, whether a supernatural tale remains altogether fantastic or eventually modulates to the uncanny or the marvelous, the reader is faced with disconcerting ontological and perceptual problems.

Indeed, the disorienting effect of the supernatural encounter in fiction seems to reflect some deeper disorientations in the culture at large. The nineteenth century, after all, was the scene of great de-

bates between faith and doubt, religion and science, transcendentalism and positivism. By revealing that ostensible ghosts were fakes,
that supernatural occurrences were illusory, writers could caution
against credulity and excessive imagination, sometimes in a topical
context attacking unorthodox claims for empirical proofs of immortality, like those of the spiritualistic movement. On the other hand,
validating a ghost, whether benevolent or horrific, could nourish the
sense of the numinous, "enhancing," as a *Harper's* writer of 1853
put it, the reader's "religious awe."[5] But the recurrent ambiguity of
the American tale of the supernatural reveals both a fascination
with the possibility of numinous experience and a perplexity about
whether there was, in fact, anything numinous to be experienced.
Writers often delighted in leading readers into, but not out of, the
haunted dusk of the borderland.

Recent studies of Victorian supernatural fiction argue that the
British were the earliest authors of the ambiguous ghost story in English. But G. R. Thompson shows in "Washington Irving and the
American Ghost Story" that Irving was first in the field with "The
Adventure of the German Student" (1824). Tracing the evolution of
the type from the Gothic novelists through the German Romantics,
Thompson shows how Irving's manipulation of complex narrative
perspectives enabled him to create the hesitation that leaves us wondering whether his German student communed with a spirit, a hallucinatory vision, or a corpse. Irving was only the first of the writers
of the American ghostly tale to recognize that the supernatural, exactly because its epistemological status is so difficult to determine,
challenged the writer to invent a commensurately sophisticated narrative technique.[6]

Gothic supernaturalism was an indication of the culture's preoccupation with death in an increasingly secular, individualistic,
and scientific age. Many of Poe's contemporaries sought to defend
against fear of death by sentimentalizing and "beautifying" the process of dying. But as J. Gerald Kennedy argues in "Phantasms of
Death in Poe's Fiction," Poe kept "the essential horror" in view by
drawing on an elaborate repertoire of supernatural motifs, the most
important of which were vampirism, metempsychosis, spiritualism,
and spectral manifestation. In "The Masque of the Red Death,"
"Metzengerstein," "MS. Found in a Bottle," "Morella," "Ligeia,"
"Mesmeric Revelation," and other stories, Kennedy discerns Poe's
four major conceptual models of death—annihilation, compulsion,

separation, transformation—all of which were combined in "The Facts in the Case of M. Valdemar." The supernatural in Poe's tales, Kennedy demonstrates, breaks disruptively into the world of experience to disclose a sign of mortality and evoke the "cosmic panic" of modern death-anxiety.

For "Mesmeric Revelation" and "Valdemar," Poe looked to the occult pseudoscience of mesmerism, so flamboyantly visible in his own times, attending lectures and reading up on the subject. Nor is his a singular case. Almost every American writer of note had some direct experience with the popular supernaturalisms of the nineteenth century, especially with mesmerism and its successors—the spiritualistic movement that began with the unearthly rappings of the Fox sisters in 1848, and the psychical research societies that sprang up later in the century. The mesmeric treatments for headaches undergone by Sophia Peabody during her courtship with Hawthorne brought to his attention the potentially sinister rapport between mesmerist and trance-maiden, upon which he would later brood in his fiction. Harriet Beecher Stowe received séance messages from the ghost of Charlotte Brontë, and her husband saw· visions throughout his life. The most famous work of Henry James, whose father was a Swedenborgian mystic, is a ghost story. His brother William founded the American Society for Psychical Research and conducted an extensive study of the famous medium Mrs. L. E. Piper. Howells suffered great embarrassment when his *Atlantic Monthly* published articles about séances that turned out to be fraudulent, but he also sought comfort in dream visions of his dead daughter and wrote a series of psychical tales. As a child, London was introduced to the occult by his mother's séances, which frightened him and left their mark on his fiction. Mark Twain knew them all—mesmerists, mediums, palmists, and psychical researchers—and treated them both straightforwardly and satirically in his work. Whatever their various attitudes toward it, all of these writers had close encounters with the occult.

Mesmerists and spiritualists often allied themselves with reform and millenarian causes—abolition, communal utopianism, feminism, vegetarianism, and others. Beginning with Hawthorne's *Blithedale Romance* (1852) and Orestes Brownson's *Spirit-Rapper* (1854) and culminating in James's *Bostonians* (1886), a long series of fictions satirized these interrelated "Isms." Carolyn L. Karcher's "Philanthropy and the Occult in the Fiction of Hawthorne, Brownson, and Melville" places *The Confidence-Man* (1857) as a variant within this tradition. Noting the evidence that links Brownson's reckless antireform fantasy both to Hawthorne's romance and to Melville's complex allegory, Karcher contends that the three works were aimed at contrasting targets: Hawthorne attacked the arrogant foolishness and cultural degeneracy in spiritualism; Brownson opposed the union of spiritualism and reform as a demonically inspired plot to overthrow Christianity; and Melville debunked the spiritualists' pretensions to social reform by showing their closer affinities with hypocritical, evangelical do-gooders. These works showed how easily the supernatural could take on ideological coloring.

Séance communications allegedly came from departed spirits; Brownson's narrator, for instance, receives a message from Benjamin Franklin. A subtype of the ghost story, the "posthumous reverie," was a logical development. As Barton Levi St. Armand shows in "'I Must Have Died at Ten Minutes Past One,'" Harriet Prescott Spofford made sensational use of such postmortem narrative in "The Amber Gods" (1860). Spofford's protagonist, Giorgione Willoughby, is totally amoral and erotic. But as an inversion of the typical Dark Lady of American romance, the blond Giorgione is allowed to tell her own story. She pays for that privilege with her life, however, and her terse report of her own death in the tale's closing sentence startled Spofford's readers. Nineteenth-century supernatural fiction provided a vehicle for the covert exploration of forbidden psychosexual themes; Giorgione's revelation of her pagan eroticism, an "unspeakable" deviation from the cultural stereotype of respectable womanhood, could be expressed only as if from beyond the grave.

After the Civil War supernatural fiction evinced an increasingly explicit concern with the hidden recesses of the human mind. Readers attuned to Romantic philosophy, to the new dynamic psychology, and to psychical research were receptive to a literature of the unconscious. While William James studied trance mediums for evidence both of the hereafter and of "subliminal consciousness," writers like his brother Henry were using the occult as a metaphor for the unconscious. In "Ghostly Rentals, Ghostly Purchases: Haunted Imaginations in James, Twain, and Bellamy," Jay Martin credits Elizabeth Stuart Phelps with mapping the new territory in her enormously popular novel of psychical consolation, *The Gates Ajar* (1868). Prompted by Phelps's example, James, Mark Twain, and Bellamy learned how to portray the unconscious in spatial terms—as the supernatural realm—in order to show a superior truth. Between 1870 and the publication of Freud's essay "The Unconscious" (1915), says Martin, the fictive depiction of the unconscious was of such great public interest that writers who had begun their careers as realists were helping to fashion a modern, psychological version of the romance.

Before Henry James could take part in these developments, he had to deal with the supernatural legacy of an earlier generation, especially with the looming presences of Hawthorne and Poe. In "James's Last Early Supernatural Tales" Howard Kerr argues that James did so in two stories of the "realistic" 1870s. In the first he rejected Hawthorne's reliance on the "magnetic miracles" of mesmerism. In the second he simultaneously parodied the melodramatic marvels of Poe's "Fall of the House of Usher" and reflected ironically on a contemporary spiritualistic scandal. In both James offered glimpses of the phenomena of psychical sensitivity and ambiguous apparition that would figure so largely in his better-known psychical fiction of the 1890s. As they challenge the tradition of Hawthorne and Poe, moreover, these early stories reveal the intense literary reflexiveness of the genre.

Like James, Howells was also a rebellious heir of Hawthorne and Poe, finally making peace with the Romance tradition by becoming part of it himself and then repointing it toward his own literary ends. As John W. Crowley and Charles L. Crow demonstrate in "Psychology and the Psychic in W. D. Howells's 'A Sleep and a Forgetting,'" he mastered the rudiments of pre-Freudian dynamic psychology, and followed the progress of psychical research. Willing to stray from the realism of the "decent average" that had made him famous and successful, he experimented with tales of the uncanny and even the fantastic. Although his late psychical fiction dwelt upon the psychopathology of everyday life and the fringe phenomena of telepathy and intimations of immortality, Howells always kept an agnostic check on his will to believe.

Mark Twain's allegiance to scientific rationalism and religious skepticism is a matter of record. But so is his unflagging curiosity about the occult. In "'When Other Amusements Fail': Mark Twain and the Occult," Alan Gribben traces that author's lifelong interest in spiritualism, phrenology, fortunetelling, palmistry, hypnotism, mental telepathy, and recurrent dreams. Always searching for humorous materials, Mark Twain as a rule ridiculed psychic fads and cults in his published writings; he also borrowed elements of the supernatural literary tradition for suspense or comedy. In private, his exploration of occult phenomena was tinged with the hope that they might withstand empirical scrutiny. The power of the spell cast by Merlin over Mark Twain's technologically adept Connecticut Yankee, the unearthly communications received by his Joan of Arc, and the dream fantasies of his late years all reveal that his positivism was often uneasy. Sharing in the ambivalence of so many of his contemporaries, he expressed the conflicting metaphysics of the nineteenth century—the pull between the "real" and the "imaginary."

Another writer whose positivism was sometimes suspect is the subject of Charles N. Watson, Jr.'s "Jack London: Up from Spiritualism." Compelled as a child to participate in his mother's séances, London as an adult embraced a scientific materialism antipathetic to any form of supernaturalism. Yet when he did exploit the popular taste for the occult in works he spoke of as mere potboilers, London inadvertently revealed that his skepticism could be shaken. The best of these efforts, *The Star Rover* (1915), is an occult novel in which a prisoner's out-of-body travels through time and space illustrate the one species of mystical experience that London believed to be genuine: the moments of transport in which one escapes the prison of the self and enters the larger currents of life. Like Henry James, Howells, and Mark Twain, moreover, London provided a bridge—in the self-hypnosis through which his prisoner separates mind from body—between supernaturalism and psychoanalysis.

There were other such bridges under construction throughout the late nineteenth century, most of them built by the philosophically minded proponents of the new discipline of psychology. Chief among these was William James, whose researches and speculations on psychical experience are the theme of Cruce Stark's "The Color of 'the Damned Thing': The Occult as the Suprasensational." Through a discussion ranging over the works of Ambrose Bierce, Henry Adams, Ignatius Donnelly, the spiritualist Isaac K. Funk, and William James himself, Stark examines some of the strategies by which *fin de siècle* intellectuals attempted to comprehend the startling expansions of psychological and physical science into worlds beyond "the limitations of the accustomed range of human experience." William James, for one, hoped to prevent a schism between positivistic psychology and psychical research, to resist yielding to the extremes either of unscientific supernaturalism or reductive materialism.

Open-minded to a fault about spiritualism, he sometimes bewildered or embarrassed his scientific colleagues, but he never betrayed their faith in the empirical method and he never ignored the threat determinism posed to human aspiration. "He was aware, as many were not," Stark observes, "that postulating a theory of the suprasensational occult suggested more about our limitations within nature than about nature's patterns themselves. Human beings could no longer dream of subjugating external reality either philosophically or imaginatively, for they could not so much as perceive all its terms."

In this knowledge and in his hope for a humane psychology grounded in science, James was close to the spirit of Freud, but he never experienced a conversion to psychoanalysis. Having heard Freud lecture at Clark University in 1909, he wrote the Swiss psychologist Theodore Flournoy that Freud's ideas "can't fail to throw light on human nature, but I confess that he made on me personally the impression of a man obsessed with fixed ideas. I can make nothing in my own case with his dream theories, and obviously 'symbolism' is a most dangerous method."[7] Freud, for his part, distrusted James's philosophical and religious proclivities. Yet long afterward he admiringly remembered how stoically James had endured the pain caused by the angina that was to kill him a year after the Clark Conference. "He stopped suddenly, handed me the bag he was carrying and asked me to walk on, saying that he would catch me up as soon as he had got through an attack."[8]

Viewed emblematically, this scene suggests why the American supernatural tale was dying out with the generation of William James. Although he told Freud's disciple Ernest Jones that "the future of psychology belongs to your work,"[9] neither James nor the other writers discussed in this book could ever have "caught up" to the psychoanalysis they had anticipated. The advent of psychoanalysis marked a change in the way consciousness was imagined by writers as well as psychologists, a change that undermined the philosophical and cultural bases both of a shared sense of reality and of a literature reflecting that reality. Another such change, as Stark's essay shows, was the realization that physical science itself was disclosing the existence of a suprasensational reality knowable to humans only in fits and starts. In the absence of the normative sense of the "real," which had always been its point of departure as well as the object of its questioning, the supernatural could no longer provoke the requisite "hesitation" in the reader. The supernatural tale evolved into either the surreal fiction of a Kafka or the psychoanalytical case history.

Psychic change, as Todorov has recognized, subverted the genre in another way, by revoking the cultural taboos, the social censorship, that had prohibited the overt treatment of psychosexual themes, which then found covert expression in the supernatural tale. "There is no need today to resort to the devil [or to posthumous reverie] in order to speak of excessive sexual desire, and none to resort to vampires in order to designate the attraction exerted by corpses: psychoanalysis, and the literature which is directly or indirectly inspired by it, deal with these matters in undisguised terms. The themes of fantastic literature have become, literally, the very themes of the psychological investigations of the last fifty years." [10]

Thus the historical line from spiritualism and psychic phenomena to dynamic psychology to psychoanalysis has its generic counterpart: from the supernatural tale to psychologism (realism psychologized) to "psychoanalytic romance" (what Freud called his study of Leonardo da Vinci). Beginning with the Romantic ambiguity of Irving's "German Student," the American supernatural tale led, through the "medicated" novels of Oliver Wendell Holmes, into the ever more explicitly psychological stories of Henry James, Howells, and others. Irving's "Strange Stories by a Nervous Gentleman" (1824), with its fireside swapping of ghost stories, became Howells's "Turkish Room" tales, in which a psychologist named Wanhope relates his riddling, semioccult case histories to a rapt audience of clubmen. [11]

From there it was only a short step to Freud and Breuer's *Studies on Hysteria* (1895). Freud, in one of his own case histories, acknowledged that he had used "detailed description of mental processes such as we are accustomed to find in the works of imaginative writers"; it struck him as "strange" but inevitable that his case histories should read like short stories. [12] The supernatural tale, a presence in America for a hundred years, dematerialized. In the clinical haunted dusk, now redefined as the boundary between the unconscious and consciousness, analyst and patient constructed the new borderland fiction of the talking-cure.

NOTES

1. Two of the essays in this volume—by Carolyn L. Karcher and by John W. Crowley and Charles L. Crow—are revised and expanded versions of articles that first appeared in *ESQ: A Journal of the American Renaissance.*

2. W. D. Howells, ed., *Shapes that Haunt the Dusk* (New York: Harper, 1907), pp. v, vii.

3. Nathaniel Hawthorne, *The Scarlet Letter*, Centenary Edition (Columbus: Ohio State University Press, 1962), p. 36.

4. Tzvetan Todorov, *The Fantastic: A Structural Approach to a Literary Genre*, trans. Richard Howard (Ithaca: Cornell University Press, 1975), p. 25.

5. "Editor's Table," *Harper's Monthly* 6 (April 1853): 699.

6. As Todorov observes, the fantastic depends for its effect on the linear nature of reading; a first reading evokes the purest form of hesitation. Thereafter, a reading of a fantastic tale is necessarily a metareading, "in the course of which we note the methods of the fantastic instead of falling under its spell" (p. 90).

7. Quoted in Nathan G. Hale, Jr., *Freud and the Americans: The Beginnings of Psychoanalysis in the United States, 1876–1917* (New York: Oxford University Press, 1971), p. 19. In *Spiritism and Psychology* (New York: Harper, 1911), Flournoy professed: "It will be a great day when the subliminal psychology of Myers and his followers and the abnormal psychology of Freud and his school succeed in meeting, and will supplement and complete each other" (p. vii).

8. Quoted in Hale, *Freud and the Americans*, p. 19. The anecdote first appeared in Freud's *An Autobiographical Study* (1925).

9. Quoted in Ernest Jones, *The Life and Work of Sigmund Freud*, vol. 2 (New York: Basic Books, 1955), p. 57.

10. Todorov, *The Fantastic*, pp. 160–61.

11. On the "Turkish Room" tales, see: John W. Crowley, "Howells' *Questionable Shapes*: From Psychologism to Psychic Romance," *ESQ* 21 (1975): 169–78; Charles L. Crow, "Howells and William James: 'A Case of Metaphantasmia' Solved," *American Quarterly* 27 (1975): 169–77.

12. *Studies on Hysteria*, trans. James Strachey (New York: Avon, 1966), p. 201. See also Freud's similar remarks in *Dora: An Analysis of a Case of Hysteria*, ed. Philip Rieff (New York: Collier, 1963), p. 77. Ernest Jones remarks, "If William James wrote textbooks of psychology as if they were novels and his brother Henry wrote novels as if they were textbooks on psychology, Freud may be said to have combined the two aims in an enchanting degree" (p. 210).

G. R. THOMPSON

Washington Irving and the American Ghost Story

In the introduction to her well-known anthology *The Supernatural in the English Short Story* Pamela Search attempts to categorize the types and modes of supernatural agency in the tale of terror, the ghost story, and the Gothic tale.[1] While she tries to keep her distinctions clear, she ends up blurring Gothic, horror, ghostly, and supernatural tales into one. Perhaps this loose classification is adequate for her purposes (and perhaps instinctively right), but along the way she makes a discovery. The "horror tale had its heyday in the earlier years" of the twentieth century, she writes; but "since then another kind of weird fiction has come into its own—the psychological ghost story" (p. 13). What she means by psychological ghost story, however, is not a tale in which apparently supernatural events turn out to be the misperceptions of a nervous narrator or distraught character. As Search defines it, the psychological ghost story is "the *inconclusive* tale of the supernatural" (p. 13), exemplified by the tales of Walter De La Mare. In fact, she implies that De La Mare invented the type.

In stories like his, a *possible* supernatural agency is balanced off against a *possible* psychological "explanation," with more or less ambiguous results. We are unsure whether the events narrated are real or misperceived; we are not concerned, however, with psychological misperception in itself but with the inconclusive character of the story. This kind of tale, Search claims, is more effective than the old-fashioned ghost story because "when the horror is left undefined it becomes all the more real to us in our imagination, and the inconclusive ending of the tale leaves us with our doubts and fears unresolved, and therefore more terrible."[2]

Now everyone knows that Henry James, not Walter De La Mare, invented the psychological ghost story. Search knows the conventional wisdom on the history of the type too. Therefore she defends her claim by suggesting that although in *The Turn of the Screw* (1898) James anticipated the technique, he did not combine "the supernatural with the psychological" nearly "so compellingly as De La Mare." At this point, Search's opinion about the quality of James's effects as compared with De La Mare's may be called into question, but we might not challenge her historical accuracy regarding the

13

ghost story proper—even if the names of Bierce, Poe, Hawthorne, and Irving come momentarily to mind. But then we are brought up short by her comment that "there have been stories of this type ever since Le Fanu wrote his famous *Green Tea.*"

Joseph Sheridan Le Fanu (1814–73) may have been the greatest British ghost-story writer of the nineteenth century, but "Green Tea" is only vaguely about a "ghost" and it came late in his career (1869). "Green Tea" tells the story of a mild-mannered and morally upright minister, Mr. Jennings, who is bedeviled by a sinister monkey with glowing red eyes. Information is filtered through the papers of one Dr. Hesselius, who has "treated" Jennings for his apparently hallucinatory demon: the monkey is visible to no one but Jennings. At times it even sits on his Bible during sermons, so that he seems to his hearers nervous and distracted, frequently breaking off in the middle of a text. Jennings tries various means of warding off the demon, and it disappears from time to time, but always returns. Jennings finally consults Hesselius, who has treated many weird cases. Hesselius concludes after Jennings's suicide that a chemical reaction, the result of recurrent overdoses of strong green tea, must have opened up some "inner eye" in the man's mind. A rift in the tissue or interface between an occult world and the ordinary, everyday world allowed Jennings a glimpse of an alien realm of being. On the other hand, we are reminded, Jennings had a family history of suicidal mania.[3] "Green Tea," Julia Briggs observes in her recent study *Night Visitors: The Rise and Fall of the English Ghost Story,* is "poised, somewhat mystifyingly, between these two explanations."[4]

"Green Tea" is the focal point of another new study of the ghost story as well. Jack Sullivan, in *Elegant Nightmares: The English Ghost Story from Le Fanu to Blackwood,* devotes to the tale a chapter entitled "The Archetypal Ghost Story."[5] Even if we grant for the sake of argument that "Green Tea" actually is an inconclusive story about a "ghost," it is still puzzling to discover that this new type is the archetype. What happened to the prototypes, where ghosts were either actual supernatural presences or were satisfactorily explained away? And how is it that the archetype is the new "variant" or a "development"? Sullivan writes that in 1839 "a new kind" of "ghost appeared in English fiction" (p. 11) with the publication of Le Fanu's "Schalken the Painter," a macabre tale about a demonic or ghostly lover who claims a living bride and transforms her into a ghost. The technique of narration, Sullivan claims, was "revolutionary"; there is a double point of view involving the perspective of the victimized young girl's befuddled uncle and that of her horrified fiancé. The plot moves toward a dream sequence, where a coffin is transformed into a Victorian four-poster. "Schalkin the Painter" is, according to Sullivan, the "promising start" of a development in ghostly fiction that culminates thirty years later in "Green Tea," which represents the new ghost story in "its most uncompromising form" (p. 12).

Sullivan seems to sense that he is on shaky ground in his claims for Le Fanu, for he is quick to disqualify Edgar Allan Poe as a ghost-story writer. He observes that 1839 was not only the publication date of "Schalkin the Painter," but also of Poe's "The Fall of the House of Usher." But in Le Fanu the ghost seems simultaneously "to emerge from within as well as invade from without" (p. 11). His concern with "Usher" implies that something similar happens in Poe. But Poe's story, he says, is an "exercise in cosmic paranoia rather than a tale of the supernatural" (p. 11). Sullivan has a point, but the same might be said of Le Fanu's "Green Tea," if it is to be read as the inconclusive tale he claims it is. Sullivan attempts to cover himself on another point as well: "As the less than reliable narrator of a horror tale, Hesselius is part of a tradition which begins with Poe's narrator in 'The Tell-Tale Heart' and culminates in the governess's account in *The Turn of the Screw*," but the "narrative problems are more complex than those in Poe" (p. 29). One wonders in what ways Poe's narrators before 1843—those of "MS. Found in a Bottle" (1833), "Berenice" (1835), "Morella" (1835), "Ligeia" (1838), and "William Wilson" (1839)—are so clearly reliable, or in what ways the double point of view of "Usher" is less complex than the editorial siftings of "Green Tea."

Sullivan, like most critics of the ghost story, admits that he uses the phrase "ghost story" as a "catch-all term." But since all the stories he deals with are, he says, "apparitional, in one sense or another . . . 'ghost story' is as good a term as any" (p. 9). If so, how then are the apparitions of Poe's tales "of a different order" from Le Fanu's in "Green Tea"? Although "horror story" is "not quite as all-inclusive" a term, Sullivan writes, "most English tales fall into the class of *both* ghost and horror story, so that the terms are almost interchangeable" (p. 9). He observes that "Lovecraft's 'supernatural horror' neatly fuses both terms," *ghost* suggesting the supernatural realm and *horror* apparently suggesting "physical mayhem and revulsion" (p. 9). Such comment echoes standard thumbnail definitions of one effect of the Gothic. Is the Gothic, then, different from the ghost story only in its wider applicability to fear-driven narrative, so that the ghost story is limited in its effect to an "apparition"? Sullivan tells us that there "is little to be gained . . . by attempting to determine precisely" what the limits are between "ghost and horror tales" (p. 9). This allows him to denigrate the Gothic tradition and claim as a novelty in the ghost story something that has already reached an apogee in the American Gothic tale as practiced by Irving, Hawthorne, and Poe.

In his eagerness to separate the ghost story from the Gothic, Sullivan claims that "the modern ghostly tale is as much a reaction against the Gothic as an outgrowth of it," for Gothic ghosts were largely "decorative," lacking the "more actively loathesome, menacing quality of modern ghosts" (pp. 5–6). Part of this menacing quality comes from the centrally inconclusive nature of the Le Fanu "archetype." Sullivan attacks "theory-obsessed critics" who would read such a work as "Green Tea" as Freudian or Christian allegory and thus miss the teasing, elusive, enigmatic quality of the tale. As the archetypal ghost story, he says, "Green Tea" is representative of a fundamentally disordered universe, incapable of rational codification. This point, Sullivan claims, is not noted by other writers on the ghost story (p. 5). If so, it must be the result of their inattention to the basic modes of the Gothic tale, for the disordered universe of the Gothic is the matrix from which the ghost story issues in its various forms.

Although it is conventional to divide the Gothic romance into two types—the supernatural and the explained supernatural—actually four modes may be usefully distinguished.[6] Historical Gothic is ontologically undifferentiated. The presence of an occasional demon or ghost is not necessarily significant for either the ontology *or* the epistemology of a text. In supernatural Gothic, the occult is in fact a central assumption. In the explained Gothic, the final assumption is that the supernatural does not, finally, interpenetrate the everyday world: all seemingly occult phenomena are the result of misinformation or misperception. But in ambiguous Gothic, it is the *tension* between the supernatural and the everyday that generates dread. Briggs does a somewhat better job than Sullivan in setting forth the development of the psychological ghost story within the Gothic tradition. Although she too sees "Green Tea" as a prime example, she traces the inconclusive tale back to the German writer, Hoffmann, a contemporary of Irving: "If any one writer can be credited with the invention of this twist it is E. T. A. Hoffmann," who, she observes, had greater impact on French and American writers than on any English writer (pp. 144–45). She mentions "The Golden Flower-Pot" (1814, rev. 1819) and "A New Year's Eve Adventure" (1814–16), neither of which is strictly a ghost story, though supernatural realms do intrude on the everyday world. But she does not mention Hoffmann's predecessors in the inconclusive supernatural, notably Ludwig Tieck and J. A. K. Musaeus, who enjoyed a certain vogue in both Britain and America. Nor does she speak of Hoffmann's contemporaries, like Clemens Brentano, "Bonaventura," Achim von Arnim, Jean Paul Friedrich Richter, and other explorers of the supernatural and psychic realms in fiction.[7] Similarly, she fails to mention key French writers, like Théophile Gautier and Prosper Mérimée, who were early concerned with the wavering line between the supernatural and the natural. She does acknowledge a later nineteenth-century writer, Maupassant, noting that "The Horla" (1887), a tale about an invisible creature haunting a possibly deranged narrator, antedates *The Turn of the Screw*. Other important omissions include major American writers: Brown, Irving, Hawthorne. Presumably this is because there are so few out-and-out ghost stories among the Americans, though the British examples cited are frequently not strict ghost stories either.

Like Sullivan, Briggs does deal with Poe, who, she says, "created the prototypes of a number of variations on the psychological ghost story" (p. 145). Why Poe is singled out as having written more ghost stories than Irving or Hawthorne is unclear; certainly those of his tales that could be said to deal with ghosts per se are as few as those of the other two American writers. Nevertheless, she identifies three prototypes of Poe's psychological ghost tales: one is the description of grotesque events in such a way as to throw doubt on the narrator's sanity; a second is the dramatization of the narrator's urge to self-destruction; a third is the indication of a particular form of mental disturbance, such as the schizophrenia of William Wilson. The only other historical commentary she offers is the observation that the psychological ghost story uses the Radcliffe method of rational explanation of seeming marvels, but with "a more open-ended effect" (p. 143). Apparently, then, the originator of the psychological ghost story in English is Poe, about whom Sullivan is so concerned. But I would like to press the matter back a generation further, to

Washington Irving, a writer who was not only deeply influenced by German romantic fiction, but who also did in fact write *ghost* stories.

II

Some of Irving's best known tales represent the range of modes for the ghost story, complicated, however, by his sportive humor.[8] A straight supernatural tale is found in "Dolph Heyliger" (1822). What seems to be an actual ghost in a haunted house leads Dolph into a series of adventures that eventually uncovers treasure, while during the course of the narrative the ghost-ship of the Hudson makes its appearance and disappearance. In "The Spectre Bridegroom" (1820), a story with a skillful blend of humor and ominous mystery, there is a central, horripilated scene where a mysterious guest at a wedding feast seems to rise up to a gigantic height to cry out that he is late for his appointment with the worms. It is all explained at the end. The bride and her family have never seen the intended groom, whose party has been ambushed on the way to the bride's castle. A survivor comes with the melancholy news of the slain bridegroom, is mistaken for the intended groom, and, before he can explain, is smitten with the beauty of the bride to be. He assumes the groom's identity, and exits with the portentous cry that he is dead so that he can later return to carry off the bride without protest from her father. "The Legend of Sleepy Hollow" (1819) exhibits what is on the surface a legitimate ghost, but it too is written in the explained mode. After the headless horseman has chased Ichabod Crane through the night and has hurled his "head" at him by the bridge, we are offered a sly innuendo that Brom Bones, the competing suitor for the beautiful Katrina, has staged the whole thing, though the remains of a shattered pumpkin are by no means conclusive evidence for the narrator—despite Bones's knowing smile. There is no particular mystery about the events of the tale, but the explanation is less overt and the effect somewhat more open-ended than that of "The Spectre Bridegroom." Whether or not the strange figures in the mountains in "Rip Van Winkle" (1819) qualify as ghosts, the story overtly presents an encounter with the supernatural, except that there is again the wink of innuendo regarding the timing of Rip's return to his village, which comes after the death of his shrewish wife. The theme of revolution becomes personal as well as political, suggesting that Rip's legendary sleep may have been the useful contrivance of a henpecked husband. Still, we are not sure but what the ghosts from the past that Rip reports seeing do in fact exist, despite all the consumption of alcohol. It is an interconnected series of lesser-known tales, however, that is Irving's main contribution to the psychological ghost story.

Although *Tales of a Traveller* (1824) is generally regarded as Irving's least successful work, its opening section, "Strange Stories by a Nervous Gentleman," undergoes a surprisingly complex progression from supernatural to explained to ambiguous ghost stories, and thence to psychological Gothic.[9] Moreover, the entire series is unified by a progressive development of an erotic theme, a central concern of the Gothic tradition. The Nervous Gentleman, we are told by the narrator-author (Geoffrey Crayon), is the very same gentleman that tells the tale of "The Stout Gentleman" in *Bracebridge Hall* (1822). After a playful introduction (in which it is suggested, though not confirmed, that the "Great Unknown" personage of that tale who so puzzles the Nervous Gentleman may be no less than Sir Walter Scott), the basic frame of the sequence of tales is established.[10] A baronet hosts a hunting dinner for an indeterminate number of guests, but it includes the second narrator (that is, the Nervous Gentleman) and several other odd persons. Among them are an Irish captain of dragoons; the Gentleman with the Haunted Head, one side of whose face does not match the other; a thin, hatchet-faced gentleman with protruding lobsterlike eyes; the Inquisitive Gentleman, who is never satisfied with a story as given; the old Gentleman with the Flexible Nose; a country clergyman; a beetle-browed barrister with a hawk's nose. The night is windy and rainy, perfect for ghost stories. The Gentleman with the Haunted Head is first to answer the call for ghost stories by relating "The Adventure of My Uncle," which is followed by accounts from the others of experiences that relatives have had (an aunt, a grandfather) until the Gentleman with the Haunted Head tells a second tale, the "Adventure of the German Student." His second tale, as we shall see, returns to and extends the Gothic ambiguity of his first.

The Gentleman with the Haunted Head sets the scene of "The Adventure of My Uncle" in an ancient château in Normandy. The uncle is given a room in the tower of the oldest part of the château, which in ancient times had been the donjon. The chamber has a "wild, crazy look," with high narrow windows in which the casements rattle with every breeze (p. 27). The door stands ajar, opening on a long, dark corridor that "seemed just made for ghosts to air themselves in, when they turned out of their graves at midnight" (p. 28). The wind springs up to a hoarse murmur through the passage. Unable to force the door completely shut against the damp, chilly breeze, the uncle piles up the bedclothes and falls asleep. He is awakened by the old clock of the château and thinks he counts thirteen strokes. He begins to fall asleep again, but then he hears the sound of footsteps approaching the doorway. The door opens ("whether of its own accord, or whether pushed open, my uncle could not distinguish") and a "figure all in white" glides in (p. 29). It is the apparition of a tall and stately woman dressed in an ancient fashion. She walks to the fireplace, where the bluish light of the flames reveals a beautiful but ghastly, pale face "saddened by care and anxiety" (p. 30). The figure casts a "glassy look about the apartment, which, as it passed over my uncle, made his blood run cold, and chilled the very marrow of his bones. It then stretched its arms toward heaven, clasped its hands, and wringing them in a supplicating manner, glided slowly out of the room" (p. 30). Since the uncle is a "man of reflection," he does not "reject a thing because it was out of the regular course of events" (pp. 30–31). But because he is also a man of firmness and is "accustomed to strange adventures" (a point that will prove important later), he goes gradually back to sleep.

The next morning, walking with the Marquis de ——, owner of the château, the uncle sees in the picture gallery "a full-length portrait," which strikes him as being "the very counterpart of his visitor of the preceding night." He remarks to the marquis, "Methinks . . . I have seen the original of this portrait." The marquis replies that "that can hardly be, as the lady has been dead for more than a hundred years" (p. 32). The marquis then tells him the long story of the Duchess de Longueville, who played a part in the civil wars in the youth of Louis XIV. Imprisoned in the château of Dieppe, she escaped through an unguarded postern gate of the castle and made her way to the sea. She nearly drowned in an attempt to board a ship through the storm-tossed surf and finally had to return to the countryside on horseback, arriving at the very château where the uncle has been spending the night. She stayed in the same apartment the uncle has just occupied. The marquis tells him he remembers the precise date because "there is a tradition—that a strange occurrence took place that night. —A strange, mysterious, inexplicable occurrence—" (p. 36). But the marquis refuses to tell more, to the great exasperation of the uncle, who finally blurts out, "I saw that lady last night." The marquis listens attentively to the details of the uncle's story and then takes a pinch of snuff and says "Bah!" (p. 37).

Here the uncle's story also breaks off, and the exasperated hearers ask the Gentleman with the Haunted Head for more details.

". . . and what did your uncle say then?"

"Nothing," . . .

"And what did the Marquis say farther?"

"Nothing."

"And is that all?"

"That is all."

At this, the "shrewd old gentleman with the waggish nose" offers an "explanation"; he surmises that "it was the old housekeeper, walking her rounds to see that all was right." To which the *narrator* now abruptly says "Bah!" (p. 37).

A subtheme of the tale is concerned with tale-telling itself, a cumulative major theme of the entire sequence of tales. During the marquis's long, digressive history of the duchess, the uncle is repeatedly exasperated with his inability to get to the point. The irony that the point is not to be revealed further underscores the metafictional concern. Moreover, each of the group brings to the *event* of the *tale* his own preconceptions. With artful symmetry, the narrator has the marquis say "Bah!" to the uncle's supernatural tale of the ghost, just as the narrator says "Bah!" to the rational explanation offered by one of the hearers.

This playful little frame has more importance for the whole series of tales than may be immediately evident. As a narrator aware of his audience, the Gentleman with the Haunted Head has a character in his uncle's narrative scoff at part of the uncle's narrative (the ghost story) in a way that will provoke dissatisfaction with the Gentleman with the Haunted Head's entire narrative. This sets up an opportunity for him to scoff at his hearers in a direct parallel with that of a character in the narrative, the marquis, who is himself also a narrator. From the point of view of the entire frame narrative, the Nervous Gentleman, as narrator of "Strange Stories" within Geoffrey Crayon's narrative *Tales of a Traveller*, has the Gentleman with the Haunted Head scoff at the response of a hearer (the Gentleman with the Flexible Nose) as a parallel with the response of the marquis as

narrator-hearer in the uncle's narrative as narrated by the Gentleman with the Haunted Head, to whom the uncle had narrated the
two tales and their frame. One of the ironies this structure generates
is that the Gentleman with the Haunted Head hereby aligns himself,
as hearer, with the skeptic of his uncle's narrative, which he himself
has just narrated, while simultaneously aligning himself, as narrator
of an actual ghost story, with its narrator (his uncle). As the distinction blurs between apparent fact (the series of narratives the group
tells, at the baron's château) and the apparent fiction (the double narrative and the denial of the facts of one, at the marquis's château), an
infinite regression almost (but not quite) opens up. He contends that
the supernatural fact of the tale is proved by the fact that his uncle
was so accustomed to strange sights that he would have no trouble
distinguishing a ghost from a housekeeper. The conclusion does not
settle anything, of course; it merely blurs subjectivity and objectivity absurdly together. As the tale dissolves into its humorous
frame of teller and hearers, it becomes poised abruptly, mystifyingly pointless, between the two poles of the supernatural and the
explained.

The hearer who asks the questions is the Inquisitive Gentleman,
described in the opening frame narrative as one who "never seemed
satisfied with the whole of a story; never laughed when others
laughed; but always put the joke to the question. He could never enjoy the kernel of the nut, but pestered himself to get more out of the
shell" (p. 20). Of course, this is precisely the ironic position to which
the reader of the interlinked series of "Strange Stories" is forced. The
Nervous Gentleman, recounting the whole sequence to Geoffrey
Crayon, then concludes that he is inclined to think the Gentleman
with the Haunted Head really does have an "after-part of his story in
reserve." But when he refuses to say anything more, there begins to
appear something in his "dilapidated countenance that left me in
doubt whether he were in drollery or earnest" (p. 38). This compli-
cates the problem of subjectivity and objectivity even further, paral-
leling the ironic narrative tone of the whole set of tales and frames.

If one compares Irving's version of this tale with the anonymously
published "Story of an Apparition" (1818) in *Blackwood's Edinburgh Magazine* or with Scott's "The Tapestried Chamber; or, The
Lady in the Sacque" (1828), the differences between the British and
the American handling of the same story are striking. Irving had vis-

ited Scott at Abbottsford in 1817, where he heard from him a story told to Scott in 1807 by Miss Anna Seward of Lichfield. Irving encouraged Scott to construct a tale from it, and perhaps the appearance of the *Blackwood's* tale the next year (though Scott's authorship is uncertain) is the result. In any case, the suggestion in Irving's opening frame narrative that the "Great Unknown" is Scott (whose protruding backside was all the Nervous Gentleman ever got to see in *Bracebridge Hall*) seems to be an oblique allusion to the challenge of constructing a ghost story from the legend. Both the Scott version and the *Blackwood's* version are straight supernatural stories about the "ghost of an unfortunate ancestress," to whom Scott attributes murder, incest, and suicide, whereas Irving's figure is more heroic and her fate totally uncertain.[11] Coleman Parsons observes that although the owner of the castle in Scott's story is a "complete skeptic on the subject of supernatural appearances" just the day before, he "does not try to explain his guest's experience as a dream, a vagary of the imagination, or an optical illusion. Instead, he believes and immediately sets about closing up the tapestried chamber."[12] In neither of the British versions is there much narrative framing, much less thematic or ontological ambiguity, and neither evidences metafictional concern for the narrative effect (serious or otherwise) on the auditors or readers of the tale.

The abrupt inconclusiveness of this first tale leads the Gentleman with the Flexible Nose to tell a more "satisfying" story, or at least what initially seems to the listeners more satisfying, "The Adventure of My Aunt." Although a brief anecdote, it is repeatedly intruded upon by the hearers. A strong-willed widow moves to a lonely house in Derbyshire. One evening while looking at herself in the mirror to see if she is still attractive enough to interest a "roistering squire" in the neighborhood, "she thought she heard something move behind her" (p. 41). But all she sees is a newly installed portrait of her dead husband. She gives a heavy sigh to his memory, whereupon her sigh is "re-echoed, or answered by a long-drawn breath" (p. 41). Momentarily, she thinks she sees one of the portrait's eyes move. But instead of being frightened, she goes downstairs and has her servants arm themselves with whatever is at a hand and leads them back to her room, herself brandishing a red-hot poker, saying, "Ghosts! . . . I'll singe their whiskers for them!" (p. 42). She orders the portrait taken down, and there in what was once a clock-niche stands a former servant of the house, armed with a knife, but trembling before the widow's ferocity. He had cut an eyehole in the portrait to watch for a chance to steal her money.

At this point, the relatively undeveloped story seems to the hearers well "concluded." But the Inquisitive Gentleman wants to know more. What did they do with the intruder—hang him? The narrator, the Gentleman with the Flexible Nose, says that the widow merely ordered him to be "drawn through the horsepond, to cleanse away all offences, and then to be well rubbed down with an oaken towel" (p. 44). Still unsatisfied, the Inquisitive Gentleman asks, "And what became of him afterwards?" The narrator suggests that perhaps he was sent to Botany Bay as a criminal. But now the Inquisitive Gentleman wants to know if the aunt had her maid sleep in the room with her afterward. No, she married the roistering squire. These questions pick up a motif introduced earlier in the telling of the tale, when the Gentleman with the Haunted Head first interrupts the narrative to comment (with a knowing look) on the aunt's being able to see the portrait's eye with the back of her head toward it. To this the narrator had replied that she saw it reflected in the mirror (p. 41). Now, despite the first consensus that this "last narrator had brought his tale to the most satisfactory conclusion," the very genre of the tale is under question. The Inquisitive Gentleman is not at all satisfied with the ontology of the tale: "But I don't see, after all . . . that there was any ghost in this last story" (p. 44). The implication, in the frame narrative, is that the explained mode is ultimately as unsatisfactory as the unexplained first tale.

The newly dominant dissatisfaction with explained ghosts leads, ironically, to "The Bold Dragoon; or, The Adventure of My Grandfather," told by the Irish captain, who says, "If it's ghosts you want, you shall have a whole regiment of them" (p. 44). The irony, of course, is that the ghosts in his tale—pieces of furniture that dance—are not necessarily any more "real" than the "ghost" behind the aunt's portrait of her husband, though the explanation is more covert. The Irish narrator's grandfather was himself a dragoon, a bold, "saucy, sunshiny fellow," who "always had a knack of making himself understood among the women" (p. 43). This last bit of information, later elaborated, at first seems digressive but is actually central to the ghostly adventure. Moreover, it also makes clearer the underlying erotic motif of the entire sequence of "Strange Stories." The grandfather stops at an "old rackety inn" with a sign "that promised good liquor." The landlord does not like his "saucy eye." Told that there are no rooms available, the Bold Dragoon determinedly slaps his thigh (in an earlier version his tight buckskins are mentioned), and the "slap went to the landlady's heart" (p. 48). He likewise charms all the ladies of the household, who hatch a plan "to accommodate him" with "an old chamber, that had for some time been shut up." The landlady's daughter remarks to him in apparent admiration, "I dare say you don't fear ghosts" (p. 49).

That night "not a female head in the inn was laid on a pillow . . . without dreaming of the Bold Dragoon" (p. 51). He himself finds "the blood in his veins . . . in fever heat," supposedly, according to the narrator, because he is "a warm-complexioned man" and the "great bags of down" both on top of him in the cover and below in the mattress begin to "melt" him (pp. 51–52). The Inquisitive Gentleman here wants to know if the maid had warmed the bed too much. "I rather think the contrary," replies the narrator, adding that for whatever the reason, his grandfather "jumped out of bed and went strolling about the house." "What for?" the Inquisitive Gentleman asks. "Why, to cool himself . . . or perhaps to find a more comfortable bed—or perhaps—But no matter what he went for—he never mentioned—and there's no use taking up our time in conjecturing" (p. 52). Having warded off this attack on his story, the narrator continues. His grandfather "had been for some time absent from his room, and was returning, perfectly cool, when just as he reached the door, he heard a strange noise within." Remembering the story of the room's being haunted, he peeps in to see "a pale weazen-face fellow, in a long flannel gown and a tall white night-cap with a tassel to it, who sat by the fire with a bellows under his arm by way of bagpipe, from which he forced . . . asthmatical music" (p. 53). Suddenly a long-backed, leather-covered chair, "studded all over in a coxcombical fashion," slides up to "an easy chair, of tarnished brocade, with a hole in its bottom, and led it gallantly in a ghostly minuet about the floor" (p. 53). Except for a great clothes-press, the rest of the furniture and other items join in the dance. To the Bold Dragoon the clothes-press seems like a female, a corpulent dowager, at a loss for a partner. Therefore, he bounces into the room and seizes the clothes-press "upon the two handles to lead her out," for he is "a true Irishman, devoted to the sex, and at all times ready for a frolic." But as soon as he does this, "whirr! the whole revel was at an end," the pieces of furniture shrink in an instant quietly into their places, and he finds himself "seated in the middle of the floor with the clothes-press sprawling before him, and the two handles jerked off, and in his hands" (p. 54).

The Inquisitive Gentleman here suggests that this is not a ghostly experience either. "This was a mere dream!" he says, explaining away the ghosts. But the Irish narrator will have none of it. "The divil a bit of a dream!" he says. "There was never a truer fact in this world" (p. 54). He continues, telling how the noise from the crash of the clothes-press brings the landlady and landlord and their daughter, along with the barmaid and all the chambermaids, up to see what is the matter. By way of explanation, the grandfather "related the marvellous scene he had witnessed." Moreover, the broken clothes-press "bore testimony to the fact." The landlady, however, "did not seem half pleased with the explanation." But her daughter "corroborates" it by recollecting that a famous juggler who died of St. Vitus's dance had been the last occupant of the chamber and must have infected the furniture (p. 55).

So the dream explanation is countered by the pseudoghostly explanation. But the tale finally comes down on the side of psychological explanation rather than remaining poised ambiguously between the two. For the tale is actually a sly account of the Bold Dragoon's sexual exploits during the night; and his vision, or drunken dream, or concocted explanation is appropriately erotic, from the bellows (traditionally a phallic symbol from the Middle Ages on), to the "coxcombical" leather-backed chair leading out the "tarnished" "easy-chair" with a hole in her bottom, to the dowager clothes-press in need of a partner. The other pieces include "a three-legged stool . . . horribly puzzled by its supernumerary leg" and a pair of "amourous tongs" which seize "the shovel round the waist" (p. 53).

The chambermaids come forward to "corroborate" the Bold Dragoon's story. They had "all witnessed strange carryings on in that room," and "declared this 'upon their honors,'" the quotation marks giving the sly wink (p. 55). Here the Inquisitive Gentleman asks if the grandfather had gone to bed again in the room. The Irish narrator says, "That's more than I can tell. Where he passed the rest of the night was a secret he never disclosed." Apparently, he had several options among the daughter, the barmaid, and the chambermaids. The narrator adds at this point that his grandfather was "apt to make blunders in his travels about inns at night," which "it would have puzzled him greatly to account for in the morning" (p. 55). Apparently missing the point, or possibly indulging further the ironic hoax, the Knowing Old Gentleman asks: "Was he ever apt to walk in his sleep?" On the surface, such a question reverts to the dream interpretation, but the amorous point is concluded when the narrator, whatever his perception of his grandfather's story, replies with finality: "Never that I heard of" (p. 56).

III

The old Gentleman with the Haunted Head now objects that the first stories have been of a burlesque turn, and he proposes to tell a real ghost story, the "Adventure of the German Student." Its place in the sequence of "Strange Stories" is significant. The first story, also told by this narrator, is an unconcluded tale of seeing a ghost that is the image of a portrait; the abrupt end and refusal to go further exasperate the hearers' desire for a more or less rational conclusion. Whether supernatural or not, the story requires for them some sort of framing in the normative world. But the Gentleman with the Haunted Head silently features a face that leaves the Nervous Gentleman in doubt as to whether there is a serious tale there or only a hoax. The second tale, "Adventure of My Aunt," is a fully explained piece that is initially satisfactory to the hearers because of the rational explanation, but subsequently unsatisfactory because the listeners want real ghosts. The third tale has both a rational psychological explanation and a supernatural explanation, but with a satiric undercurrent that finally, though somewhat subtly, makes the ghost-dance more probably the half-drunken dream, half-shrewd cover story of the amorous Bold Dragoon.

"Adventure of the German Student," the next logical step in tale-telling in the sequence of stories, is equidistantly poised between psychological explanation and the demonic. The three tales that follow the "German Student" continue the theme of the mysterious portrait in a series of Chinese-box narratives, each one seemingly explained by the next narrative, but actually finding only a partial resolution. The "German Student" is the pivotal tale of the "Strange Stories," dividing the sequence in half, fully developing the ambiguous technique, and changing the tone of the series from humorous to somber, though maintaining the irony.

Young Wolfgang, a German student in Paris during the Reign of

Terror, is initially presented as someone whose imagination has been "diseased" by his studies in "spiritual essences." He becomes obsessed by the idea that "there was an evil influence hanging over him," an "evil genius or spirit seeking to ensnare him and ensure his perdition" (p. 57). This characterization is background to a recurrent dream of a woman's face that "haunts" him both in sleeping and waking moments. This "shadow of a dream" becomes "one of those fixed ideas which haunt the minds of melancholy men, and are at times mistaken for madness" (p. 59). Thus contradictory suggestions are set up: he is mad and he is not. One stormy night he crosses the square where public executions are held and in the flashing lightning sees the guillotine. At the foot of the steps of the scaffold, revealed in a "succession of vivid flashes of lightning," is a "female figure, dressed in black," sitting on one of the steps, leaning forward (p. 59). She looks up and in "the bright glare of the lightning" reveals to Wolfgang "the very face which had haunted him in his dreams," pale and disconsolate, though beautiful (p. 60). He takes her to his apartment, where, after some soothing conversation, he suddenly asks her to pledge herself to him. He says to her:

> "I pledge myself to you for ever."
> "For ever?" said the stranger, solemnly.
> "For ever!" repeated Wolfgang.
> The stranger clasped the hand extended to her: "Then I am yours, murmured she" (p. 63).

Having spent the next morning looking for more spacious apartments, he returns to find her lying dead on the bed. When the police arrive, they inform him that "she was guillotined yesterday." Wolfgang undoes a black collar around her neck, and "the head rolled on the floor!" (p. 64). At this point the reader is confronted with two possibilities: either Wolfgang is mad and has hallucinated the experience, or he has spent the night with a ghost. On the surface, the tale seems to be in the explained mode, and critics have generally read it that way: the mad young German has carried away a corpse and made love to it. But the introductory characterization presents opposing possibilities, each equally viable. Somehow, though his imagination is diseased, he is not mad. His own response does not resolve either possibility. He returns to the obsession mentioned in the second paragraph of the tale: "The fiend! the fiend has gained possession of me! . . . I am lost for ever." The narrator then remarks: "He was possessed with the frightful belief that an evil spirit had re-animated the dead body to ensnare him" (p. 64). This observation neither confirms nor denies the actuality of supernatural manifesta-tion. Certainly, if she were in fact a ghost, Wolfgang's pledge "for ever" insures his damnation, and her response, "I am yours," also means "you are mine." Traditionally, a demonic pact drives one insane. From the moment of the pact—whatever the actuality of subsequent events—Wolfgang is damned. His "madness," whether at the scaffold or at the end, may be the sign of the pact. The story is poised, like Le Fanu's "Green Tea" thirty-five years later, between these two possibilities for a final ambiguous twist.

The wry conclusion of the narrative frame for this story under-scores the essential ambiguity. The Inquisitive Gentleman asks the narrator (the old Gentleman with the Haunted Head) if all this is "really a fact." " 'A fact not to be doubted,' replied the other. 'I had it from the best authority. The student told it me himself. I saw him in a mad-house in Paris'" (p. 64). The "madness" confirms the "fact." What fact? That the story was told? That a ghost possessed the student? That the student was mad? The ambiguous structure of the tale within a tale, providing thereby "witnesses" who testify to the central "fact" of the narrative, serves only to emphasize the essential epistemological ambiguity of the tale, thereby also underscoring its ontological ambiguity.

The German Student's adventure is followed by the "Adventure of the Mysterious Picture," told by the overall frame narrator, the Nervous Gentleman (as filtered through the "author"). After the tale of the German Student, the guests retire, and the host, the baronet, says that one of them will sleep in a haunted room, but none shall know which it is "until circumstances reveal it" (p. 66). The Nervous Gentleman is shown to a room resembling in general style and furnishings those "described in the tales of the supper-table" (p. 66). He becomes uneasy in the presence of a portrait of a young man's face "that appeared to be staring full upon me, with an expression that was startling." The "emotions it caused were strange and indefi-nite . . . something like what I have heard ascribed to the eyes of the basilisk, or like that mysterious influence in reptiles termed fascina-tion." Every time he shields his eyes in an effort to "brush away this illusion . . . they instantly reverted to the picture, and its chilling, creeping influence over my flesh and blood was redoubled" (p. 67).

The expression on the face of the young man is of the "agony of intense bodily pain" combined with a scowling "menace." The total effect is of "some horror of the mind," by which the picture awakens in the narrator an "inscrutable antipathy" (p. 68).

The next morning the Nervous Gentleman remarks on the "most singular and incomprehensible" effect the picture had on him (p. 74). The parallel with the opening story highlights important differences. Although the first story is not truly concluded, the protagonist sees or thinks he sees the ghost of the image in a portrait; this frame sequence develops a vague, amorphous unease. The other guests, being in a bantering mood, laugh at the Nervous Gentleman's apprehensiveness, whereupon the baronet reveals that the picture is well known for "the odd and uncomfortable sensations it produces in every one that beholds it" (pp. 74–75). Tantalizingly, he informs them that with this effect "there is connected a very curious story" (p. 74). The guests of course wish to hear it, and unlike the Gentleman with the Haunted Head, who refused to tell more after the first tale, the baronet obliges them. The final two tales, "The Adventure of the Mysterious Stranger" (a brief account of how the baronet met the personage in the portrait) and "The Adventure of the Young Italian" (the manuscript tale of his own life left by the Italian in the baronet's possession), do not deal with ghosts and so need not receive much discussion here. But it should be noted that the sequence moves from psychological uneasiness in the presence of the young Italian, who was afraid to be alone and kept glancing fearfully over his shoulder, to the Italian's story of his own psychological anxiety over uncertain filial affection, betrayed friendship, and romantic love. Each tale is to be explained by the next; after the young Italian's murder of a former friend, the themes of shame and guilt intertwine with the need for moral and psychological expiation.

The tales of the second half of the "Strange Stories" series gradually darken. Except for a final twist in the frame narrative, they are not humorous. But the last frame sequence does humorously or ironically extend the theme of psychological misperception. After the baronet reads the Italian's manuscript, the guests are most curious to see the mysterious portrait. Afterward, all comment that "there was a certain something about the painting that had a very odd effect upon the feelings" (p. 120). Later the host reveals to the Nervous Gentleman that actually "not one of them has seen it." For seeing that "some of them were in a bantering vein" he "did not choose that the memento of the poor Italian should be made a jest of. So I gave the housekeeper a hint to show them all to a different chamber" (p. 120). The humor of the final frame incident, which concludes the stories of the Nervous Gentleman, returns us to the tone of the opening while apparently underscoring the theme of the dominance of the subjective over the objective. Actually, however, subjective and objective are balanced off against each other. The impact of the real portrait upon the Nervous Gentleman is not necessarily explained or diminished, though, at the same time, it may be surmised that the baronet's mentioning that one of them would sleep in a haunted chamber predisposed the "nervous" gentleman to further nervousness. This possibility is given further support by his noting correspondences between his room and those of the ghost stories, and by the portrait theme of the first tales (including the dream-portrait of the face of the woman in the German's tale), which the Nervous Gentleman may have subconsciously recalled.

"Strange Stories by a Nervous Gentleman" is thus a remarkable early experiment with point of view, narrative frames, and Gothic modes, representing the range of supernatural, explained, and ambiguous techniques, while effecting a complex intertwining of epistemological and ontological ironies within a metafictional structure. The "Adventure of the German Student" is perhaps the earliest well-crafted example in English of the inconclusive psychological ghost story, strategically placed within a complicated series of ghost stories of varying modes, with thematic interruptions, frames, and shifting points of view far more complex than those of Le Fanu's "Green Tea."

IV

From the foregoing discussion it is clear that British-oriented studies of the ghost story make a historical error in attributing the origin of the inconclusive psychological ghost story to Le Fanu's "Green Tea" or "Schalkin the Painter," or to Richard Barham's "Henry Harris." The experimental fiction and drama of German Romanticists at the end of the eighteenth century antedate such techniques, and the American psychological ghost story precedes British examples by a generation or more. It is, however, apparently accurate to claim that the ambiguous mode of the Gothic, with its intricate manipulations of frames, its metafictional implications of point of view, its intrusions of humor, and its general polyphony of tone, was not much in evidence in Britain until after the publication of Le Fanu's later tales. *Wuthering Heights* (1848) perhaps presents a special case, but the major exception would seem to be James Hogg's *Private Memoirs and Confessions of a Justified Sinner* (1824), along with a handful of his tales about dream-selves. In America, however, the ambiguous mode is dominant. The early American ghost story is one manifestation of the Gothic impulse of American dark Romanticism. After Irving, the ambiguous Gothic tale reaches an apex with Hawthorne and Poe, who tend to work within the larger Gothic tradition rather than focusing on the ghost story. A reader searching for straight ghost stories in the writings of Hawthorne and Poe will in fact turn up fewer than a dozen that might qualify.

In part, this unghostly aspect of the development of American Romantic fiction may be explained by our major writers' immersion in the philosophical complexities of the Romantic movement. The conventional observation on the supposed preponderance of explained Gothicism in American Romantic fiction results from a partial misreading of such stories as Irving's "German Student." Such a reading posits the influence of the Radcliffe method of explained Gothic, without much substantiation of Radcliffe's appeal to the American mind or influence on American writers other than Charles Brockden Brown; it is related to the general proposition that a pragmatic American materialism is a national characteristic.[13] While suggestive, the assertion is finally simplistic. For one thing, such a view ignores not only the ecclesiastical history of America, but also the later influence of Scottish Common Sense School philosophy and of British empiricism, as represented by Hume and Berkeley, whose philosophical inquiries seemed to cast doubt on the existence of materiality.[14]

Just as for European writers, for Americans the human mind becomes the key element in the matter-spirit dilemma. Their speculation is marked by a recurrent apprehension that all matter may be a mental construct, just as all dreams of the spiritual world may be a delusion. Americans become obsessed with the subject-object dialectic in Kant, who is reinterpreted by German writers like Fichte, interpreted again by Coleridge, and once more reinterpreted by Carlyle—not to mention the numerous lesser translations and explications of German philosophy by Frederic Henry Hedge and other

Americans.[15] The transcendentalist writers in America—especially the later Emerson and Thoreau, but also even Whitman—grapple with the same matter-spirit-mind paradox as do the dark Romanticists, though the point of view is diametrically opposite. There is hardly any such thing as a simple American materialism discoverable in the Romantic era, and the philosophy of mind derived from Germany and Britain has a major influence on the form of American Gothic fiction.

Although a complete history of the Gothic tradition in America requires a meticulous survey of stories by minor popular writers, it seems safe to say of the major American writers that the ambiguous tale reaches another high point later in the century simultaneously with renewed interest in the ghost story as a genre. That the psychological ghost story, as defined here, does not reflect the concerns merely of the last half of the nineteenth century but those of the first half as well is a point especially pertinent to American fiction. The continuum between the earlier nineteenth century and the later as suggested by the related subgenres of the Gothic tradition deserves further examination, both for developments in literary form and for the implications for the *Zeitgeist* of a century. The century between the beginnings of Romantic fiction and the outpouring of fantastic and occult fiction in the 1880s and 90s through the 1920s suggests a continuity of aesthetic and philosophical concerns for the writer in America.

I would suggest that the development of the major modes of Gothic tale-telling by the American Romantics leads directly to the inconclusive psychological ghost story associated with later nineteenth-century writers like Bierce, Howells, and James. Their ghost stories represent the continuation of the ontological and epistemological themes of the Gothic strand of American Romanticism. If one wanted to argue for a break in a continuous line of development, I should hazard, tentatively, the suggestion that it occurs not so much in the later nineteenth century as in the obsessively "realist" fiction of the first half of the twentieth, where the Gothic seems separate from the "mainstream" in a way that it is not in the nineteenth. For even southern "Gothic" writers, like Faulkner, Welty, or O'Connor, seem to have less connection with the ghost-story writers of the popular magazines, or with writers of "weird" tales like Lovecraft, than did their predecessors two generations earlier. The later nineteenth-century writers, I would argue, continue an unbroken line. Irving, Poe, and Hawthorne are the direct ancestors of Howells's formulation of the "vague shapes of the borderland between experience and illusion" in *Shapes that Haunt the Dusk* (1907), of James's deliberate ambiguity in "The Jolly Corner" (1908), "The Friends of the Friends" (1896), and *The Turn of the Screw* (1898), of Bierce's mystification in "The Damned Thing" (1893), "The Eyes of the Panther" (1891), and especially "The Death of Halpin Frayser" (1893).

In British writing of the second half of the century, we find an exaggerated interest and belief in psychic experience transcending normal perception and cognition, and a concomitant renewed belief in scientific verifiability of an occult realm. But in America, in tension with the persisting Romanticism generated by the transcendental movement, and in the midst of the popularity of spiritualism, writers associated with the rise of realism inherit the legacy of an unresolved dilemma from the Romantic age. Perplexity persists about the fusion (or even relation) of material and spiritual worlds, of essence and perception. To see the development of the "supernatural" tale in nineteenth-century America divorced from its Romantic naturalist context (especially from the paradoxical materialist-spiritualist doctrines of transcendentalism) is to do violence to the historical record and distort our understanding of both the history of genres and the interconnection between world view and aesthetics in historical eras. For the mental apprehension of the body-spirit fusion persists as a problematic construct shaping by acceptance or denial—or by an indeterminacy in between—the world view of major nineteenth-century American writers. As a sub-genre of the Gothic tale of the "supernatural," the form of the development of the ghost story in America reveals the intellectual crises of an entire century. Unexpectedly, it reaches early full exposition in the seemingly slight, sportive sequence "Strange Stories by a Nervous Gentleman," by Washington Irving, who stands near the fountainhead of a major stream of American literary history.

NOTES

1. Pamela Search, *The Supernatural in the English Short Story* (London: Bernard Hanison Limited, 1959), pp. 7–20.

2. Ibid. Cf. Tzvetan Todorov, *The Fantastic: A Structural Approach to a Literary Genre*, trans. Richard Howard from the 1970 French ed. (Cleveland: Case Western Reserve University Press, 1973), wherein the term *fantastic* is used to indicate a "reader hesitation" principle; the reader is unsure whether the "events" of the text are to be taken as "real" or not. This narrowed use of the term *fantastic* and Search's "inconclusive" tale parallel somewhat my formulation of the "ambiguous mode" of Gothic literature, introduced below.

3. *Best Ghost Stories of J. S. Le Fanu*, ed. E. F. Bleiler (New York: Dover, 1964), pp. 178–207.

4. Julia Briggs, *Night Visitors: The Rise and Fall of the English Ghost Story* (London: Faber, 1977), p. 144; cf. p. 51.

5. Jack Sullivan, *Elegant Nightmares: The English Ghost Story from Le Fanu to Blackwood* (Athens: Ohio University Press, 1978), pp. 11–31.

6. For fuller discussion, see "Gothic Fiction of the Romantic Age: Context and Mode," the introduction to *Romantic Gothic Tales 1790–1840*, ed. G. R. Thompson (New York: Harper and Row, 1979), pp. 13–38. Like Sullivan, Briggs makes the usual bifurcation of Gothic into "two distinct types": supernatural and explained (p. 143).

7. For a fuller overview, see my discussions of "romantic irony," the "grotesque and arabesque," and the "nightside" in *Poe's Fiction: Romantic Irony in the Gothic Tales* (Madison: University of Wisconsin Press, 1973), pp. 19–38, 105–16, 139–41, 160–64, and notes. A recent article on German, British, and American Gothic is Pamela J. Sheldon and Kurt Paul's "Daylight Nightmares," *Gothic* 1 (1979): 1–6. Also see Henry A. Pochmann, *German Culture in America: Philosophical and Literary Influences 1600–1900* (Madison: University of Wisconsin Press, 1957), passim.

8. Little has been written about Irving and the ghost story, but there are a few useful works on Irving and the Gothic. See esp. John Clendenning, "Irving and the Gothic Tradition," *Bucknell Review* 12 (1964): 90–98; Donald A. Ringe, "Irving's Use of the Gothic Mode," *Studies in the Literary Imagination* 7 (1974): 51–65; and William L. Hedges, *Washington Irving: An American Study 1802–1832* (Baltimore: Johns Hopkins Press, 1965).

9. Edward Wagenknecht in *Washington Irving: Moderation Displayed* (New York: Oxford University Press, 1962) writes: "Irving himself thought *Tales of a Traveller* his best book. . . . He was developing a new theory of narrative form . . . which might have come to more than it did if further experiments had not been discouraged by the savage press the book received. . . . It is true of course that the book lacks unity" (p. 177). For a different view and for a fine, insightful discussion of the structure and effect of "Strange Stories," and of the blending of the absurd, the humorous, and the

macabre in the sequence, see Hedges's chapter, "The Way the Story Is Told," in *Washington Irving*, pp. 191–212; he and I study the material from different perspectives, but with parallel conclusions regarding unity, though he tends to hedge, somewhat nervously, about the quality of the "German Student."

10. My text for *Tales of a Traveller* is vol. 9 of *Works of Washington Irving* (New York: G. P. Putnam's Sons, 1881). This is the "Author's Revised Edition," and in it *The Sketch Book* and *Tales of a Traveller* are bound together without repagination.

11. "Story of an Apparition" appeared in *Blackwood's* in 1818 and is reprinted in *Romantic Gothic Tales*. "The Tapestried Chamber" has been widely reprinted and is conveniently found in *Short Stories by Sir Walter Scott*, with an introduction by Lord David Cecil (rpt. London: Humphrey Milsford, 1970). "The Great Unknown" was the appellation given to the then-anonymous author of *Waverly* (1814), whose identity was the subject of much speculation in Britain.

12. Coleman Parsons, *Witchcraft and Demonology in Scott's Fiction* (Edinburgh: Oliver and Boyd, 1964), p. 129; see also pp. 130–31.

13. The presumption of an "American" materialism is still widespread, especially among European critics; for a useful argument for the dominance of the explained mode in America, see Oral Sumner Coad, "The Gothic Element in American Literature before 1835," *Journal of English and Germanic Philology* 24 (1925): 72–93.

14. For a recent, concise survey of theories of the mind in America, see Rita K. Gollin's "Available Traditions," chap. 2 of *Nathaniel Hawthorne and the Truth of Dreams* (Baton Rouge: Louisiana State University Press, 1979), pp. 19–40. The present essay is part of a longer work; the concluding speculations about subject and object are elaborated in "The Apparition of This World: Transcendentalism and the American Ghost Story," in *Bridges to Fantasy: Essays from the Second Eaton Conference*, ed. Robert Scholes, Eric S. Rabkin, and George Slusser (Carbondale: Southern Illinois University Press, 1982), pp. 90–107, 207–9.

15. See Pochmann, *German Culture in America*, for a detailed survey.

J. GERALD KENNEDY

Phantasms of Death in Poe's Fiction

The tales of Edgar Allan Poe display an elaborate repertoire of supernatural motifs, so well adapted to the evocation of horror that one might suppose the *frisson* to be their exclusive object. Otherwise discerning readers have thus fixed upon such phantasmagoria as evidence of Poe's "pre-adolescent mentality"—to recall the judgment of T. S. Eliot—and concluded that his otherworldly tales amount to little more than gimcrackery. Even those with a scholarly regard for Poe's achievement sometimes assume (as the author invited us to) that mystical elements in the fiction serve mainly to secure the necessary "single effect." Collectively examined, however, his tales reveal the complex function of the supernatural, which typically introduces the predicament that his protagonists must overcome, escape, explain away, or surrender to. The intrusion of the uncanny generates "cosmic panic" (in Lovecraft's phrase) and poses the troubling paradox at the center of Poe's dark vision. Although the preternatural arrives in various shapes— as a demon-horse, a phantom ship, or a reanimated corpse—it commonly dramatizes the interpenetration of life and death, the mingling of metaphysical opposites. A passing glance at the recurrent themes of vampirism, metempsychosis, spiritualism, and spectral manifestation indicates Poe's fixation with the fate of the body and the destiny of the soul. In effect, such motifs carry a significance independent of the narrative scheme in which they emerge; they constitute an esoteric ideography and inscribe a parallel text concerned exclusively with final questions. Through a decoding of this imagery, I want to clarify the four conceptual models which dominated Poe's representation of our mortal condition.

II

Under the ostensible influence of Walpole, Radcliffe, Brockden Brown, Coleridge, Irving, and the German Romantics Tieck and Hoffmann, Poe assimilated the conventions of Gothic horror. His gravitation toward that mode was probably inevitable, for its narrative configuration seems to have embodied his fundamental percep-

tion of the human condition.[1] In his preface to *Tales of the Grotesque and Arabesque* (1840), he described the "terror . . . of the
soul" as his essential "thesis."[2] The supernatural paraphernalia of
the Gothic, particularly phantasms of death and destruction, af-
forded a means of articulating this primal fear. In a broad sense,
Poe's "terror of the soul" bears traces of the historical and intellectual crisis that produced the Gothic novel; indeed, we cannot make
sense of his preoccupation with madness, violence, perverseness,
disease, death, and decomposition without recognizing the cultural
drama inherent in what David Punter has called the "literature of
terror."[3] It is a commonplace notion that the Gothic emerged from
the rupture in Western thought between rationalism and Romanticism that occurred in the latter half of the eighteenth century. This
formulation, however crude, contains an important truth: Gothic
fiction enacts the radical uncertainty of an epoch of revolution in
which nearly all forms of authority—neoclassicism, Right Reason,
religious orthodoxy, and aristocracy—came to be seen as constrict-
ing systems. Ghosts and crumbling castles, wicked lords and diabolical monks served as fictive emblems of a collapsing order. Alone
in a landscape of nightmare, the Gothic hero experienced the dark
side of Romantic freedom: existential disorientation, wrought by the
loss of defining structures. The Gothic paradigm dramatized for the
first time the quintessential modern predicament—the plight of an
alienated being whose rational skepticism had vitiated his capacity
for belief, while paralyzing dread had betrayed the insufficiency of
science and logic. It was the peculiar achievement of the Gothic
(and, one imagines, the basis of its appeal) to express in playful,
imaginative terms the latent fears of Western culture in an urban,
industrial, post-rational, and post-Christian era. If this species of fiction presented a search for answers, an elucidation of mysteries, its
real force lay, as Punter observes, in the evocation of doubt, in its
capacity for "removing the illusory halo of certainty from the so-
called 'natural' world."[4]

Through its own illogic, Gothic supernaturalism exposed the limits of reason as an explanatory model. The proliferation of occult
themes in eighteenth-century literature amounted, in the view of
Patricia Meyer Spacks, to a recognition that "the mind of man is naturally subject to secret terrors and apprehensions" and that supernatural motifs possess a "real and universal" validity.[5] Writers of
Gothic fiction, even those like Ann Radcliffe who were committed
to an ultimately rational vision, felt the need to widen the range of

narrative possibility and draw upon the imagery of dreams. But the insurgence of literary supernaturalism expressed more than a resistance to Augustan aesthetic constraints; it also manifested a curious response to the rationalizing of religious thought in the eighteenth century. In effect, writers of Gothic novels salvaged elements of popular belief—devils, curses, and spiritual visitations—that had been jettisoned by Christian humanist thought. And their use of supernatural imagery appears to have one other major implication: as a response to death in the face of religious skepticism. Glen St. John Barclay has argued that "any story which in any sense refers to the intervention of the supernatural in human affairs necessarily affirms that the supernatural exists. It holds out the reality of alternative modes or realms of existence beyond the physical limitations of our material life. In doing so, it responds directly to what is certainly man's most abiding concern, the prospect of his own personal annihilation and oblivion in death."[6] One must question the inference that any literary representation of the supernatural affirms its existence in the experiential world—a blatant confusion of art and life— but Barclay's perception of the uncanny in fiction as a response to the fear of "personal annihilation" seems astute. When we consider that the Gothic movement derived much of its impetus from the graveyard school of poetry, we perceive that in the midst of other revolutions in taste, belief, and thought in the eighteenth century, a wholly new and powerful consciousness of death had begun to emerge. In place of the calm acceptance of mortality we might expect in the verse of a clergyman-poet, we find in Young's *Night Thoughts on Death* and Blair's *The Grave* a deepening anxiety about extinction. Such poetry excited curiosity about death and decomposition; it introduced dreams and fantasies about dying; and it conferred upon the tomb and the cemetery a peculiar new importance. The abode of death became associated with preternatural phenomena, as instanced by Blair's depiction of a weird procession:

> Roused from their slumbers,
> In grim array the grisly spectres rise,
> Grin horrible, and obstinately sullen
> Pass and repass, hushed as the foot of night. (ll. 39–42)

Such images proliferated in the mid-eighteenth century as a funereal sensibility infused popular literature; death was no longer simply an event or moment in writing but its very object.

The association of supernaturalism and mortality acquires broader significance in light of the monumental study of Philippe Ariès, *The Hour of Our Death*. Through research into the burial practices, wills, and memorial sculpture of France (and Western culture generally) since the Middle Ages, Ariès demonstrates that, far from being a universal and static phenomenon, our conception of mortality has undergone vast changes, from the serene, public leave-taking of the medieval "tame death" to the lonely despair of our contemporary "invisible death"—the institutional concealment of the final hour.[7] Perhaps the most striking of Ariès's general conclusions is the observation that before the end of the seventeenth century, "human beings as we are able to perceive them in the pages of history [had] never really known the fear of death" (p. 405). Initially this seems a baseless proposition, for the phrase "fear of death" involves an apparent conflation of several distinct responses—to the idea of death, its imminence, its bodily effects, and its psychic consequences. As a historical judgment, this also seems doubtful; we know, for example, that the deadly plagues of the late Middle Ages inspired terror throughout Europe. But we must bear in mind that the medieval fear of an immediate threat and its spiritual corollary fear of eternal judgment are both quite different from the modern dread of mortality, the crux of the general claim. Ariès associates the onset of contemporary death-anxiety with three broad developments: the secularization of death and the erosion of belief in an afterlife; the growth of self-consciousness and individualism, which diminished the communal aspect of death and made it a private, personal experience; and the advent of science and modern medicine, which converted the corpse into an object of study and death into a physiological process. As indices of these changes, we see in the eighteenth century the appearance of public cemeteries and the abandonment of services once provided by the church; the practice of erecting funerary monuments to commemorate the existence of the common folk; the exhuming of bodies for experimental purposes; and, as noted earlier, the appearance of literary and artistic productions concerned with mortality and grief.

One result of scientific attention to the physiology of death was a mounting curiosity about the connection between the body and the soul. The medieval idea of the *homo toto*, the whole and indissoluble man, was supplanted during the Enlightenment by the concept of a self that divided at death. But what part did the soul play in the agony of dying, and where did it go at the moment of extinction? Ariès notes that "this question, which is at the heart of the medical interest in death, is also one of the central preoccupations of the age" (p. 354). Investigations of cadavers exerted a "profound impact on the imagination of the time" (p. 367), feeding speculation about residual sentience in the corpse and about the prospect of galvanic reanimation. Such research demanded fresh anatomical specimens and thus gave rise to the atrocity of grave-robbing. This clandestine industry swiftly generated a folklore of violated tombs and reviving corpses; it must have contributed to the appearance, about 1740, of a terror hitherto unexpressed in Western culture—the fear of premature burial (p. 397).

III

This upheaval in attitudes touches almost every facet of cultural experience. With respect to Gothic fiction, the ubiquity of corpses (often bleeding preternaturally) reminds us, as Freud would much later, that the ultimate source of all terror is death itself. In effect, the haunted castle, the subterranean passageway, the secret vault, and the sealed room—all the conventional scenes of Gothic mystery—evoke anxiety because they pose the implicit threat of fatal enclosure. In an age that witnessed what Ariès calls "the first manifestation of the great modern fear of death" (p. 403), we discover a literary form given over to the recurrent staging of ultimate vulnerability. But the Gothic did not remain a static form; when we come upon its recognizable contours in the fiction of Poe, we also encounter new resonances and motifs indicative of changes in the cultural consciousness of death.

Perhaps in reaction to the eighteenth century's prolonged contemplation of the unshrouded corpse and the gaping grave, the dark imaginings once poetically associated with death had shaded into a bland sentimentality about time and transience, about loss and separation. By the early nineteenth century, as Ariès points out, the sense of mortality as "pure negativity" accompanied a fascination with the idea of a spiritual reunion beyond the grave. The ghastly image of death created by the procurement and dissection of cadavers yielded to an extravagant, romanticized vision of "the beautiful death"—a tender, well-planned departure, in which the prospect of an other-

worldly rendezvous loomed large. Religious sentiment enjoyed a su-
perficial resurgence in consolation literature, as the hour of death
became a fetishized event. Ann Douglas has called attention to the
necrolatry inherent in these works: "Such writings inflated the
importance of dying and the dead by every possible means; they
sponsored elaborate methods of burial and commemoration, communication with the next world, and microscopic viewings of a sentimentalized afterlife."[8] The poetry of Felicia Hemans and her
American admirer, Lydia Huntley Sigourney, epitomized the movement in popular culture toward an ethereal image of mortality,
purged of gross physical detail. Ariès summarizes the prevailing attitude: "Since death is not the end of the loved one, however bitter the
grief of the survivor, death is neither ugly nor fearful. On the contrary, death is beautiful, as the dead body is beautiful. Presence at the
deathbed in the nineteenth century is more than a customary participation in a social ritual; it is an opportunity to witness a spectacle that is both comforting and exalting" (p. 473). But this new perception involves aesthetic contrivance: "This death [was] no longer
death, it [was] an illusion of art." Indeed, the preoccupation with
mortality so evident in magazines, annuals, and contemporary en-
gravings betrays massive cultural self-deception: "In life as well as in
art and literature, death [was] concealing itself under the mask of
beauty" (p. 473).

What these shifts in sensibility reveal most clearly is the essential
instability of Western ideas about mortality since roughly 1700. The
reassuring model of "familiar and tame" death, prevalent until the
late seventeenth century, vanished with the rise of the modern, in-
dustrialized, secular city. In its place emerged a multiplicity of conflicting attitudes and assumptions, producing radical confusion
about the nature and meaning of death. The Christian message of
resurrection continued to be heard, but clergymen as frequently ex-
tolled the beauty of dying, outlined the spiritual benefits of grief, or
described the amenities of a domesticated heaven. Proponents of
spiritualism grew numerous and by the mid-nineteenth century had
established an organized movement. Those still influenced by a
deistic or pantheistic perspective saw death as Bryant had painted it
in "Thanatopsis": a beatific return to the bosom of nature, that
"mighty sepulchre" of humanity. Attitudes originating in eighteenth-
century graveyard verse continued to obtrude upon the popular consciousness; as I have shown in another essay, the fear of premature

burial sustained a flourishing fictional subgenre in contemporary periodicals.[9] Medical experiments upon corpses still excited a horrified fascination, as the popularity of Mary Shelley's *Frankenstein* (1819) suggests. The rise of scientific positivism prompted widespread doubts about the existence of an immaterial soul, to the chagrin of ministers and spiritualists alike.

But amid the welter of contending viewpoints, David Stannard has discerned the "overriding national treatment of death" between the Revolution and the Civil War: "In large measure, if not entirely in response to the growing individual anonymity brought on by changes in their social world, Americans sought a return to their lost sense of community in the graveyard and the heavenly world of the dead; in the process, paradoxically, they effectively banished the reality of death from their lives by a spiritualistic and sentimentalized embracing of it."[10] That is, the death fetish of the early nineteenth century grew from a need to reestablish bonds of commitment in an increasingly impersonal, urban society. But in order for death to become the great Meeting Place, it had to be disinfected and prettified. The effort to invest death with sentimentalized beauty drew the support of many leading writers; Washington Irving's tales "The Pride of the Village" and "The Broken Heart" (in *The Sketch-Book*) epitomize the tearful fare that flooded the publishing scene, promoting the Beautiful Death. This was the very society that, in Mark Twain's *Huckleberry Finn*, produced the lachrymose Emmeline Grangerford: "She warn't particular, she could write about anything you choose to give her to write about, just so it was sadful. Every time a man died, or a woman died, or a child died, she would be on hand with her 'tribute' before he was cold." With respect to popular gift book poetry, there is less exaggeration in Twain's caricature than one would suppose.

IV

Such was the literary and cultural environment in which Poe endeavored to sustain himself as a writer in the early 1830s. That he found the funereal sentimentality of the day a valid rhetorical mode may be surmised from his appreciative regard for Mrs. Sigourney, Letitia E. Landon, Mrs. E. Clementine Stedman, and other purveyors of maudlin stuff. In 1842 he did score the "namby-pamby character" of *Graham's Magazine* in a moment of pique,[11] but there is no evidence that he found the cultural preoccupation with mortality unhealthy, inappropriate, or laughable. By temperament and mournful personal experience, Poe was drawn into the contemporary cult of death. But if he respected the muse of sentiment, he avoided in his tales the conventional sad-but-joyful departure, and he clearly saw through the "mask of beauty" that concealed the grim features of human dissolution. In his "Marginalia" series Poe observed trenchantly: "Who ever *really* saw anything but horror in the smile of the dead? We so earnestly *desire* to fancy it 'sweet'—that is the source of the mistake; if, indeed, there ever was a mistake in the question."[12] Unlike his contemporaries, he refused to soften or idealize mortality and kept the essential "horror" in view; but he also moved beyond the Gothic formula to explore divergent conceptions of death. Through the symbolic notation provided by supernatural motifs, we can identify the features of four principal paradigms: annihilation, compulsion, separation, and transformation.

Annihilation. In his illuminating study *The Denial of Death*, Ernest Becker builds his argument upon a fundamental insight: "This is the meaning of the Garden of Eden myth and the rediscovery of modern psychology: that death is man's peculiar and greatest anxiety."[13] This comment goes far in explaining the stunning contemporaneity of Poe's fiction and poetry. Becker's analysis demonstrates that we experience death as a "complex symbol" that changes as human beings pass through successive stages of consciousness. But the primal, embedded meaning of death, which all of our "immortality projects" seek to overcome, is that of terrifying annihilation. Initially encountered in childhood through the permanent disappearance of loved ones, this terror develops finally into a concept of personal extinction, a recognition of one's creaturely condition—that one is trapped within a body that "aches and bleeds and will decay and die" (p. 26). This elemental anxiety informs much of Poe's fiction; it manifests itself in the wild, deathbed protest of Ligeia: "O God! O Divine Father!—shall these things be undeviatingly so?—shall this Conqueror be not once conquered?" (2 : 319). The Conqueror Worm, its "vermin fangs / In human gore imbued," provides a graphic reminder of our bodily fate. An acute interest in the physiology and physical imagery of death in fact typifies Poe's annihilation model. Visible signs of disease, impending death, or dissolution assume importance as reminders of the ultimate naturalistic process.

Poe also draws attention to traditional emblems of death—the skull, the skeleton, the "grim reaper," the moldering corpse—to intensify the anxiety of his protagonists (cf. "The Pit and the Pendulum"). As a metaphorical reminder that one is, to borrow the later phrase of Yeats, "fastened to a dying animal," the annihilation paradigm in Poe frequently involves physical entrapment aboard a ship, inside a house, within a vortex, behind a wall, or (most revealingly) in the tomb itself.

Elements of this model can be found in most of Poe's tales, but its purest expression occurs in "Shadow—A Parable" and in the more impressive sequel, "The Masque of the Red Death." [14] These works have in common an atmosphere of brooding anticipation. Both represent the deliberate immurement of a group fearful of pestilence, and both depict the physical intrusion of death. Each tale implicitly suggests that our most ingenious strategies cannot protect us from this fate, nor can we entirely repress the dread to which that awareness gives rise. Significantly, I think, neither story raises the prospect of a happy reunion in another world. "Shadow" closes with the perception by the "company of seven" of a multitude of spirit voices, "the well remembered and familiar accents of many thousand departed friends" (2:191), but far from providing reassurance, these voices cause the assemblage to start from their seats "in horror, and stand trembling, and shuddering, and aghast" (2:191). The annihilation model presents a stark encounter with the death-anxiety from which our "neurotic shield" of repression ordinarily protects us.

As the headnote to "Shadow" makes clear, the title figure is the shadow of death, whose presence imposes a palpable depression: "There were things around us and about of which I can render no distinct account—things material and spiritual—heaviness in the atmosphere—a sense of suffocation—anxiety—and, above all, that terrible sense of existence which the nervous experience when the senses are keenly living and awake, and meanwhile the powers of thought lie dormant. A dead weight hung upon us . . . ; and all things were depressed, and borne down thereby" (2:189). Death weighs upon the group because it is thrice present: first in the pallid countenances of the men themselves as reflected on the ebony table; then in the corpse of "young Zoilus," whose unclosed eyes reveal a "bitterness" (even though the body is "enshrouded"); finally in the "dark and undefined shadow" that issues from the sable draperies and fixes itself upon the door. Here, the supernatural impinges upon the natural world to signify an important concept. The "vague, and formless, and indefinite" shadow, a manifestation "neither of man, nor of God, nor of any familiar thing" (2:190), projects a view of death as terrifying absence and absolute difference. Its horror derives from its complete unintelligibility. Poe's conception of the shadow also relates mortality to the idea of evil, for the inscription sets up an inherent contrast between the Psalmist, who will "fear no evil" in the valley of the shadow of death, and the narrator Oinos, who suffers "the boding and the memory of evil" within the sealed room. According to Ariès, death lost much of its sacral quality in the eighteenth century when men ceased to believe in hell and "the connection between death and sin or spiritual punishment" (p. 610). No longer a moment of religious significance, the hour of reckoning, death itself became evil, a thing to be avoided. (We begin to see the importance of this association for Poe when we note the elements of the human tragedy specified in the "The Conqueror Worm": Madness, Sin, and Horror.)

A slightly different emphasis develops in "The Masque of the Red Death," where the situation adumbrated in "Shadow" acquires complexity and dramatic effect. There is no need here to review extant interpretations of the tale's color symbolism, nor should we be detained by the "ebony clock," with its too-obvious linking of time and death. What demands closer scrutiny is Poe's characterization of the dreadful intruder and the implications of that portrayal. Cutting through a tangle of critical conjecture, Joseph Patrick Roppolo has called the work "a parable of the inevitability and universality of death." Death cannot be barred from the palace, he argues, because it is in the blood, part and parcel of our humanity, not an external invader. Hence, according to Roppolo, the spectral figure is not a representation of mortality (which is already present) but a figment of the imagination: man's "self-aroused and self-developed fear of his own mistaken concept of death." [15]

This approach has a certain validity—death is indeed in our blood, coded in our genes—and it leads to the interesting hypothesis that Prospero succumbs to his own terror, to the "mistaken" idea that death is a tangible enemy. But it also collapses the supernaturalism of the story and reduces the intriguing figure to a simple misconception, thus distorting the allegorical signification. The notion of the specter as self-delusion loses credibility when we realize that all of the revellers observe "the presence of a masked figure" (2:674). Either everyone deludes himself in precisely the same way, or else there *is* a figure. Poe's careful description of the "spectral image," as he is seen by "the whole crowd," supports the latter view.

> The figure was tall and gaunt, and shrouded from head to foot in the habiliments of the grave. The mask which concealed the visage was made so nearly to resemble the countenance of a stiffened corpse that the closest scrutiny must have had difficulty in detecting the cheat. And yet all this might have been endured, if not approved, by the mad revellers around. But the mummer had gone so far as to assume the type of the Red Death. His vesture was dabbled in *blood* —and his broad brow, with all the features of the face, was besprinkled with the scarlet horror. (2:675)

In choosing to symbolize the unmentionable, the "mummer" has violated a taboo and brought death into the open. But why does Poe insist upon the particularity of the Red Death imagery? In the opening paragraph he describes the plague as extraordinarily fatal and hideous: "there were sharp pains, and sudden dizziness, and then profuse bleeding at the pores, with dissolution." Even more terrible, "the whole seizure, progress and termination of the disease, were the incidents of half an hour." That is, the Red Death produces grotesque disfiguration and almost instantaneous decomposition (the horror of M. Valdemar). The putrefaction of the grave becomes a public spectacle as the plague transforms a vibrant individual into a loathsome object. Belief in the uniqueness of personality and the immortality of the soul crumbles at the sight of human carrion. The Red Death evokes dread because it exposes our creatureliness and raises the question at the core of naturalistic thought: are we finally nothing more than the biological organization of our own perishable flesh?

Such appears to be Poe's conclusion, at least in this parable of annihilation, for when the masqueraders fall upon the stranger, they discover an emptiness behind the corpselike mask.

> Then, summoning the wild courage of despair, a throng of the revellers at once threw themselves into the black apartment, and, seizing the mummer, whose tall figure stood erect and motionless within the shadow of the ebony clock,

gasped in unutterable horror at finding the grave cerements
and corpselike mask which they handled with so violent a
rudeness, untenanted by any tangible form. (2 : 676)

This discovery reenacts the nineteenth-century perception of death
as "pure negativity," a nullity resulting from the "separation of the
body and the soul" (Ariès, p. 360). Poe's portrayal of pure absence sig-
nifies "the presence of the Red Death"; the revellers fall, the clock
stops, and "the flames of the tripods" expire. Pestilence holds do-
minion with "Darkness and Decay" over the realm of human experience. The silence of the mummer reigns, and for Poe, silence nearly
always implies both the death of the body and the extinction of the
soul. In "Sonnet—Silence," written three years before "The Masque
of the Red Death," Poe distinguished between "the corporate Silence," which has "no power of evil . . . in himself," and "his shadow," the nameless and (by implication) evil silence that is the death
of the spirit. The wordless figure who comes "like a thief in the
night," bringing silence to Prospero's domain, presents but a sem-
blance of physical death; he is actually the more dreadful incor-
poreal silence that affirms the annihilation of the soul.

   Compulsion. In "The Imp of the Perverse," Poe accounts for the
irrational urge to cast one's self from a precipice, to plunge into an
abyss: "And this fall—this rushing annihilation—for the very reason that it involves that one most ghastly and loathsome of all the
most ghastly and loathsome images of death and suffering which
have ever presented themselves to our imagination—for this very
cause do we now the most vividly desire it" (3 : 1223). This passage at
once epitomizes the compulsion paradigm and suggests its relationship to the model already discussed. Death-as-compulsion draws
upon the terror of annihilation but finds within it an irrational plea-
sure, "the delight of its horror." The disgusting character of death,
which generates anxiety and aversion in the previous form, now becomes an object of fascination and longing. In *The Narrative of
Arthur Gordon Pym* and "A Descent into the Maelstrom," Poe associated the "perverse" with the image of the abyss, a self-evident
symbol of engulfing mortality, and thus indicated its patently suicidal nature. In other works dramatizing the perverse—"The Tell-
Tale Heart," "The Black Cat," and "The Cask of Amontillado"—the
literal abyss becomes an implied figure disclosed by temptation: the
"unfathomable longing of the soul *to vex itself*—to offer violence to

its own nature" (3:852) through displaced self-destructiveness. In each of these tales, an act of murder leads to obsessive revelation; "The Imp of the Perverse" makes explicit the suicidal impulse of the confession: "They say that I spoke with a distinct enunciation, but with marked emphasis and passionate hurry, as if in dread of interruption before concluding the brief but pregnant sentences that consigned me to the hangman and to hell" (3:1226).

Although the death-wish theory of Freud has been largely discredited, the longing for an end to life has (as Eliot's headnote to *The Waste Land* suggests) a persistent tradition of its own. Since the rise of Romanticism, the will to die has become increasingly conspicuous in Western culture. Roughly concurrent with the rise of the Gothic novel and the valorization of "sensibility," Goethe's *Sorrows of Young Werther* (1774) "swept over eighteenth-century Europe like a contagious disease,"[16] initiating a vogue for suicide—or, more precisely, unleashing an impulse that had long been held in check by reason, faith, and social convention. Four years before *Werther*, the self-induced death of Thomas Chatterton had had only a limited impact, but in the wake of Goethe's novel and its literary progeny, Chatterton's death became an important symbol: he was, for the Romantics, "the first example of death by alienation."[17] The outbreak of suicide in life and literature in the late eighteenth century expresses far more than a passing fashion; it seems to manifest an intriguing response to the modern dread of death. At first glance, this seems an illogical supposition: how does the wish for death follow from the fear of mortality? We now know that in some cases thanatophobia paradoxically drives the individual toward death as a means of release from the burden of death-anxiety. We understand too that the act on some basic level involves a rejection of the fated biological creature; the mind or self directs violence against the body to eradicate the pain and despair inevitably experienced in the viscera. Hence the Romantic vogue for suicide, which finds expression in Poe, reflects yet another aspect of the quintessential modern affliction that Kierkegaard called the "sickness unto death."

Two of Poe's early tales, "Metzengerstein" and "MS. Found in a Bottle," use supernatural motifs to illuminate the inner world of suicidal compulsion. In "Metzengerstein" a "mysterious steed" seems to embody the soul of the hated Count Berlifitzing, and by carrying the Baron Metzengerstein to his death, it enforces a curse and completes the revenge pattern. But attention to detail indicates that the

horse actually embodies the fiendish malignancy of the baron himself, whose "perverse attachment" to the animal stems from an in-
trinsic likeness: "the young Metzengerstein seemed riveted to the
saddle of that colossal horse, whose intractable audacities so well accorded with his own spirit" (2:27). The beast inspires an instinctive
dread: Metzengerstein "never vaulted into the saddle, without an
unaccountable and almost imperceptible shudder" (2:28); he never
names the horse and never places his hand "upon the body of the
beast." His fear originates from his first perception of the horse as a
tapestried image. Significantly, Poe writes that the baron feels an
"overwhelming anxiety" that falls "like a pall upon his senses"
(2:22). The nature of his terror becomes explicit when a preternatural change in the horse's features discloses its symbolic function: "The eyes, before invisible, now wore an energetic and human
expression, while they gleamed with a fiery and unusual red; and
the distended lips of the apparently enraged horse left in full view
his sepulchral and disgusting teeth" (2:23). Once again, Poe associates evil (the fiery, hellish eyes) with death (the sepulchral teeth) in
contriving an image of Metzengerstein's inescapable doom. But here
is the essence of the compulsion model: far from banishing the symbol of his future destruction, Metzengerstein compulsively surren-
ders himself to the creature (and the horror he inspires), finally allowing the horse to carry him into the all-consuming flames.

"MS. Found in a Bottle" adds a significant dimension to this conception of death by suggesting that the narrator seeks more than his
own perverse annihilation: he longs to enter the abyss, the vortex, to
glimpse the *mysterium tremendum* it contains. In the tale's most
frequently cited passage, Poe juxtaposes the terror of extinction and
the yearning to pierce the veil of mortality: "To conceive the horror
of my sensations is, I presume, utterly impossible; yet a curiosity to
penetrate the mysteries of these awful regions, predominates even
over my despair, and will reconcile me to the most hideous aspect of
death. It is evident that we are hurrying onwards to some exciting
knowledge—some never-to-be-imparted secret, whose attainment is
destruction" (2:145). The story's dense supernaturalism virtually
obliges one to understand "these awful regions" as a reference to
death, for the voyage itself is a parable of the passage toward it.
Shortly after its departure from Java, the freighter on which the narrator sails is becalmed in a manner reminiscent of the ship in Coleridge's *Ancient Mariner*. The stillness, a foretoken of death's fixity,

expresses itself in two signs: "The flame of a candle burned on the poop without the least perceptible motion, and a long hair, held between the finger and thumb, hung without the possibility of detecting a vibration" (2:136). Readers of Poe's day would have recognized in these details two familiar methods of verifying death in cases of suspended animation. The analogy becomes more apparent when the sun is suddenly "extinguished by some unaccountable power," plunging the ship into the "pitchy darkness" of "eternal night" and the narrator into a condition of anxiety and "utter hopelessness" (2:138–39). Poe's introduction of the phantom ship—appropriately colored a "deep dingy black"—contributes images of aging to the increasingly complex death symbolism; the spectral sailors personify decay, the ineluctable failure of the flesh: "Their knees trembled with infirmity; their shoulders were bent double with decrepitude; their shrivelled skins rattled in the wind; their voices were low, tremulous, and broken; their eyes glistened with the rheum of years; and their gray hairs streamed terribly in the tempest" (2:143). Yet these wasted figures, phantasms of the narrator's own never-to-be-reached senescence, inspire a "sentiment ineffable," for they approach the fatal vortex with "more of the eagerness of hope than of the apathy of despair" (2:145). Their immense age and acceptance of death fill the narrator with a sense of novelty and expectation, and so despite irrepressible sensations of horror, he awaits a potential revelation. In this sense the tale of compulsion looks forward to two other models—separation and transformation—in which death is both an end and a beginning.

Separation. In an age that cultivated the idea of "the Beautiful Death," the last hour became a matter of extravagant preparation. Those stricken with a lingering illness (tuberculosis was the fashionable malady) made the most of their invalidism by composing letters, poems, diaries, and meditational works, filled with reflections upon earthly life and hopes for the hereafter.[18] Belief in a spiritual rendezvous introduced an element of joyous expectancy to the deathbed scene, Ariès notes, but it also caused death itself to be regarded as "an intolerable separation" (p. 435). The parting became a ritualistic event; the offering of flowers—to beautify the image of death—entered into common usage, as did the creation of commemorative jewelry, needlework, and painting (pp. 419, 460–62). Ariès characterizes this pattern of funereal idolatry as "the death of the Other" because in an important sense, death became an object of scrutiny and the dying person a kind of aesthetic component, an element in the tableau of "the Beautiful Death." This transformation could only have occurred through a suppression of the physiology of decay and the dissociation of mortality from a concept of hell. Ariès remarks: "No sense of guilt, no fear of the beyond remained to counteract the fascination of death, transformed into the highest beauty." Without the threat of damnation, the notion of heaven also changed, becoming "the scene of the reunion of those whom death has separated but who have never accepted this separation" (p. 611).

Poe's valorization of "the death of a beautiful woman" as "the most poetical topic in the world" thus exploited a common theme in nineteenth-century culture. In poem after poem, his persona experiences the death of a woman as a radical separation from the beloved Other, an estrangement inducing guilt, grief, madness, and lonely visits to the tomb of the deceased. The sequence of stories from "Berenice" through "The Oval Portrait" uses the same poetic premise but with some intriguing modifications: in fiction, the woman's death excites horror, even perverse impatience in the narrator, who observes disgusting physical changes; in place of the beatific reunion of spirits envisioned in consolation literature, Poe dramatized an implicit antagonism, sometimes culminating in a frenzied, mad encounter with the buried woman. The notable exception to this scheme is "Eleonora," a tale that embodies fairly conventional ideas of death and spiritual communion. More representative of Poe's separation paradigm, however, are "Morella" and "Ligeia," works that depict death not as absolute annihilation but as an ambiguous, temporary parting. In a monstrous parody of the death of the Other, Poe represents the return of the beloved not in spiritual terms but as a ghastly reincarnation tinged with vampirism. Through such supernaturalism, he implies that death is neither an extinction of the self nor admission to a heavenly social club. Rather, it is a condition of spiritual confinement and unrest, a dream world where one acts out the desires and hostilities of an earlier existence.

"Morella" dramatizes a metaphysical question that troubled Poe's generation: his narrator ponders the fate of individual essence—the *"principium individuationis,* the notion of that identity *which at death is or is not lost forever"* (2:231). The tale seems to confirm the survival of personal entity when the dying wife ostensibly returns in the person of the daughter whom she has delivered upon her deathbed; the empty tomb, discovered at the story's end, implies the transmigration of the mother's soul. But the story also raises a doubt about the idea of an enduring, transferable identity, for death of the "second Morella" apparently brings to a close the cycle of resurrection. Less ambiguously, the narrative demonstrates Poe's characteristic attraction-repulsion pattern: the narrator's "singular affection" for Morella and the abandon with which he enters into a mystical apprenticeship give way at length to "horror" and "alienation." As in "Berenice," the onset of physical decline obsesses the narrator: "In time, the crimson spot settled steadily upon the cheek, and the blue veins upon the pale forehead became prominent; and, one instant, my nature melted into pity, but, in the next, I met the glance of her meaning eyes, and then my soul sickened and became giddy with the giddiness of one who gazes downward into some dreary and unfathomable abyss" (2:232). This is a fascinating passage: the narrator observes the signs of his wife's impending death and feels himself caught helplessly in a mechanism of self-destruction (the compulsion model). Her extinction somehow entails his own.

Here Poe touches upon the human tendency to feel jeopardized by the vulnerability or aging of one's partner. Ernest Becker notes that "if a woman loses her beauty, or shows that she doesn't have the strength and dependability that we once thought she did," men may experience an ultimate threat: "The shadow of imperfection falls over our lives, and with it—death and the defeat of cosmic heroism. 'She lessens' = 'I die'" (p. 167). The narrator's revulsion should be understood not as a response to Morella herself but to her mortality; we can trace his disgust back to her "cold hand," to the voice whose melody is "tainted with terror," to the "melancholy eyes"—all signs of the fate she anticipates and symbolizes. His abhorrence of the process of dissolution and his eagerness for the moment of release foreshadow the twentieth-century concept of unspeakable, invisible death—the hidden shame we encounter, unforgettably, in Tolstoi's "The Death of Ivan Ilych."

In effect, "Morella" presents a grotesque inversion of the sweet parting idealized as "the Beautiful Death." The dread evoked by the death of the Other seems central to this model: in "Berenice" the narrator's "insufferable anxiety" leads to the unconscious defilement of his cousin's body; in "The Fall of the House of Usher" Roderick's terror prevents him from voicing his suspicion that Madeline has been interred prematurely; in "The Oval Portrait" the

painter grows "tremulous and very pallid, and aghast" as he perceives the fate of his wife. Fear and loathing enter the scheme of
"Ligeia" in a different way. After witnessing his wife's fierce struggle
to overcome death through a sheer act of will, the narrator remarries
and projects his repressed disgust upon Rowena. The image of his
second wife's "pallid and rigid figure upon the bed" brings to mind
Ligeia's death and "the whole of that unutterable woe with which
[he] had regarded *her* thus enshrouded" (2 : 326). During the "hideous
drama of revivification," Rowena's morbid relapses produce two associated effects: the narrator's shudder of horror at "the ghastly expression of death" and his "waking vision of Ligeia." The mingling
of past and present pushes the narrator to the brink of madness: the
woman before him is both living and dead, Lady Rowena and Ligeia,
an impossible fusion of irreconcilable opposites. Privately, Poe dismissed the idea that the story affirmed the soul's immortality, and
he underscored the finality of death: "One point I have not fully carried out—I should have intimated that the *will* did not perfect its
intention—there should have been a relapse—a final one—and
Ligeia (who had only succeeded in so much as to convey an idea of
the truth to the narrator) should be at length entombed as Rowena—
the body alterations have gradually faded away." [19] Notwithstanding
Poe's omission, the tale as published hardly implies a joyous or last-
ing reunion; apart from "Eleonora," he rigorously resisted any ide-
alizing of the death of the Other.

  What then is the meaning of the apparently supernatural return
staged in the separation pardigm? In "Morella" Poe intimates that
the reincarnation completes a curse; Morella warns the narrator:
"thy days shall be days of sorrow . . . thou shalt bear about with thee
thy shroud on earth" (2 : 233), perhaps as retribution for the contempt she has received from him. The return of Madeline Usher also
savors of revenge; after a bloody and "bitter struggle" to escape her
tomb, she destroys the brother who buried her prematurely, bearing
him to the floor "a corpse, and a victim to the terrors he had anticipated" (2 : 417). The return of Ligeia seems to victimize Rowena
rather than the narrator, but we must remember that, unlike Eleonora, Ligeia never sanctions or encourages her husband's remarriage.
Note the avoidance in the gesture by which she signals her reap-
pearance to the narrator: "*Shrinking from my touch*, she let fall
from her head the ghastly cerements which had confined it" (2 : 330,
emphasis mine). The point is subtle but important, for we see that

the parting marks an irreversible alienation, to which the horrific reunion bears witness. The ultimate implication of the separation model becomes clear: death makes us strangers to each other. In Poe's fiction, the dramatized return of the Other also suggests, paradoxically, that human ties continue to exert a claim and that loss haunts us in the midst of life. If the death of a beautiful woman grants a certain immunity to Poe's protagonist (dissolution is what happens to someone else), the very task of watching and waiting intensifies the consciousness of his own mortality and destroys his hold upon life and reason. Only in "Eleonora" does the narrator accept the death of the Other and commune happily with her spirit. But that situation more nearly resembles a fourth figuration of human destiny.

Transformation. In his 1844 tour de force, "The Premature Burial," Poe wrote: "the boundaries which divide Life from Death, are at best shadowy and vague" (3: 955). Describing one of those "cessations . . . of vitality" known to result in accidental burial, he mused, "where, meantime, was the soul?" The question of the soul's whereabouts during sleep and after death has a long tradition in Western philosophy, stretching back to Plato and Aristotle. But this enigma aroused profound uncertainty for Poe's generation, as gathering religious doubt inevitably came to center on the problem of mortality. The traditional notion of an immortal, individual essence had come under attack from two fronts. Developing medical knowledge had by the early nineteenth century charted the human anatomy so precisely that the venerable belief in a physical seat of the soul (held by Descartes, for example, who exalted the pineal gland) could no longer be sustained. Indeed, skepticism about the soul's very existence increased in direct ratio to physiological understanding. Meanwhile, the Romantic movement, influenced by German idealism, had popularized a transcendental view of man and nature: a world suffused by an over-soul that animated human beings (as it did all living things) but that returned unto itself at death, bearing no trace of personal essence. In the face of these popular ideologies, belief in an individuated soul persisted, mainly because that concept was bound up with the individualism that had undergirded Western culture since the early Renaissance. But the apparent failure of religious dogma channeled belief in the soul into secular occultism, both organized and informal.

Matters of death and the soul were never very far from Poe's thoughts. As we have seen, his writing emphasizes the physiological and psychological aspects of dying, suggesting his greater responsiveness to the threat of oblivion than to the prospect of an afterlife. Yet in early poems like *Al Aaraaf* and "Israfel" (as well as tales like "Eleonora"), he could occasionally entertain fancies of transcendence. In a series of four works, which began with "The Conversation of Eiros and Charmion" and ended with "The Power of Words," Poe depicted death as metamorphosis and through supernatural dialogues projected scenes of spiritual reunion and cosmic discovery. In "The Colloquy of Monos and Una," the transformation of the title entities makes possible a retrospective view of death and burial, in which the "evil hour" of separation now appears as a "passage through the dark Valley and Shadow" toward "Life Eternal": a rebirth. After delivering a harangue on earthly problems, Monos relates the "weird narrative" of his own decease, noting the sensory impressions of his last moments, the lamentations of his survivors, preparations for his burial, and the interment itself. He insists that the "breathless and motionless torpor" which was "termed Death by those who stood around [him]" (2: 612) did not deprive him of "sentience." But gradually his senses dim, and Monos becomes aware of a new mode of consciousness, the "sentiment of *duration,*" which he terms "the first obvious and certain step of the intemporal soul upon the threshold of the temporal Eternity" (2: 615). Finally the "consciousness of being" yields to a simple sense of place: "The narrow space immediately surrounding what had been the body, was now growing to be the body itself" (2: 616). In reporting this transformation, Poe propounds the idea that the soul and body do not separate at death, that the spirit remains within the mortal frame, still in effect a prisoner of sensation, until the process of decay reduces the body to dust. Yet Poe's final, troubling sentence implies that not even the soul survives this disintegration; what remains is pure absence, "nothingness." But we have the dialogue itself as evidence of an "immortality." Poe appears to suggest that the total annihilation of body and soul must take place before the rebirth or transformation alluded to at the beginning of the work. The self must endure "many lustra" of decomposition ("corrosive hours") before reaching the condition of nullity preliminary to "Life Eternal."

This vision of infinity becomes somewhat clearer in "Mesmeric Revelation." Here the dialogue occurs between Vankirk, a patient dying of tuberculosis, and P., the narrator-mesmerist. On the point of death, Vankirk summons P. to place him in a sleep-waking state, so that he may explore his own "psychal impressions" about the soul. Articulating what may have been Poe's own uncertainties, the dying man admits: "I need not tell you how sceptical I have hitherto been on the topic of the soul's immortality. I cannot deny that there has always existed, as if in that very soul which I have been denying, a vague half-sentiment of its own existence" (3: 1031). Under mesmeric influence, and speaking (in the latter portion of the tale) from the beyond, Vankirk elaborates a transcendental theory of God as an all-pervasive spirit, of which the human being is an individualized expression. He affirms of man: "Divested of his corporate investiture, he were God. . . . But he can never be thus divested—at least never *will* be—else we must imagine an action of God returning upon itself—a purposeless and futile action" (3: 1036). According to this hypothesis, each of us is trapped within a body that is coextensive with and inseparable from the soul. How then do we escape the tomb? Here is the key to Poe's theory of immortality (and the concept of death as transformation): "There are two bodies—the rudimental and the complete; corresponding with the two conditions of the worm and the butterfly. What we call 'death,' is but the painful metamorphosis. Our present incarnation is progressive, preparatory, temporary. Our future is perfected, ultimate, immortal. The ultimate life is the full design" (3: 1037). If we understand "present incarnation" to encompass both flesh and spirit, the metaphysics of "The Colloquy of Monos and Una" becomes intelligible. The temporal body falls away like a chrysalis, revealing the intemporal, "complete" body, the astral body. But Poe is no systematic thinker; in "Mesmeric Revelation" he drops the idea of a season in limbo (called "the alloted days of stupor" in "The Conversation of Eiros and Charmion") and says that "at death or metamorphosis, these creatures, enjoying the ultimate life—immortality" inhabit "SPACE itself" as "nonentities" invisible to the angels (3: 1038). Unfortunately, the final tale in the sequence, "The Power of Words," sheds no light on these mysteries, defining the soul merely as a "thirst" for ultimate knowledge.

These philosophical inconsistencies are perhaps beside the point. What seems significant about the cycle of spiritualized dialogues is Poe's inclination to see body and soul as inextricably bonded. Despite the conception of an unearthly, astral form, an odd materialism informs Poe's notion of the spirit world; "Aidenn" is simply a place where things, substances, are less densely constituted. God is "un-particled matter," souls have bodies, and words have a "physical power." It is as if, for all of his mystical inclinations, Poe cannot escape an empirical vision of a bounded world. His depiction of an afterlife seems to express a yearning for a realm "out of space, out of time," beyond the contingencies of mortal existence. Yet in fact his spirit figures carry with them a good deal of earthly baggage—memories, affections, beliefs, political opinions—and spend much of their time (if one can thus speak of the eternal) reflecting upon personal experiences or explaining celestial phenomena according to mundane scientific principles. In short, Poe's visionary texts (and here I include the monumentally confused *Eureka*) project a false transcendence, a phantasmic existence after death, conceptually embedded in a cosmos of matter and energy, a system that culminates in irreversible dissolution: entropy.

V

Among Poe's manifold representations of death and dying, we discern no single formulation that might confidently be described as the essential design. His object as a writer was not, of course, to construct a programmatic analysis of human fate; his thematic diversity and penchant for irony complicate even further an identification of his "real" conceptual matrix. Nevertheless, the imagery of death recurs with such insistence that its imaginative priority seems self-evident. Edward Davidson once described Poe as a "verbal landscapist of death,"[20] and in an early poem, "The City in the Sea," we encounter the characteristic scene of silence and desolation, upon which "Death looks gigantically down" (1: 202). For Poe, death was indeed gigantic, not in crude physical terms but as a ubiquitous and oppressive presence. Personal experience, popular culture, and intellectual history conspired to make it so. The pathetic facts of his own life—the successive deaths of his parents, his surrogate mother (Mrs. Jane Stith Stanard), his foster mother (Mrs. Allan), and his child bride, Virginia—describe a pattern of loss that must have haunted him like a specter. His inveterate melancholy also fed upon the funereal spirit of the age, as manifested in the sentimental offerings of the gift books and ladies' magazines. And his fear and trembling (to use the phrase of his contemporary, Kierkegaard) further derived from the crisis of authority and understanding that shook

Western culture in the eighteenth century. Among other consequences, this crisis seriously challenged or destroyed traditional ways of accepting death and introduced a welter of new, secular conceptions that necessarily contributed further uncertainty. To use the phrase of Becker, it was at this moment that the "eclipse of secure communal ideologies of redemption" (p. 193) produced the anxiety characteristic of the modern age. Since 1700 rapidly changing conceptions of death, symptomatic of a decentered culture, have failed to mitigate or resolve the underlying dread. It is a mark of Poe's genius that he perceived the central problem of death and sensed in his own dubiety the confusion of our existential plight. As Sarah Helen Whitman shrewdly perceived in 1859, the "unrest and faithlessness of the age culminated in him"; Poe was the saddest and loneliest writer of his generation because he "came to sound the very depths of the abyss," to plumb the nature of modern despair.[21]

No story in the Poe canon sounds the depths more effectively than "The Facts in the Case of M. Valdemar," a tale that incorporates elements of all four models previously discussed. A sequel to "Mesmeric Revelation," "Valdemar" further illuminates the disjunction between body and soul as disclosed by mesmeric experiment; it postulates the threshold experience of a man *in articulo mortis*. Like the tales of separation, it portrays mortality as an object of scrutiny; the narrator furnishes expert observations on the physiological decline of his friend. Like characters in the tales of compulsion, M. Valdemar expresses the desire for death ("Do not wake me—let me die so") and longs for release from the mesmeric trance so that his dissolution may be completed. The ensuing spectacle of immediate putrefaction ties the story to the annihilation model and exemplifies the naturalistic horror inherent in death. This is not to suggest that "Valdemar" involves a conscious manipulation of these patterns; rather, the synthetic, composite effect seems the result of an intense concentration of anxiety, a focusing, as it were, of Poe's ambivalent perceptions of mortality.

Despite the fact that Poe in correspondence acknowledged the tale to be a "hoax," "Valdemar" demands serious attention as a conceptualization of death. With excruciating precision, it records the grotesque "facts" of the protagonist's apparent demise:

> The eyes rolled themselves slowly open, the pupils disappearing upwardly; the skin generally assumed a cadaverous hue, resembling not so much parchment as white paper; and

> the circular hectic spots which, hitherto, had been strongly
> defined in the center of each cheek, *went out* at once. . . .
> The upper lip, at the same time, writhed itself away from the
> teeth, which it had previously covered completely; while the
> lower jaw fell open with an audible jerk, leaving the mouth
> widely extended, and disclosing in full view the swollen and
> blackened tongue. (3: 1239)

The disappearance of the "hectic spots" brings to mind, appropriately, the sudden extinction of the sun in "MS. Found in a Bottle," while the revelation of the writhing lip recalls "Metzengerstein," "Berenice," and other Poe tales in which teeth function as a sign of death. This moment of apparent decease has its counterpart in the tale's unforgettable final image, the instantaneous decomposition of Valdemar: "Upon the bed, before that whole company, there lay a nearly liquid mass of loathsome—of detestable putridity" (3: 1243). Apart from effecting our revulsion, these details serve a figurative purpose, for "Valdemar" dramatizes the scientific effort—undertaken in the eighteenth century and continuing in our era of medical technology—to understand, control, and perhaps finally conquer the major causes of death. From an empirical viewpoint, cessation of life results from physiological processes that can theoretically be halted or reversed. Even aging has proved susceptible to retardation, and recent developments in genetic engineering and organ replacement bring ever closer the possibility of a technologically guaranteed immortality. However improbable or undesirable this idea seems, one can scarcely deny that the great dream of our scientific utopia lies in the direction of extending life beyond its traditional limits and converting death into a manageable, discretionary experience. Like Hawthorne's Dr. Rappaccini, the narrator of "Valdemar" uses scientific (or pseudoscientific) methods to control the processes of life artificially. His ultimate object is to determine "to what extent, or for how long a period, the encroachments of Death might be arrested" (3: 1233) by mesmerism. The stratagem succeeds in postponing Valdemar's dissolution, but when the man is awakened from his vegetative stupor, the grotesque final scene betrays the limitation of human efficacy and reaffirms the sovereignty of death. In effect, the illusion of a scientifically insured immortality disintegrates with Valdemar.

Another key to the symbolic ramifications of the tale lies in the supernatural voice, the "harsh, and broken and hollow" sound that seems to emanate from some deep or distant source, producing a "gelatinous" impression. When the voice declares, "I *have been* sleeping—and now—now—*I am dead*" (3: 1240), it perpetrates what Roland Barthes has called a "scandal of language, . . . the coupling of the first person (*I*) and of the attribute '*dead*'"; it "asserts two contraries at the same time (Life, Death)"; and it effects a "scandalous return to the literal" when "Death, as primordial repressed, erupts directly into language."[22] The last point seems especially pertinent: the tale violates language, logic, and cultural taboo, allowing the unspeakable to speak, the unbearable sight to be seen. It compels us to confront death in all of its visceral repulsiveness, unsoftened by the effusion of sentiment or the prospect of a spiritual afterlife.

As noted earlier, Poe rejected the illusion of "the Beautiful Death" which beguiled his generation, and through the preternatural voice in "Valdemar" he expresses the hard physical and psychological truth at the core of modern consciousness. In this work as in so many others, supernaturalism intrudes upon the world of reason and experience to deliver the message of mortality. The uncanny produces a disruption, shatters the illusion of one's control over the flow of existence; it rivets the consciousness of Poe's protagonists like the first undeniable sign of a mortal illness. It arrives as a threat to the quest for knowledge, beauty, and godlike dominance, driving home a perception of the existential paradox summarized by Becker: "Man is literally split in two: he has an awareness of his own splendid uniqueness in that he sticks out of nature with a towering majesty, and yet he goes back into the ground a few feet in order blindly and dumbly to rot and disappear forever. It is a terrifying dilemma to be in and to have to live with" (p. 26). While Poe could entertain visions of transcendence, he was finally too much the victim of our own crisis of death to exorcise its dread. Yet he faced the "terrifying dilemma" with remarkable tenacity and acuity, producing a literature that seems, in our age of "invisible death," more than ever disturbing and menacing. Little wonder that for many, Poe cannot be taken seriously: to do so is to confront the fearful yet vitalizing truth that our century has done its best to deny.

NOTES

1. An idea ably developed by Stephen L. Mooney, "Poe's Gothic Waste Land," in *The Recognition of Edgar Allan Poe*, ed. Eric W. Carlson (Ann Arbor: University of Michigan Press, 1966), pp. 278–97.

2. Preface to the *Collected Works of Edgar Allan Poe*, ed. Thomas Ollive Mabbott (Cambridge: Harvard University Press, 1978), 2: 473. All subsequent references to Poe's poetry and fiction correspond to the Mabbott edition, cited parenthetically by volume and page.

3. David Punter, *The Literature of Terror: A History of Gothic Fictions from 1765 to the Present Day* (London: Longman, 1980).

4. Ibid., p. 404. I have characterized the modern age as "post-Christian" in the sense defined by Alan D. Gilbert: "A post-Christian society is not one from which Christianity has departed, but one in which it has become marginal. It is a society where to be irreligious is to be normal, where to think and act in secular terms is to be conventional, where neither status nor respectability depends upon the practice or profession of religious faith." See *The Making of Post-Christian Britain: A History of the Secularization of Modern Society* (London: Longman, 1980), p. ix.

5. Patricia Meyer Spacks, *The Insistence of Horror: Aspects of the Supernatural in Eighteenth-Century Poetry* (Cambridge: Harvard University Press, 1962), pp. 196, 200.

6. Glen St. John Barclay, *Anatomy of Horror: The Masters of Occult Fiction* (New York: St. Martin's Press, 1978), p. 9.

7. Philippe Ariès, *The Hour of Our Death*, trans. Helen Weaver (New York: Alfred A. Knopf, 1981). Subsequent references to Ariès all derive from this work, with page references noted parenthetically.

8. Ann Douglas, *The Feminization of American Culture* (New York: Alfred A. Knopf, 1977), pp. 201–2.

9. J. Gerald Kennedy, "Poe and Magazine Writing on Premature Burial," *Studies in the American Renaissance* 1 (1977): 165–78.

10. David Stannard, *The Puritan Way of Death* (New York: Oxford University Press, 1977), p. 185.

11. Letter to Frederick W. Thomas, 25 May 1842, in *The Letters of Edgar Allan Poe*, ed. John Ward Ostrom (1948; rpt. New York: Gordian Press, 1966), 1 : 197. A vexed Poe thus rationalized his break with the journal.

12. "Marginalia," in *The Complete Works of Edgar Allan Poe*, ed. James A. Harrison (1902; rpt. New York: AMS Press, 1965), 16:42.

13. Ernest Becker, *The Denial of Death* (New York: Free Press, 1973), p. 70. All further citations from Becker derive from this work, with page references noted parenthetically.

14. The relationship is discussed by Burton R. Pollin, "Poe's 'Shadow' as a Source of His 'The Masque of the Red Death,'" *Studies in Short Fiction* 6 (Fall 1968): 104–7.

15. Joseph Patrick Roppolo, "Meaning and 'The Masque of the Red Death,'" in *Poe: A Collection of Critical Essays*, ed. Robert Regan (Englewood Cliffs, N.J.: Prentice-Hall, 1967), pp. 142, 144.

16. Herbert Ross Brown, *The Sentimental Novel in America, 1789–1860* (Durham, N.C.: Duke University Press, 1940), p. 155.

17. A. Alvarez, *The Savage God: A Study of Suicide* (New York: Bantam, 1973), p. 195.

18. A classic instance of such writing is the deathbed poetry of young Margaret Miller Davidson, preserved in Washington Irving's *Biography and Poetical Remains of the late Margaret Miller Davidson* (Philadelphia: Lea and Blanchard, 1841).

19. Letter to Philip P. Cooke, 21 September 1839, *The Letters of Edgar Allan Poe*, 2: 687.

20. Edward Davidson, *Poe: A Critical Study* (Cambridge: Harvard University Press, 1957), p. 115.

21. Sarah Helen Whitman, *Edgar Poe and His Critics* (New York: Rudd and Carleton, 1860), p. 6.

22. Roland Barthes, "Textual Analysis of a Tale by Edgar Poe," trans. Donald G. Marshall, *Poe Studies* 10 (June 1977): 10.

CAROLYN L. KARCHER

Philanthropy and the Occult in the Fiction of Hawthorne, Brownson, and Melville

he extraordinary spate of religious and social movements that swept the United States during the first half of the nineteenth century has long intrigued historians. One question in particular has elicited much speculation: what common features could have attracted so many thousands of antebellum Americans to the seemingly diverse causes, cults, and philosophies they successively or concurrently embraced—revivalism, organized benevolence, Mormonism, adventism, transcendentalism, utopianism, abolitionism, pacifism, women's rights, temperance, vegetarianism, hydropathy, phrenology, Swedenborgianism, mesmerism, and spiritualism.[1] Recently literary critics have discovered that these interrelated "Isms," as contemporary scoffers called them, also inspired a body of fiction, amounting to a virtual genre, that satirized the "follies and delusions of the nineteenth century" and caricatured the leading figures in heterodox religious and reformist circles as deluded fanatics or diabolical humbugs.[2] The chief originators of the genre, which would culminate late in the century with Henry James's *The Bostonians* (1886), were Nathaniel Hawthorne, Orestes Brownson, and Herman Melville. All three aimed some of their most pointed shafts at the cult of spirit-rapping launched by the Fox sisters in 1848, but incorporated their satire of spiritualism into wider-ranging indictments of American society. Examining the ways in which their indictments overlap and diverge helps place them ideologically with respect to each other and to their culture's dominant creed—the belief in a dawning millennial age that in one form or another underlay every "Ism" nineteenth-century Americans patronized.

The genre of antireform satire seems to have had its birth in the 1840s with Hawthorne's sketches "The Hall of Fantasy," "The Procession of Life," and "Earth's Holocaust." Among the butts they whimsically poke fun at are "the abolitionist, brandishing his one idea like an iron flail"; the transcendentalist, dissolving into a "misty apparition"; the teetotaler, seeking to ban "all the spice of life"; the pacifist, attempting to eliminate war by eliminating weapons; and the adventist, prophesying the end of the world in 1843, who "with one puff of his relentless theory scatters all [other reformers'] dreams like so many withered leaves upon the blast."[3]

69

It was the spiritualist craze of the 1850s, however, that played the primary role in popularizing and shaping the genre. As Howard Kerr has shown, a host of satiric poems, sketches, and novels by both major and minor writers sprang up in response to spiritualism. The satirists targeted three main aspects of the cult: its trivial revelations and wonders, which inadvertently parodied Christian doctrines and the miracles authenticating them; its occult manipulation of the human psyche, as exemplified by the trance states that mediums and their mesmerist precursors induced in themselves and their subjects; and its association, through overlapping constituencies, with radical causes like abolitionism, utopianism, and above all women's rights, which had made its fomal début at Seneca Falls the same year that spirits had possessed the Fox sisters of nearby Hydesville and consecrated them as the high priestesses of a new, female-dominated religion.

In *The Blithedale Romance* (1852), a fictionalized post mortem of the transcendentalist, Utopian community Brook Farm, Hawthorne provided the model that most of the satires provoked by spiritualism would follow.[4] Linking a cross-section of reformers—the feminist Zenobia and her sister Priscilla, the prison reformer Hollingsworth, and the Utopians of the Blithedale community to which they all belong—with a sinister mesmerist who mouths the same rhetoric the reformers do about brotherhood in a coming millennial era (*BR*, p. 200), Hawthorne implies that social reformers and traffickers in the occult alike merely exploit their compatriots' desire for a better world as a means of advancing their own selfish aims. The reformers either betray the causes they profess to believe in, as Zenobia betrays her feminism, her sisterly obligations toward Priscilla, and her commitment to Blithedale when she falls in love with the rabidly antifeminist Hollingsworth; or else, like Hollingsworth himself, they pervert their philanthropic projects into monuments to their own egos, to which they sacrifice everyone and everything that stands in their way, including their own humanity (pp. 218, 243). The occult operators violate the whole moral being, so that if the feats they boast of are genuine, "the individual soul [is] virtually annihilated, and . . . the idea of man's eternal responsibility . . . made ridiculous, and immortality rendered, at once, impossible, and not worth acceptance" (p. 198). *The Blithedale Romance* thus conveys a triple message: that the nineteenth century's cherished belief in "human progress" is but a chimera ("Let them believe in it who can," shrugs Hawthorne's narrator, Coverdale, as he winds up his account of the Blithedale débacle); that the humanitarian reformers' schemes for perfecting society are as delusive as the prestidigitations of the charlatans with whom they fraternize; and that the occult phenomena cited in proof of mesmerism and spiritualism—"miraculous power of one human being over the will and passions of another, . . . tables, upset by invisible agencies, bells, self-tolled at funerals, and ghostly music, performed on jewsharps"—merely betoken the moral depths to which the civilization of the nineteenth century has sunk and the "downward course" it is pursuing (pp. 246, 198–99).

II

Hawthorne's blanket indictment of the "Isms" to which his contemporaries subscribed struck a responsive chord in an acquaintance from Brook Farm days, Orestes Brownson. Though never a full-fledged member of the Utopian community in which Hawthorne had spent a year, Brownson had been an intimate friend of its founder, George Ripley, and a vociferous supporter of the Workingmen's Party, led by Frances Wright and Robert Dale Owen.[5] Since his conversion to Catholicism in 1844, however, Brownson had led the attack against social and religious radicalism by editing the influential quarterly that bore his name. Hence he immediately recognized in *The Blithedale Romance* a powerful propagandistic weapon. Reviewing the book in his quarterly, Brownson praised its "quiet satire . . . on all philanthropic and communitarian enterprises" and exulted: "Nothing has been written among us better calculated to bring modern philanthropists into deserved disrepute, and to cure the young and enthusiastic of their socialistic tendencies and dreams of world reform."[6]

Nevertheless, Brownson apparently felt that Hawthorne, who had assigned the satanic mesmerist Westervelt a minor part in *The Blithedale Romance* and exposed his conjurations as fraudulent, underestimated the sinister role that occult forces played in fostering world reform; for soon afterward he set out to write an antireform satire of his own, which promoted the occult operator to the status of title character. *The Spirit-Rapper: An Autobiography* (1854) purports to be the deathbed confession of a Faustian scientist who kin-

dled the spiritualist movement in order to subvert Christianity. As
the subtitle suggests, the novel can be read on one level as a spiritual
autobiography in the Puritan tradition—a tradition that also lies
behind *The Blithedale Romance*. Like Hawthorne, Brownson is
exploring a past on which he has come to look back with embarrassment. But whereas Hawthorne assesses that past from the perspective of the alienated artist unable to sympathize with his compatriots' dreams, Brownson assesses it from the perspective of a
Catholic convert who now perceives those dreams as heretical. On
another level, the past *The Spirit-Rapper* explores is not Brownson's
alone, but America's, viewed through Brownson's eyes. The Spirit-
Rapper's career recapitulates the history of religious heterodoxy, social radicalism, and occult experimentation in America from the
1830s through the mid-1850s. It also exemplifies the baleful relationship Brownson sees between philanthropy and the occult.

Like the nation, the future Spirit-Rapper is introduced almost simultaneously to mesmerism and social reform. The visiting French
lecturer who first arouses the Spirit-Rapper's interest in mesmerism, "Dr. P——" (Charles Poyen, who, as Brownson recalls in his
genuine autobiography, *The Convert*, "initiated me and so many
others in New England into [its] mysteries"),[7] happens to be a Saint
Simonian, thus uniting occultism and socialism in his own person.
And the Spirit-Rapper's associates, a disparate set of "philanthropists and world-reformers," ranging in religious persuasion from
Unitarianism and Universalism to Hicksite Quakerism and Swedenborgianism, belong to "the very circles where Animal Magnetism
[another name for mesmerism], as well as all conceivable novelties
and absurdities, were the order of the day."[8]

As was the case for Brownson, however, the Spirit-Rapper receives
his most memorable lessons in philanthropy and world reform not
from Poyen, but from a feminist freethinker modeled primarily after
Frances Wright.[9] Naming her Priscilla, doubtless with a nod in the
direction of *The Blithedale Romance*, Brownson has her invite the
Spirit-Rapper to become her partner in world reform, as Wright had
invited him to join with her and Owen in the Workingmen's Party.
The invitation, of course, has strong sexual overtones, since Brownson, like Hawthorne, believes that women embrace world reform
and feminism out of sexual frustration, and that feminism inevitably breeds the free love which Frances Wright was unjustly reputed
to have advocated and practiced.[10] Like Hawthorne, Brownson also

drives home the message that women cannot violate the sexual pro-
prieties with impunity. After Priscilla's seduction of the Spirit-
Rapper she will lose her freedom; he will exercise over her the power
that Hawthorne's Westervelt exercises over Zenobia and Priscilla.

The course on which Brownson proceeds to set his fictionalized
persona represents his attempt to show how the impulses to dabble
in the occult and to reform society converge, and how they lend
themselves to a satanic conspiracy against Christianity. At first the
Spirit-Rapper experiments with mesmerism out of curiosity and a
Faustian desire to "master nature" (*SR*, p. 52). In the process, he
finds that he can "at will paralyze the whole body of another . . . and
force it to obey my bidding," that he can exert such mesmeric dominance at a distance and unbeknown to the person mesmerized, via
inanimate objects, and that he can even make inanimate objects
themselves serve as oracles (pp. 61–62). Although a Calvinist clergyman whom Brownson calls Increase Mather Cotton warns the
Spirit-Rapper that he is "forming a league with the devil," the rationalistic and optimistic assumptions the Spirit-Rapper shares with
most nineteenth-century Americans prevent him from taking the
warning seriously (p. 124). Confident that the phenomena brought
into play by mesmerism are "forces of nature," rather than of the
devil, he infers that they must be good, "as nature was good, [and] as
it worked always to a good end." If so, he reasons, "I could hope to
avail myself of [mesmerism] only in proportion as I myself became
good and devoted to the end to which nature herself works" (p. 69).

At a climactic stage of his experiments, the occult forces the Spirit-
Rapper has conjured up confirm these postulates and inform him ex-
pressly that in order to master mesmerism fully, he must harness
himself and it to the cause of philanthropy by associating himself
"heart and soul with the movement party of the times"—the party
in which Priscilla plays such a prominent role: "I had only partially
imbibed the spirit of the age, and took no part in the great movements of the day; felt no interest in the great questions of social
amelioration and progress. I had no sympathy with the poorest and
most numerous class, and made no efforts to emancipate the slave,
or to elevate woman to her proper sphere in social and political life. I
did not properly love my race, and had no due appreciation of humanity. I had great talents, great abilities, and might, if I would,
make myself the Messiah of the nineteenth century" (*SR*, pp. 67–
68).[11] Accompanying this directive is a revelation of what Brownson

considers to be the reformers' underlying creed: "Man could really become as a god, but the priests had invented the prohibition to prevent him. The god of the priests, then, could not be the true God, and Satan, instead of being regarded as the enemy, should be . . . loved and honored as the friend of man. . . . The world had hitherto worshipped a false god; it had called evil good, and good evil" (p. 70). Thus the Spirit-Rapper throws himself into philanthropy for the sake of acquiring godlike powers, and his goal of promoting world reform becomes synonymous with that of overthrowing Christianity.

"The devil, when he would seduce, can disguise himself as an angel of light," comments Brownson, speaking through the Reverend Cotton. "The devil knows . . . the weak side of every one, and he adapts his temptations accordingly. The weak side of our age is a morbid sentimentality, a sickly philanthropy, and the devil tempts us now by appealing to our dominant weakness. He comes to us as a philanthropist, and his mouth full of fine sentiments, and he proposes only what we are already prepared to approve" (SR, pp. 128–29).

In the first phase of his satanic mission, the Spirit-Rapper tries to achieve his goal directly, by fomenting anti-Christian social revolutions through "mesmeric batteries in every country in Europe" (SR, p. 172). The failure of these European revolutions in 1848 convinces him, however, that "Christianity could be eradicated only by means of a rival religion . . . which could appeal to a supernatural origin, and sustain itself by . . . what the vulgar would regard as miracles" (p. 229). Recent history offers the Spirit-Rapper two prototypes for such an endeavor: the Church of Jesus Christ of Latter-day Saints, founded by the Mormon prophet Joseph Smith, and the Church of the New Jerusalem, founded by the Swedish seer Emanuel Swedenborg, both based on revelations the founders claimed to have received from spirits or angels while in a state of mediumistic trance (pp. 164–66, 229). Yet neither Mormonism nor Swedenborgianism can be made to serve the Spirit-Rapper's purpose, since neither has "sufficiently provided for the progressiveness of the race, or with sufficient explicitness consecrated the principle of innovation and change" that rules the nineteenth century (pp. 229–30). At last the Spirit-Rapper hits on the answer: spiritualism, which he unleashes by magnetizing a bunch of flowers and handing them to the subsequently "world-renowned Misses Fox" (pp. 135–36).

Henceforth working through mediums like the Fox sisters, the Spirit-Rapper undermines Christianity by having the spirits seem to confirm doctrines that nineteenth-century Americans take to be Christian, but that Brownson deems ruinous departures from orthodoxy. Thus instead of testifying to the resurrection of the body—the true keystone of Christian faith—the spirits will claim to attest to the immortality of the soul, a heathen notion modern Christians confuse with carnal resurrection. Instead of inculcating charity— the "distinguishing trait of Christian morality," in Brownson's view correctly understood as a "supernaturally infused virtue"—the spirits, "under the name of charity," are to "teach a philanthropic, sentimental, and purely human morality . . . appealing to the morbid spirit of the age" (*SR*, pp. 234–35). Instead of promulgating the orthodox Christian doctrine of final reward and punishment at the Last Judgment, the spirits are to substitute for it the totally incompatible idea of progress that had become the "dominant doctrine of our age" (pp. 235–36); progress, they are to assert, governs celestial as well as terrestrial life, so that souls eternally rise from lower to higher states of being. Soon, the Spirit-Rapper hopes, these dubious revelations of "alleged denizens of another world, bearing the imposing names of William Penn, George Washington, Benjamin Franklin," and so forth, will supersede those of "Moses and the prophets, our Lord and his Apostles." By eclipsing Christianity, the spurious religion will automatically "open the way for that 'good time a coming,' for which all our philosophers and reformers are looking" (pp. 237–38).

In short, Brownson sees spiritualism as nothing less than the consummation of all the heretical tendencies exhibited in contemporary reform movements, and the most insidious threat to Christianity devised by the devil in modern times. Here he parts company with Hawthorne, who merely uses spiritualism and the devil as literary symbols of the moral decadence and self-deception that made nineteenth-century Americans seek shortcuts to salvation and panaceas for evils rooted in human nature. Unlike Hawthorne, Brownson does not suspect "humbug at the bottom" of the supernatural prodigies that had attracted so many converts to spiritualism (*BR*, p. 199). On the contrary, he insists that they constitute genuine instances of demonic possession. Brownson repeatedly cites the annals of witchcraft, including Cotton Mather's *Magnalia Christi Americana*, for analogues to the trance states, clairvoyant prophecies, poltergeist visitations, and communications from departed spirits reported by acolytes of the new cult. Interpreting all such phenomena

as evidence "that there is a devil, and that there are evil spirits, who
. . . interfere with men, harass them, and sometimes take literal possession of them" (SR, p. 157), he contends that to deny the "reality of
demonic intervention" is to deny Christianity itself: "If it were
proved that the Bible in the time of Pharaoh mistook . . . poor charlatans for *enchanters*, a few knavish and lying priests for the false
gods of the Gentiles, . . . delirious cataleptics for spirits of Python,
&c; if it were proved that Jesus Christ, in granting to his disciples
the gift, and prescribing to them the rules, of expelling demons, mistook a fact of pure physiology; if it were proved that the Church, in
instituting exorcism, . . . and, moreover, practising it for eighteen
centuries, has been deceived during all that period, —we should feel
that it is all over with Christianity" (pp. 158–59).

III

With its characterization of spiritualism as a satanic travesty of
Christianity, and with its dangerous reliance on a long discredited
theory of demonism to prove the truth of Christianity, *The Spirit-
Rapper* must have presented tempting bait to a skeptic of Melville's
bent. Both in his spoof of spiritualism, "The Apple-Tree Table; or,
Original Spiritual Manifestations" (1856), and in his full-scale indictment of the nation that had hailed the rappings as another sign
of its millennial destiny, *The Confidence-Man: His Masquerade*
(1857), Melville shows indications of having read *The Spirit-Rapper*
and having found it a rich trove of ideas for satirizing American religion and society from an ideological perspective very different from
Brownson's and Hawthorne's.

In contrast to Brownson and Hawthorne, Melville sympathized
wholeheartedly with the egalitarian ideals of the reformers so frequently caricatured as confederates of diabolical mesmerists and
spirit-rappers. He had explicitly taken issue, in a letter reaffirming
his own "ruthless democracy on all sides," with the "aristocracy of
feeling" that led Hawthorne to look down on reformers.[12] It might
appear "ludicrous," Melville admitted, to proclaim that "a thief in
jail is as honorable a personage as Gen. George Washington." Nevertheless, he moralized, "Truth is the silliest thing under the sun."
That was precisely why those who preached the truth always appeared silly. "It can hardly be doubted," he went on, slyly disregarding

Hawthorne's often expressed doubts on the subject, "that all Reformers are bottomed upon the truth, more or less." Why, then, he asked rhetorically, are reformers "almost universally laughingstocks?" His answer was not flattering to a writer who prided himself on revealing the truth of the human soul: "Truth is ridiculous to men." In short, Melville was arguing that the very charge Hawthorne leveled against reformers—that they were ridiculous—proved them to be in the right.

Melville expressed the same fervent egalitarianism in the fiction he wrote during this period. Indeed his letter to Hawthorne echoes two of the most famous passages in *Moby-Dick* (1851), which Melville was then in the throes of finishing. The first is the description of Queequeg as "George Washington cannibalistically developed," a description Melville feared might "seem ridiculous"; the second is the invocation to the "just Spirit of Equality, which hast spread one royal mantle of humanity over all my kind," and which "ever cullest Thy selectest champions from the kingly commons."[13]

By the mid-1850s, however, Melville had come to despair of seeing his vision of egalitarian brotherhood fulfilled in America. Under the presidency of Hawthorne's friend Franklin Pierce, slaveholders and their northern allies had gained complete control of the government and were imposing the law of slavery on the entire country. Meanwhile, the racial prejudice Melville had long recognized as a major factor in the country's inability to resolve the problem of slavery was visibly on the rise.[14] Confronting a society that held itself up as a beacon to the world while its policies violated every tenet of the creed it professed, Melville turned from celebrating the ideals of democracy, equality, and Christian charity to exposing the nation's monstrous betrayal of them. That is, he turned from the epic mode of *Moby-Dick* to the satiric mode of *The Confidence-Man* and of sketches like "The Apple-Tree Table."

Ironically, in trying his hand at topical satire of the nostrums that sinister confidence-men were peddling to a gullible public, Melville was availing himself of a literary tradition shaped by social conservatives, whose hostility to humanitarian reformers he did not share. Hence he faced the challenge of adapting their conventions to a two-pronged attack on the watered-down Christianity and hollow philanthropy that conservative satirists lampooned, and on the ossified orthodoxy and callous social creed they promulgated in its place. These conventions, which Hawthorne had developed and bequeathed to Brownson, were the treatment of spiritualism and philanthropy as twin symptoms of the nineteenth century's moral degeneracy, the association of both movements with the devil, and the dramatization of the folk belief that the devil seduced people by masquerading as a lover of humanity and preaching a counterfeit Christianity in harmony with contemporary tastes. Melville would draw on all of these conventions in *The Confidence-Man*. But while working on that ambitious summation of his case against nineteenth-century America, he wrote a witty takeoff on the orthodox view of spiritualism that Brownson had presented in *The Spirit-Rapper*.[15]

"The Apple-Tree Table; or, Original Spiritual Manifestations" describes an eruption of mysterious ticking or rapping much like that which had occurred in the Fox household. At first circumstances seem to point toward a demonic explanation of the phenomenon. The ticking begins around midnight while the narrator is reading Cotton Mather's *Magnalia*, one of Brownson's chief authorities on demonism, and it emanates from a cloven-footed, "satanic-looking" old table, which had lain hidden for close to a century in the family's reputedly haunted garret (the Spirit-Rapper had conducted his earliest occult experiments with a similarly "necromantic" table).[16] Yet neither the fears of witchcraft that the narrator has imbibed from Mather nor the belief in spirits that his more up-to-date daughters espouse turns out to be warranted. Instead, a natural explanation for the ticking emerges when the narrator discovers that it issues from two bugs trying to eat their way out of the table. So much for Brownson's contention that such "spiritual manifestations" as the Fox sisters' rappings were supernatural phenomena produced by satanic agency.

More subversive than Melville's satire on supernatural explanations of spiritualism, however, is the parallel he suggests between the dubious origins of the spiritualist movement and those of Christianity itself, between the "miracles" that, according to spiritualists, testified to the soul's continued life after death, and the miracle of Christ's resurrection, which, according to Christian doctrine, testified to Christ's divinity and promised a future resurrection for all human beings. It is the narrator's daughters who personify this parallel. Forced to recognize that the "spirits" to which they had attributed the table's unaccountable ticking are mere insects, they do not abandon their belief in spirits, but resort to a practice contemporary transcendentalists had derived from the Puritans—that of seeking allegorical meanings in nature. Though not a spirit, they conclude, the "seraphical" bug whose "glorious" rebirth they have witnessed "yet teaches a spiritual lesson. For if, after one hundred and fifty years' entombment, a mere insect comes forth at last into light, . . . shall there be no glorified resurrection for the spirit of man?" (pp. 380, 382).

The lesson they formulate, moreover, fuses three main strands of nineteenth-century American Christianity: orthodox, transcendentalist, and spiritualist.[17] Like the orthodox Brownson, the narrator's daughters specifically refer to the doctrine of the resurrection, based on the story of Christ's resurrection from the tomb. Like the transcendentalist Thoreau, whose peroration to *Walden* they echo, they find their "faith in a resurrection and immortality strengthened" by an analogy from nature.[18] Like the spiritualists, the narrator's daughters speak in terms of the spirit, rather than the body, even when they use the orthodox term *resurrection*. Thus when the narrator informs us two sentences later that the "mysterious insect did not long enjoy its radiant life," but "expired the next day," he is simultaneously undercutting all three of the bases on which nineteenth-century Christians relied for their hope of immortality: the story of Christ's resurrection, the testimony of nature, and the existence of spirits. Melville's final shaft seems to be aimed directly at the form of orthodoxy to which Brownson subscribed—Catholicism; for the dead insect ends up as a relic, "embalmed in a silver vinaigrette" and regularly exhibited to those who, like doubting Thomas, demand tangible proof.

In "The Apple-Tree Table" Melville confined himself to turning Brownson's and Hawthorne's indictment of spiritualism on its head: instead of using spiritualism as a gauge of the nineteenth century's declension from true Christianity, he used it as a mirror of Christianity's own questionable foundations. In *The Confidence-Man*, Melville went on to explore the relationship between spiritualism and philanthropy that occupied such a prominent place in *The Blithedale Romance* and *The Spirit-Rapper*. Once again, as we shall see, his analysis of that relationship and his diagnosis of America's moral ills differed radically from Hawthorne's and Brownson's.

On a first reading, nevertheless, one can easily lose sight of the differences between *The Spirit-Rapper* and *The Confidence-Man* because of the affinities they exhibit. Edwin Fussell long ago pointed out the remarkable parallels betraying Melville's probable debt to

Brownson: the comparable caricatures of Emerson, the chapter titles that reverberate from one work to the other—"A Lesson in Philanthropy" (*The Spirit-Rapper*) and "A Philanthropist Undertakes to Convert a Misanthrope . . ." (*The Confidence-Man*), "Worth Considering" (*The Spirit-Rapper*) and "Worth the Consideration of Those to Whom It May Prove Worth Considering" (*The Confidence-Man*)—and above all, the satanic characters who masquerade as philanthropists.[19]

This last feature of *The Spirit-Rapper* may have suggested to Melville the daring revision of antireform satiric convention that became the basis for *The Confidence-Man*: replacing the simplistic figure of the devil with that of an apocalyptic Confidence-Man who would appear on Judgment Day to try American society by the moral values it professed, while seeming to endorse its travesty of those values. Although Melville's Confidence-Man plays a more complex role than Brownson's Spirit-Rapper, he burlesques many of the same tenets of nineteenth-century American Christianity. Like the Spirit-Rapper, who had postulated that "nature was good [and] . . . worked always to a good end" (*SR*, p. 69), the Confidence-Man advocates faith in the beneficence of nature. "Nature cannot work ill," he pontificates. "As little can she work error. Get nature, and you get well."[20]

Like the Spirit-Rapper, the Confidence-Man also promotes a Christianized version of the secular belief in progress and carries it to an extreme that reveals its dangerous moral implications. Claiming that progress is inherent in nature, he describes it as a process of "natural advance" in which "all creatures . . . bury themselves over and over again in the endless resurrection of better and better" (*CM*, p. 172). Thus, he argues, moral progress too is inevitable: bad children automatically grow into good adults, and the rake is but "crude material for the saint" (p. 173).

Like the Spirit-Rapper again, the Confidence-Man hails the "advance of the humanitarian spirit" and looks forward to a millennial age "when the whole world shall have been genialized, [and] it will be as out of place to talk of murderers, as in a Christianized world to talk of sinners" (*CM*, pp. 251–52). The evidence he cites of an approaching millennium, however, ironically belies the popular notion that American society is on the brink of attaining perfection. "Our age [is] the age of joint-stock companies and free-and-easies," he announces, thumbing his nose at the churches and benevolent organizations generally regarded as the chief symbols and agents of the nineteenth century's advance over "former and less humanitarian ages." That is, capitalism rather than humanitarianism is its ruling spirit, and money and drink rather than religion are the sources of its vaunted geniality.

Melville's satire of nineteenth-century American Christianity even encompasses one of Brownson's minor targets, Mormonism, which had furnished the Spirit-Rapper with a prototype for the spurious revelations of spiritualism. In his first guise as a lamblike deaf-mute, the Confidence-Man reminds one observer of a "green prophet from Utah" (CM, p. 10). When he later reappears as the President of the Black Rapids Coal Company, the Confidence-Man offers investors a choice between shares in his firm, with its overtones of hell, or in the New Jerusalem, a "new and thriving city, . . . originally founded by certain fugitive Mormons" (pp. 70–71).

It is in his treatment of Brownson's major targets—spiritualism and philanthropy—that Melville's profound disagreement with him becomes apparent, however. Through the Confidence-Man's two most important avatars, the mute who inaugurates his apocalyptic April Fools' Day masquerade and the cosmopolitan who climaxes it, Melville subverts the distinction Brownson makes between spiritualism and "true" Christianity, discredits the evidence on which Brownson bases his belief in demonic possession, exposes the fraudulence of the occult powers that Brownson concurs with spiritualists in pronouncing genuine, and redefines spurious philanthropy (which Brownson like Hawthorne associates with spiritualism) not as humanitarian social reform, but as its opposite—a Christian orthodoxy blind to the wrongs reformers sought to redress.

The mute strikes most of the characters who come into contact with him as either a lunatic or an impostor. One of them, indeed, explicitly suspects him of being a "spirit-rapper" (CM, p. 10). The mute's main activity—writing Saint Paul's pronouncements about charity on his slate—may well identify him as a slate-writing medium, since they too transcribed on slates messages dictated from the other world.[21] Coupled with his fleecy hat, "lamb-like figure," and mysterious "advent," on the other hand, the mute's silent preaching of charity seems more obviously to identify him with Christ, returned to try his followers on the day of reckoning. If so, he may be acting as a spirit-rapper in the most literal sense, by summoning the spirits of the dead for the Last Judgment. Melville's fusion of the two roles suggests that the difference between the spirit-rapper and the true Christ he impersonates is harder to discern than Brownson would admit. Whatever the mute's identity, his function is to expose the absence of Christian charity in a society that claims to be establishing Christ's kingdom on earth. The crowd on board the ironically named *Fidèle* not only rejects his message, but "thrust[s] him aside" with "epithets and . . . buffets" culminating in a symbolic crucifixion (*CM*, pp. 7, 9).

The mute's last avatar, the cosmopolitan, likewise makes an apocalyptic advent and plays the role of a spirit-rapper while preaching charity and philanthropy. He first manifests himself to the avowed misanthrope Pitch, whom he will vainly attempt to convert to philanthropy, as a "voice, sweet as a seraph's," speaking out of a "spicy volume of tobacco-smoke" (*CM*, p. 183), like the voice of God issuing from the clouds of smoke on Mount Sinai. During his subsequent encounters with other misanthropes, the cosmopolitan will seek to enforce charity on his interlocutors through both verbal exhortation and mesmeric influence. In each case, his transparent burlesque of mesmerism will simultaneously explode Brownson's demonic theory and reveal American society's imperviousness to philanthropy.

In the chapter "Showing That the Age of Magic and Magicians Is Not Yet Over," the cosmopolitan assumes the part of a "necromancer," literally, one who conjures up the spirits of the dead. The dead spirit in question is that of his erstwhile bosom friend, the Mississippi operator Charlie, who has just undergone a "metamorphosis more surprising than any in Ovid." Surrounding Charlie with a "magic-ring" of ten five-dollar gold pieces, waving "his long tasseled pipe with the air of a necromancer, an air heightened by his costume," and murmuring "cabalistical words," the cosmopolitan enjoins his "former friend" to "reappear, reappear, reappear." In the process of summoning his friend back from the dead, the cosmopolitan also performs an act of exorcism—the rite of driving evil spirits out of a possessed person—by banishing the "hideous apparition" that has taken possession of Charlie's "blest shape." That is why Melville describes the Mississippi operator as being "restored" to "self-possession" and "lost identity."

Obviously, the cause of Charlie's metamorphosis from an ingratiating friend into a venomous enemy is not an evil spirit, but disappointed greed: the cosmopolitan, whom he had intended to milk for money, has asked for a loan himself, thus beating Charlie at his own game. Similarly, the spell that restores Charlie to "self-possession" is not an authentic rite of exorcism or necromancy, but the sight of the very substance he covets—gold—in the very amount the cosmopolitan has asked to borrow. The episode thus parodies the cases of possession Brownson had cited in *The Spirit-Rapper* as evidence that evil spirits really exist.[22] It also offers Brownson an unwelcome confirmation of his view that it would be "all over with Christianity" if it could be proved that Jesus Christ, in instituting exorcism, and the Catholic Church, in "practising it for eighteen centuries," had been "deceived." Belying its title, the chapter shows that Brownson notwithstanding, the age of magic and magicians *is* over—if it ever existed. Ironically, however, the cosmopolitan's feigned necromancy and exorcism have accomplished the usual purposes of these occult rites—to divine hidden things and to rout demons. They have uncovered the Mississippi operator's true character and put to flight the "hideous apparition" of demonism that Brownson has identified with Christianity.

A later episode, the cosmopolitan's encounter with the barber, follows much the same pattern of intertwining satire on spiritualism with criticism of a society that cannot be infused with charity, even by supernatural means. Like the cosmopolitan's first interlocutor, Pitch, the barber rejects philanthropy in favor of a philosophy summed up in the sign he hangs over his door to discourage impecunious customers: "NO TRUST." Despite his lack of faith in humanity, the barber, like Brownson, proves credulous enough to believe in spiritualism and mesmerism. When the cosmopolitan approaches him as a disembodied voice, pronouncing a benediction "in tones not unangelic," the barber takes him for "a sort of spiritual manifestation" (*CM*, pp. 312–13). The circumstances, classic for a ghostly encounter, recall those of "The Apple-Tree Table." Here, too, the supposed "spiritual manifestation" occurs shortly before midnight, although the barber is not reading Cotton Mather, but dozing and dreaming "with back presented to the glare of his lamps, and so to the door." As it was in "The Apple-Tree Table," the illusion seems dispelled by a natural explanation, when the barber awakens to discover that the "spiritual manifestation" is "only a man." The cosmopolitan, however, counters this explanation with arguments reminiscent of Brownson's. "Don't be too sure what I am," he tells the barber, reminding him that angels and devils assumed human form in biblical times.

The words Melville uses to describe the barber's awakening— "disenchanted," "regained self-possession"—echo those applied to Charlie and suggest a parallel with the cosmopolitan's earlier simulation of necromancy and exorcism to expose Charlie's pretense of philanthropy for what it is. This time the cosmopolitan resorts to mesmerism to impose philanthropy on the barber, all rational and moral appeals having failed. By adopting a "magical" manner, "not wholly unlike the manner, fabled or otherwise, of certain creatures in nature, which have the power of . . . holding another creature by the button of the eye, as it were, despite the serious disinclination, and, indeed, earnest protest, of the victim," the cosmopolitan "irresistibly" impels the barber to "agree to try, for the remainder of the present trip, the experiment of trusting men, as both phrased it" (CM, p. 323).

Once again, the outcome of this episode serves at once to contradict Brownson and to comment wryly on the hopelessness of trying to convert the American public to philanthropy. Unlike the mesmeric powers Brownson attributes to the Spirit-Rapper, which hold his victims in thrall wherever they may be, even without their knowledge,[23] the cosmopolitan's mesmeric influence over the barber ceases to operate outside of his presence. No sooner is the barber left to himself, than he is "restored to his self-possession and senses" (another echo of the scene with Charlie), which he evinces by forthwith violating his agreement with the cosmopolitan and putting his "NO TRUST" sign back on the wall. "In fascination as in natural philosophy," concludes Melville, obviously taking issue with Brownson, "nothing can act where it is not" (CM, pp. 327–28).

IV

If the opposing views of spiritualism presented in The Spirit-Rapper and The Confidence-Man reveal the two authors' fundamental disagreement over religious principles, the contrasting targets they single out for opprobrium in attacking spurious philanthropy reveal a still more fundamental disagreement over social issues. Here it is useful to include Hawthorne in the comparison, since Brownson borrowed so heavily from him in formulating his analogous critique of reformers. Both Brownson and Hawthorne direct their harshest gibes at the humanitarian social reformers, whom they vilify by association with spiritualists. Both charge the advocates of such causes as prison reform, Utopian socialism, abolition, and women's rights with perverting the spirit of Christianity and restricting the tide of their benevolence to "one exclusive channel," as Hawthorne says of Hollingsworth, "so that there was nothing to spare for other great manifestations of love to man, nor scarcely for the nutriment of individual attachments, unless they could minister, in some way, to the terrible egotism" that reformers generally "mistook for an angel of God."[24] In all these respects, Melville conspicuously departs from the conventions of antireform satire. Far from linking spiritualism with humanitarian reform, he links it instead, as we have seen, with orthodox Christian beliefs and practices. Reserving his chief barbs for the opponents of humanitarian reform, and for their clerical allies, he centers his own indictment of America's religious hypocrisy on the oppression of blacks and Indians sanctioned by the church.

The leading embodiment of Christian hypocrisy in *The Confidence-Man* is the sanctimonious, long-faced man in gray. A veteran of the "charity business," he advertises an "invalid's easy-chair" promising relief to "the most restless body, . . . the most tormented conscience" (*CM*, pp. 54–55). The causes he promotes turn out to be variants of such easy-chairs for invalid consciences. The "Widow and Orphan Asylum recently founded among the Seminoles" (p. 42) allows the nation that has just produced these widows and orphans by waging a bloody territorial war against the Seminoles to congratulate itself on its benevolence. On a larger scale, the World's Charity Society the man in gray hopes to create would advance capitalism and imperialism in the name of Christianity, through missions injected with the "Wall street spirit." By taxing the entire population of the planet, "the pauper not less than the nabob" and "the heathen not less than the Christian," the man in gray proposes to raise funds for appeasing the London poor with "twenty thousand bullocks and one hundred thousand barrels of flour" and for sending "ten thousand missionaries in a body" to convert the Chinese "*en masse* within six months of the debarkation" (pp. 56–59).

Significantly, abolition is *not* one of the causes the man in gray promotes. In fact, while soliciting contributions from a wealthy slaveholder, the man in gray pointedly overlooks the manner in which this gentleman keeps his hands clean—through a "negro body-servant," whose hands do "most of his master's handling for him; having to do with dirt on his account, but not to his prejudices" (*CM*, p. 51). On a moral level the man in gray and the clerical establishment he represents fulfill much the same function as the gentleman's "negro body-servant": by lending him their moral sanction, they, too, help the slaveholder to retain his "spotlessness."

Like the cosmopolitan, however, the man in gray plays a dual role in the apocalyptic masquerade that Melville's Confidence-Man stages when he confronts America on the day of reckoning. Not only does he caricature the spokesmen of Christian orthodoxy, nearly all of whom had sided with southerners in suppressing abolitionist agitation, but he forces his interlocutors to reveal the hollowness of their charity. Even without bringing up the subject of slavery, for example, the man in gray unmasks the gentleman slaveholder as one of those Saint Paul referred to when he wrote, "though I bestow all my goods to feed the poor . . . and have not charity, it profiteth me nothing" (1 Cor. 13:3), for this gentleman, who contributes so generously to distant causes, yet feels nothing for his slave, displays a heart harder than the "granite" ones that the man in gray's eloquence "might crumble into gravel" (*CM*, p. 60).

In the guise of the man in gray, the Confidence-Man illustrates the churches' complicity with slaveholders in tacitly excluding slavery from the list of Christian concerns. In his later guise as the herb-doctor, he explicitly burlesques the position the churches had taken on slavery. Asked if he is an abolitionist, the herb-doctor responds by trying to express sympathy for his fellow man while dissociating himself from abolitionism and steering clear of condemning slavery: "If by abolitionist you mean a zealot, I am none; but if you mean a man, who, being a man, feels for all men, slaves included, and by any lawful act, opposed to nobody's interest, and therefore, rousing nobody's enmity, would willingly abolish suffering (supposing it, in its degree, to exist) from among mankind, irrespective of color, then am I what you say" (*CM*, p. 155).

This brilliant parody of the temporizing statements moderate churchmen issued from the pulpit also sums up Hawthorne's and Brownson's views on abolition. Both had pronounced slaves to be better off than laboring whites, and Hawthorne, in his campaign biography of Franklin Pierce, had advocated looking upon slavery "as

one of those evils which divine Providence does not leave to be rem-
edied by human contrivances, but which, in its own good time, by
some means impossible to be anticipated, but of the simplest and
easiest operation, when all its uses shall have been fulfilled, it causes
to vanish like a dream."[25] Through the mouth of the herb-doctor's
interlocutor Pitch, Melville delivers a stinging rebuke: "You are the
moderate man, the invaluable understrapper of the wicked man.
You, the moderate man, may be used for wrong, but are useless
for right" (CM, p. 155). Melville thus turns the weapons conservative satirists had used against reformers back on the conservatives
themselves.

The Confidence-Man's focus on slavery as the central moral issue
of the day furnishes the most clear-cut evidence of the deep humanitarian sympathies that ranged Melville with reformers, rather than
with the conservative satirists who lampooned them, in the ideological war the two parties were waging to determine the future shape
of American society. The Blithedale Romance and The Spirit-Rapper, of course, focus instead on women's rights, prison reform, utopianism, and the regnant transcendentalist philosophy of Brook
Farm, all of which they satirize in conjunction with spiritualism.
"Woman's-rights women," the prison reformer Elizabeth Gurney
Fry, and caricatures of Emerson and Thoreau likewise come up for
review in The Confidence-Man. Initially, Melville's treatment of
these reformers appears more consonant with Hawthorne's and
Brownson's. Closer examination, however, reveals that Melville is
satirizing rather than echoing their vilification of "woman's-rights
women" and criticizing Fry and Emerson for reasons entirely different from Hawthorne's and Brownson's.

The question of women's rights crops up in a highly ambiguous
interpolated tale of conjugal strife, told from the viewpoint of the
aggrieved husband. Its title, "Story of the Unfortunate Man, from
Which May Be Gathered Whether or No He Has Been Justly So Entitled," unmistakably warns readers to exercise judgment and to beware of uncritically accepting the testimony of the alleged unfortunate. The warning acquires direct relevance to the controversy over
women's rights when we realize that the story contains nearly all
the clichés of antifeminist literature.[26] Besides portraying a domi-
neering wife appropriately named Goneril and describing her perse-
cution of her husband, the "Story of the Unfortunate Man" attributes to this harridan the various traits male detractors commonly

attributed to "strong-minded," or feminist, women: "independence of mind" (Goneril deems it "honesty, to fling people's imputed faults into their faces"); masculine proclivities ("a trace of moustache," a relish for "brawn of ham" and "little dried sticks of blue clay, secretly carried in her pocket," and a corresponding "natural antipathy to such things as the breast of chicken, or custard, or peach, or grape"); nymphomaniac or "free love" tendencies ("a strange way of touching, as by accident, the arm or hand of comely young men"); and most damning of all in a woman, an utter lack of maternal feeling (CM, pp. 83–85).

According to her husband, Goneril conceives a "deranged jealousy" of their seven-year-old daughter, his "consolation and pet," and treats the child so viciously that he feels impelled to rescue it from her clutches by "accompanying it into domestic exile" (CM, pp. 85–86). The antifeminist animus of his tale becomes explicit when he proceeds to blame his ensuing misfortunes on "woman's-rights women." As a result of their making Goneril a cause célèbre and inciting her to file suit against him, he claims, she wins such a settlement as "not only to recover custody of the child, but . . . to make penniless the unfortunate man (so he averred)" (p. 86).

As the ironic qualifier in the last sentence implies, however, the unfortunate man is not a reliable witness. Indeed, Melville undermines his story in a number of ways: by telling it through a third-person narrator, in order not to "do better justice to the man than the story" (CM, p. 81); by emphasizing its virulently biased point of view at the outset (the very first sentence characterizes Goneril as "anomalously vicious"); by hinting at an Oedipal attachment between the unfortunate man and his daughter as a possible cause of the family's dissensions; and by ascribing the story to one of the sleaziest avatars of the Confidence-Man, the man with the weed, whose manifest purpose in telling this tale of woe is to wheedle charity out of the male auditor to whose masculine sympathies, antifeminist sentiments, and paranoid fears of women's rights he appeals.

There is considerable evidence, moreover, that Melville based the "Story of the Unfortunate Man" on an actual domestic imbroglio, the notorious divorce case of the Shakespearean actress Fanny Kemble (hence the name Goneril) and her husband, Pierce Butler, a Georgia slaveholder.[27] If so, he deliberately reversed the roles of the two parties—in reality the husband, rather than the wife, had shown what might be termed "deranged jealousy" in quarrels over the children, and after sending his wife into "domestic exile," had filed suit against her, winning custody of their two daughters. The effect is to underscore the absurdity of depicting men as victims of their wives in a society that concentrates all legal power in male hands.

The "Story of the Unfortunate Man" thus satirizes antifeminism in much the same way that other episodes of *The Confidence-Man* satirize spiritualism and abolitionism. It suggests that the masculine, nymphomaniac, henpecking harpy portrayed by antifeminist writers is nothing but the fabrication of a diseased male mind, and that the nightmare these writers obsessively conjured up, of women reducing men to impotence and destitution if granted the rights for which they were agitating, is nothing but the paranoid *lex talionis* fantasy of being subjected to the crippling legal disabilities they themselves impose on women. Once again, Melville has appropriated a convention of antireform satire and turned it against the conservative opponents of reform.

In the episodes of *The Confidence-Man* that deal with spiritualism, slavery, and women's rights, Melville seems to have addressed himself primarily to answering antireform satirists and polemicists. In the chapter he centers around the question of prison reform, on the contrary, he seems to be speaking directly to reformers and warning them against taking a narrow or "sentimental" approach toward the evils they are seeking to remedy.

Significantly, it is an ex-prisoner named Thomas Fry who brings up the issue. Asked by the herb-doctor if he is "anyway connected with *my* Mrs. Fry," the celebrated English prison reformer, Thomas Fry retorts: "Blister Mrs. Fry! What do them sentimental souls know of prisons or any other black fact? I'll tell ye a story of prisons. Ha, ha!" (*CM*, pp. 131–32).

To understand why Thomas Fry considers his illustrious namesake sentimental, we need to remember that Elizabeth Gurney Fry was most famous for her moral reformation of criminals, in which preaching and reading the Bible to them played the largest part. Although she also propagandized for improving physical conditions in the prisons, she regarded her main mission to be that of saving the prisoners' souls.[28] Implicit in her whole concept of prison reform was the assumption that prisoners were guilty of the crimes with which they had been charged and that it was the state of their souls, rather than the nature of the criminal justice system, much less the class structure of the society it served, that needed to be changed.

The "story of prisons" Thomas Fry proceeds to tell specifically challenges this assumption; for he claims to have been unjustly imprisoned as witness to a murder, while the murderer himself, a rich gentleman with influential "friends," was allowed out on bail and subsequently acquitted. Hence the "unhandsome notions" he now flaunts about "'free Ameriky,' as he sarcastically called his country" (CM, p. 136). Given a society in which money buys justice and poverty is punished as a crime, he implies, to talk of reforming prisoners, or even of upgrading prisons, is merely to delude oneself.

Whereas Melville criticizes prison reform as a sentimental substitute for social justice, Hawthorne flippantly dismisses it as "impracticable." Referring to the plan that his fictional philanthropist Hollingsworth has formulated "for the reformation of criminals, through an appeal to their higher instincts"—a plan much like Mrs. Fry's—Hawthorne comments: "He ought to have commenced his investigation of the subject by perpetrating some huge sin, in his proper person, and examining the condition of his higher instincts, afterwards" (BR, p. 36). In contrast to Melville, and even to Mrs. Fry, Hawthorne is arguing not only that prisoners are criminals, but that they are depraved beyond redemption. The ideological positions from which Hawthorne and Melville call prison reform into question could hardly be further apart.

V

The contemporary prophet who becomes the final touchstone for distinguishing among the varieties of antireform satire that Hawthorne, Brownson, and Melville produced is Emerson, whom all three recognize as the voice of nineteenth-century America personified. The portraits of Emerson that appear in "The Hall of Fantasy," The Spirit-Rapper, and The Confidence-Man bear a definite family resemblance. All highlight the peculiar amalgam of the practical and the mystical in Emerson's character and philosophy. All likewise place Emerson in relation to other transcendentalists and attempt to assess the impact his philosophy had on those who embraced it.

Nevertheless, the three portraits accentuate different facets of Emerson, each revealing its artist's distinctive angle of vision.

Of the three, Hawthorne's portrait is the least unflattering. He introduces Emerson into "the Hall of Fantasy"—a palace of dreams frequented by poets and philosophers, "real or self-styled reformers," religious leaders, inventors, and stock-exchange speculators—amid a circle of admirers including the Utopians of Brook Farm.[29] (The latter, Hawthorne remarks facetiously, "seem so far advanced . . . in the realization of their idea, that their sunburnt faces and toil-hardened frames may soon be denied admittance into the Hall of Fantasy.") Describing Emerson as transcendentalism's most powerful intellect, Hawthorne credits him with attempting to ground his philosophy in reality, even if he does not always succeed. Unlike his foil Alcott, for example, whom Hawthorne characterizes as "a dreamer, a bodiless idea" on the brink of "vanish[ing] into the sunshine," Emerson has "come into the hall in search . . . either of a fact or a real man." Still, Hawthorne hints, there is something of Alcott in Emerson. To search for facts or reality in the Hall of Fantasy, after all, seems doomed at the outset. Indeed in his notebooks, Hawthorne frankly calls it a "vain search."[30] Truth sometimes "assumes a mystic unreality and shadowyness in [Emerson's] grasp," complains Hawthorne, reiterating in his published sketch the opinion he had confided to his notebook the previous year. It is this tendency toward "mysticism" that constitutes Emerson's chief failing, in Hawthorne's eyes.

What Hawthorne disparages as mysticism, Brownson denounces as heresy. Caricaturing Emerson in *The Spirit-Rapper* as "Mr. Edgerton, a New England Transcendentalist, a thin, spare man, with a large nose, and a cast of Yankee shrewdness in his not unhandsome face," Brownson parodies his essays "Self-Reliance," "Nature," and "The Over-Soul." "Plant yourselves on your imperishable instincts," he has Mr. Edgerton preach. "Form no plan, . . . seek no moral, but . . . build as builds the bee her cell, sing as sings the bird, the grasshopper, or the cricket" (*SR*, p. 93). When the Catholic spokesman whom Brownson ranges against Mr. Edgerton accuses him of thinking that "the nearer men approach to birds and insects the better it will be for the world," Edgerton retorts: "I never dispute. . . . I utter the word given me to utter, and leave it as the ostrich leaveth her eggs. . . . If it is true, . . . it will prove itself. If it approves not itself to

you . . . it is not true for you" (p. 94). Obviously this relativistic philosophy is anathema to Brownson. As his Catholic spokesman
points out, it implies that "truth varies as vary individual minds,"
and consequently, that the Bible and the Church have no absolute
authority.

On first acquaintance, Melville's Mark Winsome looks and sounds
almost exactly like Brownson's Mr. Edgerton. "A blue-eyed man,
sandy-haired, and Saxon-looking . . . tall, and, but for a certain
angularity, well made," he too displays "one-knows-not-what of
shrewdness and mythiness, strangely jumbled," so that he seems "a
kind of cross between a Yankee peddler and a Tartar priest" (CM,
p. 265). And in his colloquy with the cosmopolitan, he too speaks in
accents parodying Emerson's essays and mimicking the master's
show of erudition. Throughout the six chapters devoted to reevalu-
ating Emerson's philosophy, however, Melville focuses on its ethical
rather than its doctrinal implications, on its practical rather than
its "mystical" tendencies. For all its seeming mysticism, Melville
charges, Emerson's philosophy is firmly rooted in the "cold-blooded"
ethic of laissez-faire capitalism, which draws "a red-ink line" between business and friendship and postulates that "there is something wrong about the man who wants help" (pp. 284, 288–89). That
is why Melville poses, as the ultimate test of this philosophy, whether
it will permit the exercise of charity, even in the form of a "friendly
loan." It is no accident that in the "hypothetical" case he formulates,
Melville has Mark Winsome's "practical disciple" assume the name
of Charlie. Charlie, of course, was also the name of the Mississippi
operator whose response to a loan request had been to metamor-
phose into a snake, for the icy-hearted transcendentalist merely provides a philosophical rationale for recoiling in disgust from anyone
who asks for charity.

VI

In their reactions to Emerson, as in their attitudes toward spiritualism and humanitarian reform, Hawthorne, Brownson, and Melville
thus typify three different forms of dissent from nineteenth-century
America's dominant millennial creed, all of which contributed to
defining and shaping the genre of antireform satire. Hawthorne's is
the dissent of a secular conservative, who has translated his Calvin-

ist ancestors' belief in innate depravity into a social philosophy that distrusts innovation, be it religious or political, and grimly denies the possibility of improving human life. Brownson's is that of a religious conservative, who sees the devil lurking behind every contemporary deviation from orthodoxy and who founds his opposition to social reform on a literal interpretation of the Bible. Melville's, finally, is that of a radical deeply committed to humanitarian values and outraged by the hypocrisy and cynicism of those who mouth Christian precepts, yet oppress their fellow human beings.

As a genre that arose in response to the concatenation of religious and social "Isms" culminating in spiritualism and women's rights, antireform satire serves to illuminate a persistent cultural pattern: the interpenetration of occultism and radical social protest. Antebellum America, where such leading reformers as William Lloyd Garrison, Horace Greeley, the Owens, and Paulina Wright Davis took a friendly interest in spiritualism and devoted space to it in their publications, while such leading spiritualists as Andrew Jackson Davis, LaRoy Sunderland, Giles Stebbins, and Mary Davis advocated socialism, abolitionism, and feminism, has not been exceptional in manifesting this pattern.[31] One historian, for example, has found a similar interpenetration between revolutionary and mesmerist circles in France during the 1780s and 1840s.[32] And the 1960s, of course, witnessed the meshing of the antiwar movement with the hippie cult of drugs, Eastern religions, and astrology.

To some extent, antireform satirists were raising a question that has engaged historians of these periods: why occultism and radical politics have so often sprung up side by side, and whether they have reinforced or diluted each other in converging on a common target. From opposing ideological standpoints, both Hawthorne and Melville were advancing the thesis most historians have propounded: that occultism represents a substitute for genuine efforts to promote social justice.[33] Yet this explanation of the appeal spiritualism held for antebellum Americans during a time of acute conflict over slavery, women's rights, and other humanitarian issues accounts mainly for those who retreated from social activism to private pietism, or who turned to spiritualism for reasons unrelated to their ideological convictions. It does not shed much light on why even such unremittingly active crusaders for abolition and women's rights as Garrison and Susan B. Anthony also flirted with spiritualism. Brownson suggests an intriguing answer. Because he not only execrated the social changes these reformers sought, as did Hawthorne, but attributed genuine power to the occult forces the spiritualists were invoking, as Hawthorne and Melville did not, Brownson sensed that spiritualism and mesmerism may have attracted reformers as potent means of aiding the transformation of society by altering individual and mass consciousness. In this he may not have been wholly wrong. The aim of promoting a change in attitude toward blacks, women, and the working class was certainly an important part of the abolitionist, feminist, and socialist programs for perfecting American society. Although most reformers relied on a combination of religious conversion and rational persuasion to bring about such change, some may well have hoped that the testimony of departed spirits would help to hasten it.[34] If so, the conjunction of antebellum spiritualism and reform may exemplify a dialectical relationship that has also characterized the reform movements of the twentieth century: the relationship between remolding attitudes and restructuring society.

NOTES

1. This essay adds a consideration of Hawthorne and antireform satire in general to my earlier article "Spiritualism and Philanthropy in Brownson's *The Spirit-Rapper* and Melville's *The Confidence-Man*," *ESQ* 25 (1979): 26–36, which is here substantially revised and expanded. For the history of antebellum reform, see Alice Felt Tyler, *Freedom's Ferment: Phases of American Social History from the Colonial Period to the Outbreak of the Civil War* (1944; rpt. New York: Harper and Row, 1962); Whitney R. Cross, *The Burned-Over District: The Social and Intellectual History of Enthusiastic Religion in Western New York, 1800–1850* (1950; rpt. New York: Harper and Row, 1965); and Ronald G. Walters, *American Reformers, 1815–1860* (New York: Hill and Wang, 1978).

2. See Howard Kerr, *Mediums, and Spirit-Rappers, and Roaring Radicals: Spiritualism in American Literature, 1850–1900* (Urbana: University of Illinois Press, 1972); and Taylor Stoehr, *Hawthorne's Mad Scientists: Pseudoscience and Social Science in Nineteenth-Century Life and Letters* (Hamden, Conn.: Archon Books, 1978). The quotation is from the subtitle of a satiric novel discussed by Kerr, the pseudonymous Fred Folio's *Lucy Boston; or, Women's Rights and Spiritualism, Illustrating the Follies and Delusions of the Nineteenth Century* (Boston: Shepard, Clark, 1855).

3. Quotations are from the original, uncut version of "The Hall of Fantasy," published in *The Pioneer* 1 (1843): 53, and from "Earth's Holocaust," in *The Works of Nathaniel Hawthorne*, Centenary Edition, ed. William Charvat et al. (Columbus: Ohio State University Press), vol. 10, *Mosses from an Old Manse* (1974), pp. 387, 389–91.

4. Page references to *The Blithedale Romance* will be to vol. 3 (1964) of *The Works of Nathaniel Hawthorne*, Centenary Edition, ed. William Charvat et al. (Columbus: Ohio State University Press), and will be given in the text, keyed to the abbreviation *BR*. Kerr traces the lineage of antireform satire from *The Blithedale Romance* to Brownson's *The Spirit-Rapper*, Folio's *Lucy Boston*, Bayard Taylor's *Hannah Thurston: A Story of American Life* (1864), and James's *The Bostonians* (1886).

5. See Arthur M. Schlesinger, Jr., *Orestes A. Brownson: A Pilgrim's Progress* (Boston: Little, Brown, 1939), chaps. 2, 5.

6. Orestes A. Brownson, *"The Blithedale Romance," Brownson's Quarterly Review*, n.s. 6 (October 1852), p. 564.

7. *The Works of Orestes A. Brownson*, ed. Henry F. Brownson, 20 vols. (Detroit: H. F. Brownson), vol. 5, *The Convert* (1882), p. 93.

8. Orestes A. Brownson, *The Spirit-Rapper: An Autobiography* (Boston: Little, Brown, 1854), pp. 4, 46. All further page references to this edition will be given in the text, keyed to the abbreviation *SR*.

9. See *The Convert*, pp. 57–63, for Brownson's reminiscences of Frances Wright.

As Kerr points out in *Mediums, and Spirit-Rappers, and Roaring Radicals*, p. 86, Brownson also drew on Lucretia Mott and Elizabeth Cady Stanton as models for his feminist freethinker.

10. Compare *The Blithedale Romance*, pp. 120–21, 224, and *The Spirit-Rapper*, p. 80. For a biographical sketch of Frances Wright, see the entry on her in *Notable American Women, 1607–1950: A Biographical Dictionary*, ed. Edward T. James, Janet Wilson James, and Paul S. Boyer (Cambridge, Mass.: Harvard University Press, 1971), 3:675–79.

11. In *The Convert*, chaps. 8–9, Brownson offers a parallel account of his dream of becoming the "Messiah of the nineteenth century."

12. Merrell R. Davis and William H. Gilman, eds., *The Letters of Herman Melville* (New Haven: Yale University Press, 1960), pp. 126–27.

13. Herman Melville, *Moby-Dick; or, The Whale*, ed. Harrison Hayford and Hershel Parker (New York: Norton, 1967), pp. 52, 105.

14. I have discussed these issues more fully in *Shadow over the Promised Land: Slavery, Race, and Violence in Melville's America* (Baton Rouge: Louisiana State University Press, 1980).

15. On the dating of "The Apple-Tree Table" and *The Confidence-Man*, see Merton M. Sealts, Jr., "The Chronology of Melville's Short Fiction, 1853–1856," *Harvard Library Bulletin* 28 (1980): 402–3; and Elizabeth Foster's introduction to *The Confidence-Man: His Masquerade* (New York: Hendricks House, 1954), p. xxiii.

16. Herman Melville, "The Apple-Tree Table," in *Great Short Works of Herman Melville*, ed. Warner Berthoff (New York: Harper and Row, 1969), pp. 362, 366–67. The Spirit-Rapper describes his experiments with "table turning" in the chapter by that title.

17. This interpretation is a refinement of the one I presented in "The 'Spiritual Lesson' of Melville's 'The Apple-Tree Table,'" *American Quarterly* 23 (1971): 108–9, where I argued that the daughters' language was merely orthodox.

18. The echo of *Walden* was first pointed out by Frank Davidson, "Melville, Thoreau, and 'The Apple-Tree Table,'" *American Literature* 25 (1954): 483–84, 487. Thoreau tells the story of the apple-tree table, which he and Melville both derived from other sources, in the next to last paragraph of *Walden*.

19. Edwin Fussell, *Frontier: American Literature and the American West* (Princeton: Princeton University Press, 1965), p. 308n.

20. Herman Melville, *The Confidence-Man: His Masquerade*, ed. H. Bruce Franklin (Indianapolis: Bobbs-Merrill, 1967), p. 112. All further page references to this edition will be given in the text, keyed to the abbreviation *CM*.

21. On writing mediums in general, see Kerr, *Mediums, and Spirit-Rappers, and Roaring Radicals*, pp. 5, 15–18; on slate-writing mediums, see Frank Podmore, *Modern Spiritualism: A History and Criticism*, 2 vols. (London: Methuen, 1902), 1:248, 2:87–90, 204–22.

22. See *The Spirit-Rapper*, chaps. 11, 18–19.

23. See *The Spirit-Rapper*, chap. 6.

24. Compare *The Spirit-Rapper*, pp. 49–50, 91–92, with *The Blithedale Romance*, pp. 55, 243. The quotation is from the latter, p. 55.

25. For Brownson's views on slavery, see *The Spirit-Rapper*, pp. 100–101; *The Convert*, pp. 117–18; and his essay "The Laboring Classes," *Boston Quarterly Review* 3 (1840): 368–71; also Schlesinger, *Orestes A. Brownson*, pp. 79–80, 90–91,

240–46. For Hawthorne's views, see Allen Flint, "Hawthorne and the Slavery Crisis," *New England Quarterly* 41 (1968): 393–408, and Hawthorne's *Life of Franklin Pierce*, in the Riverside Edition of *The Complete Works of Nathaniel Hawthorne*, ed. George Parsons Lathrop, 12 vols. (Boston: Houghton Mifflin, 1888), 12:414–17. The quotation is from the latter, p. 417.

26. For an example of the antifeminist literature Melville is parodying, see Folio's *Lucy Boston*. Many of the same clichés also appear in Taylor's *Hannah Thurston* and James's *The Bostonians*.

27. Egbert S. Oliver, "Melville's Goneril and Fanny Kemble," *New England Quarterly* 18 (1945): 489–500, notes the similarities between the two cases, but concludes that Melville's intent was to vilify Fanny Kemble. Foster, ed., *The Confidence-Man*, pp. 311–14n. points out the differences between the two cases in order to show that Melville could not have been "guilty of savage, malicious personal satire." An examination of Butler's testimony reveals that Melville is burlesquing it in the manner in which he burlesques James Hall's writings in the Indian-hater chapters. See Pierce Butler, *Mr. Butler's Statement, Originally Prepared in Aid of His Professional Counsel* (Philadelphia: J. C. Clark, 1850); also the newspaper clippings from the *New York Evening Post*, December 7 and 14, 1848, assembled in Pierce Butler, *Pierce Butler vs. Frances Anne Butler, Libel for Divorce, with Answer and Exhibits* (Philadelphia: n.p., 1848). Fanny Kemble also published her own version of the story: *The Answer of Frances Anne Butler to the Libel of Pierce Butler, Praying a Divorce from the Bonds of Matrimony* (Philadelphia: n.p., 1848). The judge who ruled in Pierce Butler's favor ordered her narrative stricken from the record on the grounds that it was "extraneous."

28. See W. G. Blaikie's article in the *Dictionary of National Biography* s.v. "Fry, Elizabeth"; and Michael Ignatieff, *A Just Measure of Pain: The Penitentiary in the Industrial Revolution, 1750–1850* (New York: Pantheon Books, 1978), pp. 143–74. Ignatieff brilliantly analyzes the politics of prison reform and contrasts philanthropists like Elizabeth Fry with their radical contemporaries, whose views resemble Thomas Fry's.

29. Nathaniel Hawthorne, "The Hall of Fantasy," *The Pioneer* 1 (1843): 52–53.

30. Nathaniel Hawthorne, *The Works of Nathaniel Hawthorne*, Centenary Edition, ed. William Charvat et al. (Columbus: Ohio State University Press), vol. 8, *The American Notebooks* (1972), pp. 336, 357.

31. On the alliance between spiritualists and reformers, see R. Laurence Moore, *In Search of White Crows: Spiritualism, Parapsychology, and American Culture* (New York: Oxford University Press, 1977), chap. 3; Walters, *American Reformers*, pp. 167–72; and Cindy S. Aron, "Levitation and Liberation: Women Mediums in Nineteenth-Century America," M.A. thesis, University of Maryland, 1975, chap. 3.

32. See Robert Darnton, *Mesmerism and the End of the Enlightenment in France* (Cambridge, Mass.: Harvard University Press, 1968).

33. See, for example, Moore, *In Search of White Crows*, pp. 74, 88, 100, and Walters, *American Reformers*, pp. 167–72.

34. Walters, *American Reformers*, pp. 169–70, and Robert H. Abzug, *Passionate Liberator: Theodore Dwight Weld and the Dilemma of Reform* (New York: Oxford University Press, 1980), pp. 251–53, advance a similar hypothesis.

BARTON LEVI ST. ARMAND

"I Must Have Died at Ten Minutes Past One": Posthumous Reverie in Harriet Prescott Spofford's "The Amber Gods"

Emily Dickinson was not the only protégée of that extraordinary reformer and man of letters, Thomas Wentworth Higginson. Another author who was equally entitled to call Higginson "Master" or "Dear Preceptor" because of his unstinting help, advice, and promotional efforts on her behalf was the young Harriet Prescott. A "demure little Yankee girl" whom Higginson had encouraged during his tenure as minister of the First Religious Society of Newburyport in the 1850s, Miss Prescott, later Mrs. Spofford, made her early reputation as the author of extravagant and sensational narratives.[1] Her first effort in this line, "a tale of crime and espionage in the very highest circles of French and British society," was called "In a Cellar," and it caused much consternation to the editor of the *Atlantic Monthly*, James Russell Lowell, when Prescott submitted it to him through the good offices of Higginson. So authentic did the details of "In a Cellar" seem that Higginson had to assure Lowell that the story was not simply a clever translation from the French. It duly appeared in February of 1859, launching Harriet Prescott Spofford on a long-lived and notable career. Higginson, a gregarious and genial man, tried to interest his even demurer and more retiring correspondent, Emily Dickinson, in Spofford's work, but she shied away, claiming that Spofford's grim narrative of a pioneer woman worried by a ferocious mountain lion, entitled "Circumstance" and published in the *Atlantic* for May of 1860, "followed me, in the Dark—so I avoided her."[2] Yet of the same story the poet wrote to her sister-in-law, Susan Huntington Dickinson, that it "was the only thing I ever saw in my life that I did not think I could have written myself," while she begged that Sue send her forthwith "everything she writes."[3]

As a faithful reader of the *Atlantic*, Dickinson would have read not only "Circumstance" but also Spofford's "The Amber Gods," a florid exercise in posthumous reverie that was published in January and February of 1860, as well as her supernatural novel, *Sir Rohan's Ghost*, which appeared the same year and was reviewed by Lowell himself in the February number. Even if Dickinson had denied herself any further taste of Spofford's work by April of 1862, the date of her letter to Higginson, she would have imbibed enough of the rich

vintage of 1860 to last a lifetime. For Harriet Prescott Spofford is a
representative in fiction of a native American Della Cruscan school,
a mannered Romanticism that we usually sample only in the more
frenzied passages of Harriet Beecher Stowe's work or in the calculated perversities of Herman Melville's *Pierre*. That this school had
great power is undeniable, but that it was also—to use a favorite ad-
jective of both Spofford and Dickinson—"phosphorescent" in its
effect is demonstrated by the reminiscences of one of its most devoted readers. Writing in the *Century Magazine* in November of
1910, Elizabeth Stuart Phelps, author of the phenomenally successful *The Gates Ajar*, took as her topic the subject of "Stories That
Stay." When she discusses "The Amber Gods," Phelps speaks like
one who has been struck by lightning. She calls that tale "a story
which took a grip upon something deeper than taste or imagination
in me," but also confesses that

> the interesting thing about it is that the controlling power
> lay in a single sentence. At this time I can recall nothing
> about the story except its closing words. The essential art of
> the work converged upon its last sentence; this has outlived
> the plot or action or style, and has survived within me for
> the large and active part of a life. . . . What happened? Who
> *were* the amber gods? Who was the hero? Who the heroine?
> What were their accidents and incidents, their woes and
> joys? It may be small credit to me that I cannot answer one
> of these elementary questions.[4]

A modern reprint of "The Amber Gods" misses Phelps's point entirely by leaving off the last sentence and the whole section that precedes it, falsely calling it an "absolutely conventional" sequel.[5] In
fact it was this very dénouement that most startled contemporaries
like Phelps with its "alien chill" and its suggestion of "something
pagan, something pantheistic . . . that smote the young Christian in
the face of her faith." What Spofford accomplishes in her narrative is
a complete inversion of Poe's theory of the well-made tale. "The
Amber Gods" is consummately a tale of effect, but it does not progress through a honing of plot and language toward a single, preconceived end. Rather, Spofford builds startling contrasts to her tight,
premeditated closure through extravagance of diction, imagery, and
metaphor. In his review of Hawthorne's *Twice-Told Tales*, Poe
writes in a justly famous passage:

A skillful literary artist has constructed a tale. If wise, he has not fashioned his thoughts to accommodate his incidents; but having conceived, with deliberate care, a certain unique or single *effect* to be wrought out, he then invents as may best aid him in establishing this preconceived effect. If his very initial sentence tend not to the outbringing of this effect, then he has failed in his first step. In the whole composition there should be no words written, of which the tendency, direct or indirect, is not to the one pre-established design. And by such means, with such care and skill, a picture is at length painted which leaves in the mind of him who contemplates it with a kindred art, a sense of the fullest satisfaction. The idea of the tale has been presented unblemished because undisturbed: and this is an end unattainable by the novel. Undue brevity is just as exceptionable here as in the poem; but undue length is yet more to be avoided.[6]

"The Amber Gods" is, for a short story, unduly long, unduly rambling, and unduly indirect, yet it appropriates two of Poe's favorite themes: posthumous reverie and the death of a beautiful woman. Rather than a dialogue like "The Colloquy of Monos and Una" or "The Conversation of Eiros and Charmion," Spofford's narrative is a monologue, a passionate declamation, confessional in nature and remarkable in its anticipation of stream-of-consciousness technique. As Lee Edwards and Arlyn Diamond describe it, "The Amber Gods" is "an extended monologue by the heroine, Giorgione Willoughby, expressing an intense sensuality which is both compelling and terrifying in its self-absorption" (p. 16). It is a ghostly tale, but one of the secrets of its power is how it challenges the reader to ascertain the nature of the spirit that tells it.

Perhaps it is misleading to consider Giorgione Willoughby as the heroine of "The Amber Gods," for she emerges as a modern emblem of Luxuria or Vanitas, her destiny to a great extent decreed by her own voracious appetites. There is nothing "spirituelle" about her, and by putting a sensual Dark Lady in the skin of a typical, sentimental Blond Maiden, Spofford accomplishes another inversion that was calculated to send shivers up and down the spine of her mid-Victorian audience.[7] Yone, as she calls herself for short, using her "baby name," revels in her perverse blondness, and while posturing before a symbolic mirror dwells on her own paradoxical nature:

Sunbeams like to follow me, I think. Now when I stand in one before this glass, infiltrated with a rich tinge, don't I look like the spirit of it just stepped out for inspection? I seem to myself like the complete incarnation of light, full, bounteous, overflowing, and I wonder at and adore anything so beautiful; and the reflection grows finer and deeper while I gaze, till I dare not do so any longer. So, without more words, I am a golden blonde.[8]

Yone is a psychic vampire who feeds largely upon herself and the praise of others, and her childlike narcissism takes on darker resonances when we remember that Bram Stoker's Van Helsing compares Count Dracula to an infant in his immature longing for life pure and simple.[9] "I am used to admiration, now, certainly," Yone declares. "It is my food; without it I should die of inanition, but do you suppose I care any more for those who give it to me than a Chinese idol does for whoever swings incense before it?" (p. 19).

Like Dracula, Yone clings to mere being for its own sake, and so is spiritually stillborn. Yet like Nathaniel Hawthorne's Phoebe in *The House of the Seven Gables*, she at first seems to be an animated sunbeam, a wonder-working light bearer. Beneath this fair exterior, however, lurks a Lilith, a Cleopatra, a Medusa. Yone herself describes her hair as "Lucrezia Borgian, spun-gold, and ought to take the world in its toils"; she makes other pointed references to Clytemnestra and Isis (p. 5). The horror of her inverted nature is best expressed by Herman Melville in *Pierre*, when he meditates on "that sweetest, most touching, but most awful of feminine heads—The Cenci of Guido." Melville writes:

The wonderfulness of [this] head consists chiefly, perhaps, in a striking, suggested contrast, half identical with, and half analogous to, that almost supernatural one—sometimes visible in the maidens of tropical nations—namely, soft and light blue eyes, with an extremely fair complexion, veiled by funerally jetty hair. But with blue eyes and fair complexion, the Cenci's hair is golden—physically, therefore, all is in strict, natural keeping; which, nevertheless, still the more intensifies the suggested fanciful anomaly of so sweetly and seraphically *blonde* a being, being double-hooded, as it were, by the black crape of the two most horrible crimes (of one of which she is the object, and of the other the agent) possible to civilized humanity—incest and parricide.[10]

As a tropical exotic growing in stony New England soil, Giorgione Willoughby does not approach the enormity of the Cenci's transgressions, but given the Puritan roots of her surroundings, her sins are no less spectacular and unpardonable. They consist of her total amorality and single-minded worship of self. Yone's pride is almost sublime in its egotistical vastness: "I'm not good, of course; I wouldn't give a fig to be good. So it's not vanity. It's on a far grander scale; a splendid selfishness,—authorized, too; and papa and mamma brought me up to worship beauty,—and there's the fifth commandment, you know" (p. 7). That she does not hesitate to use the fifth commandment ("Honor thy father and thy mother") as a means of justifying her continual breaking of the first ("I am the Lord thy God: Thou shalt not have strange Gods before me") is the least of Yone's blasphemies, for her entire life is an affront to orthodox piety. The strange gods that Yone prefers above all others, including herself, are the beads of the amber necklace which gives the story its title. This necklace has been transmuted into a rosary, but even the fact that it has been blessed by the pope cannot exorcise its primordial evil.

Yone, who can "wear only concretions and growths" rather than the "crystallizations" represented by precious stones, feels a natural affinity with the grotesque, carved gods of the necklace. Her orphan cousin Lu is drawn to the purity of aquamarine, which reflects back her own soft nature. "What is your idea of a Louise?" Yone asks. "Mine is,—dark eyes, dark hair, decided features, pale, brown pale, with a mole on the left cheek,—and that's Louise. Nothing striking, but pure and clear, and growing always better" (pp. 21–22). The amber necklace by contrast is both a totem and a talisman, a throwback to that oceanic pagan consciousness that Yone represents:

> Why, observe the thing; turn it over; hold it up to the window; count the beads,—long, oval, like some seaweed bulbs, each an amulet. See the tint; it's very old; like clots of sunshine,—aren't they? Now bring it near; see the carving, here corrugated, there faceted, now sculptured into hideous, tiny, heathen gods. You didn't notice that before! How difficult it must have been, when amber is so friable! Here's one with a

chessboard on his back, and all his kings and queens and pawns slung round him. Here's another with a torch, a flaming torch, its fire pouring out inverted. They are grotesque enough;—but this, this is matchless: such a miniature woman, one hand grasping the round rock behind, while she looks down into some gulf, perhaps, beneath, and will let herself fall. O, you should see *her* with a magnifying-glass! You want to think of calm satisfying death, a mere exhalation, a voluntary slipping into another element? There it is for you. They are all gods and goddesses. They are all here but one; I've lost one, the knot of all, the love of the thing. Well! Wasn't it queer for a Catholic girl to have at prayer? (pp. 7–8)

The emblematic images that Yone catalogues are all indicative of the transient quality of existence, and convey a sense of fatality: the puppetlike game of life, the certainty of death, the imminence of the void. But since Yone is herself an emblem of life without consequence, her own hollow being is absorbed into the vacant space where the true lover's knot should be. The amber gods are a potent charm, and Yone is the amber witch who conspires with them to draw a magic circle around her cousin, depriving Lu of the man they both love, Vaughan Rose. Yone and the necklace are of one substance, symbolically united in an unholy marriage, for when she first sees the bauble and is asked why she should possess it rather than her cousin, she replies, "Why, to wear, too,—to look at,—to have and to hold, for better, for worse,—to say my prayers on" (pp. 8–9).

The necklace itself originates in the sinister East, where it is first brought into the family by a "little islander, an Asian imp, six years old, wilder than the wind," who is imported by Yone's great-grandfather, a sea captain who is also a slave trader. The owner of the amber gods is found to be too untamable for New England and so is packed off to New Holland by the Willoughbys, where she is subsequently shipwrecked and finally adopted by a rich Florentine family. In the Willoughby family these events assume mythic proportions: "In my great-grandmother's home, however, the tradition of the Asian sprite with her string of amber gods was handed down like a legend, and, no one knowing what had been, they framed many a wild picture of the Thing enchanting all her spirits from their beads about her, and calling and singing and whistling up the winds with them till storm rolled round the ship, and fierce fog and foam and drowning fell upon her capturers" (p. 13).

It is only years later that Yone's father sees a young girl telling her beads on the amber necklace; the place is ancient Fiesole above Florence, and the girl is accompanied by an ancient Asian slave. At the same moment a ray of light illuminates a painting by Giorgione, the subject for which Yone says could have been a Venus or a Magdalen or a Madonna or "something I fancy the man painted for himself, and christened for others." Yone's father returns to America, but, haunted by his experience in the church, is compelled to seek out the girl, eventually winning her as his wife. He overcomes the "sundry belligerent demonstrations" of the little Asian by confronting her with the only two words she had learned during her New England exile: "Willoughby" and the town's name. These act as runes of power controlling the "rancorous hate" of the dwarf, but in good fairy-tale fashion she curses the marriage, declaring that the new Mrs. Willoughby's charms would never cross the water, "that all their blessing would be changed to banning, and that bane would burn the bearer, should the salt-sea spray again dash round them" (pp. 14–15).

This intricate Gothic ritual sets the stage for Yone's entrance into the plot, for she is inextricably linked to the vignette of the painting, the beautiful girl, the withered dwarf, and the amber rosary that her father beholds in the Florentine church. It is as if her being is conceived at this moment, a mingled product of sensual delight and occult malediction, for only years later, like Venus, is she actually "born upon the sea, in a calm far out of sight of land, under sweltering suns." Moreover, Yone is "twice-born" in a way that again emphasizes the vampire side of her strange nature: "Not that I was always what I am now," she declares:

> Oh, bless your heart! plums and nectarines and luscious things that ripen and develop all their juices, were green once, and so was I. Awkward, tumble-about, near-sighted, till I was twenty, a real raw-head-and-bloody-bones to all society; then mamma, who was never well in our diving-bell atmosphere, was ordered to the West Indies, and papa said it was what I needed, and I went, too . . . when I reached the islands my sight was as clear as my skin; all that tropical

luxuriance snatched me to itself at once, recognized me for
kith and kin; and mamma died, and I lived. (pp. 15–16)

Recalling the plot of Poe's "Ligeia," Yone's metamorphosis from a
demonic raw-head-and-bloody-bones nightmare into a seductive
blond temptress is dependent on the sacrifice of another woman—in
this case, her own mother. Symbolically, then, Yone rivals Beatrice
Cenci by committing an unpremeditated matricide, while the Cenci's act of incest is sublimated into her appropriation of Vaughan
Rose, the lover she wrests away from Cousin Lu, her sister in everything but temperament. As if it were alive, the string of amber beads
breaks when Lu and Yone exchange their jewelry at an evening party,
with Yone looking like "the moon in a halo" decked out in her
cousin's aquamarine and a "cruel, savage dress, very like, but ineffa-
bly gorgeous." Like a priestess of Hecate, Yone conspires with the
moonlight to work her witchery on all about her. "A full moon is
poison to some; they shut it out at every crevice, and do not suffer a
ray to cross them; it has a chemical or magical effect; it sickens
them. But I am never more free and royal than when the subtle ce-
lerity of its magic combinations, whatever they are, is at work" (p.
44). The shattered necklace releases its perverse aroma as one of the
charms is crushed; along with Yone these narcissistic and cannibalis-
tic gods offer up worship to their own selves. Vaughan Rose "breathed
the penetrating incense of each separate amulet," and Yone sees that
"from that hour, when every atom of his sensation was tense and
vibrating, [Louise] would be associated with the loathed amber in his
undefined consciousness, would be surrounded with an atmosphere
of its perfume, that Lu was truly sealed from him in it, sealed into
herself" (p. 45). The amber gods trap Lu like an unwary fly.
    But flies are not the only objects to be trapped in amber, and Yone
suggests the possibility of something else that could be sealed in its
golden time capsule. "What if in some piece of amber," she asks during a conversation with Rose on the properties of that strange substance, "an accidental seed were sealed; we found, and planted, and
brought back the lost aeons? What a glorious world that must have
been where even the gum was so precious!" (pp. 28–29). Rose has a
virulent antipathy toward amber, calling it "unnatural" and comparing its acrid perfume to that of a putrid relic. It is precisely this antipathy that causes him unconsciously to reject Louise when she
wears the amber gods. Yone's attraction for them and her specula-

tion that there are "hidden relations between us and certain sub-stances" indicates that she herself is a primeval seed that has broken out of its golden husk and fructified in the tropics, a strange exotic, who, as her father puts it, sailed to the West Indies "persimmon" and returned "apricot" (p. 18).

That is, she went to the West Indies red as a persimmon (unripe, raw, hard) and came back refined, mellow, peach-colored. Spofford is again archetypal in her conjuration of this lost, predatory realm of which Yone is the bad seed. Rose recognizes that the images of the amber gods are in fact "all those very Gnostic deities who assisted at Creation," archons and demiurges only temporarily imprisoned. As he explains, amber is fundamentally evil because "when we hold it in our hands, we hold also that furious epoch where rioted all mon-sters and poisons,—where death fecundated and life destroyed,—where superabundance demanded such existences, no souls, but fiercest animal fire—just for that I hate it" (p. 29).

Yone sees a different trance-vision of this lost primeval world, which is an integral part of her own consciousness. Rose tries to de-mythologize amber by calling it merely "fossil gum," but Yone de-scribes its formation in terms of a phenomenology that combines all that symbolism of extravagance, sorcery, and savage beauty that characterizes her own being:

> Can you say those words and not like it? Don't it bring to you a magnificent picture of the pristine world,—great seas and other skies,—a world of accentuated crises, that sloughed off age after age, and rose fresher from each plunge? Don't you see, or long to see, that mysterious magic tree out of whose pores oozed this fine solidified sunshine? What leaf did it have? what blossom? what great wind shivered its branches? Was it a giant on a lonely coast, or thick low growth blistered in ravines and dells? That's the witchery of amber,—that it *has* no cause,—that all the world grew to produce it, maybe,—died and gave no other sign,—that its tree, which must have been beautiful, dropped all its fruits,— and how bursting with juice must they have been— (p. 28)

Yone's overwrought rhetoric is itself an objective correlative of that luxuriance that is to doom her, for with her superabundant fluen-cies, she, too, is like an exotic fruit "bursting with juice" that decays as soon as it drops to the ground. The first segment of "The Amber Gods" is entitled "Flower o' the Peach," and perhaps we can be excused if the stylistic analogue that springs immediately to mind is Melville's parodic description in *Pierre* of the gift-book prose that Spofford was to cultivate to overripe perfection: "a volume bound in rose-leaves, clasped with violets, and by the beaks of humming-birds printed with peach-juice on the leaves of lilies" (p. 45). While Melville, writing eight years before the appearance of "The Amber Gods," was consciously exaggerating the Sentimental-Gothic style for purposes of satire, Spofford was equally conscious of the opulence (if not the absurdity) of her escalated language. Yet the style of "The Amber Gods" is "organic" in the sense that it perfectly reflects the tropical prodigality of Yone's tawny and tigerish nature, of what she herself calls "my florid health, my rank redundant life." And this leads us to a consideration of the meaning of the character of Giorgione Willoughby, both as an aberrant type in American fiction and as a particular kind of supernatural narrator.

We could classify "The Amber Gods" as either a ghost story or as an abortive Gothic romance, for it is obvious by this point that Yone is fated to submit to her greatest enemy and her greatest fear, the "wasting disease of death." She is not alone in being "hostile" to "focal concentration and obscure decomposition," for again we have in American literature the example of Poe's "Ligeia," an equally extravagant personality who chants of the horrors of "The Conqueror Worm" and who seeks to avoid the necessary dissolution of death. In Yone's own last name is encoded a message about the imperative nature of human volition (will, oh be!) that recalls Poe's pun on the duplicity of selfhood in "William Wilson" or Ligeia's own passionate quotation of Joseph Glanvill: "Who—who knoweth the mysteries of the will, with its vigor? Man doth not yield him to the angels, *nor unto death utterly*, save only through the weakness of his feeble will" (p. 216). The frustration of Yone's profane worship of a life totally dedicated to overbred self-indulgence might even tempt us to think of the tale as "The Fall of the House of Willoughby," since she boasts that "I am the last of the Willoughbys, a decayed race, and from such a strong decay what blossom less gorgeous should spring?" (p. 58). Nor is Yone the only Fatal Woman to be found in American fiction. What makes "The Amber Gods" such a startling exotic in native nineteenth-century literary history is once more Spofford's prevailing technique of inversion: Yone tells her own story and allows us to participate in an inside narrative of her sensual life, even if she has to do so from beyond the grave.

If the Court of Charlemagne can be looked upon as a "little Renaissance" that heralded the greater classical revival of the fifteenth and sixteenth centuries, then "The Amber Gods" is a potent foretaste of that late nineteenth-century decadence which effloresced in such foreign works as the novels of Flaubert and the poetry of Swinburne. I need not trace the archetype of the Fatal Woman in European literature, since that task has already been so well accomplished by Mario Praz in *The Romantic Agony*,[11] but even given the fact that the figure of "La Belle Dame Sans Merci" could have originated in Spofford's beloved Keats or in any of those protodecadent works that Keats and the early Romantic poets inspired—Gautier's *Une Nuit de Cléopâtre* (1845) or Mérimée's *Vénus d'Ille* (1837)— Giorgione Willoughby remains one of the most original female characters in our literature. It is as if *The Blithedale Romance* were told not by the self-deluded and pathetic Miles Coverdale but by the haughty and tragic Zenobia, speaking after her suicide from the other world, or, better, as if Spofford has perversely combined the sunny spontaneity of Hawthorne's Phoebe from *The House of the Seven Gables* with the pulsating energy of his doomed and darker heroine. Recently, Nina Baym has helped us to understand this duality by observing that "sexual and poetic energy are varying forms of the same drive. In her symbolic function Zenobia stands for the creative energy of both nature and self." She also remarks that "one astute critic of *The Blithedale Romance* has observed that Zenobia is linked to Phoebe through frequent sun images, and the point is certainly valid; but Phoebe's is a capacity for decorating the surface, while Zenobia can radiate from within."[12]

One doubts that the demure and retiring Harriet Prescott, in spite of her intuitive sympathy with French customs and the French language, could have even obtained such risqué foreign sources as Gautier or Mérimée in provincial Newburyport. Hawthorne she did have access to, and her other immediate models were the Brontë sisters, who inspired her to climb to rhapsodic heights, as they did her unknown compatriot, Emily Dickinson. The extravagance of Spofford's conception of a totally free female nature found tortured expression in her prose if not in the actions of her main character, whose only overtly cruel deed is to marry Rose in order to satisfy the demands of an overpowering ego. Although "The Amber Gods" is

technically a New England romance as far as locale goes, there is
no act of total self-sacrifice and renunciation such as we find in the
archetype of this genre, Harriet Beecher Stowe's *The Minister's
Wooing.* The only thing that really anchors Spofford's tale to New
England is a prolonged discussion of the native Mayflower or trailing
arbutus, which becomes an apt emblem of Lu's purity and long-
suffering. The jealous Yone naturally detests these "fair little Puritans" and tears them up by myriads, calling them "a cheat."

But Yone's passionate outbursts and fabulous reveries take on
added significance when we ignore local color and again relate her to
Mario Praz's discussion of the Fatal Woman. Praz reminds us that
"the exotic and the erotic ideals go hand in hand, and this fact also
contributes another proof of a more or less obvious truth—that is,
that a love of the exotic is usually an imaginative projection of a sexual desire" (p. 197). The admitted decadence of Mrs. Spofford's prose
expresses the erotic through a descriptive exoticism that blooms as
if forced in a hothouse. This exoticism finds its most immediate cultural analogue in the lush tropical landscapes of the American artist
Frederic Edwin Church, painter of such grandiose panoramas as *The
Heart of the Andes* (1859). Church's work was described by a contemporary as "throbbing with fire and tremulous with life,"[13] and it
is no accident that Yone hopes to transform Rose from a painter of
"gray, faint, half-alive things" to an artist who "abound[s] in color."
Among the "rich, exhaustless" scenes that Yone imagines Rose producing through her inspiration are such Church-like subjects as
"wild sea-sketches,—sunrise,—sunset,—mountain mists rolling in
turbid crimson round lofty peaks, and letting out lonely glimpses of
a melancholy moon,—South American splendors,—pomps of fruit
and blossom,—all this affluence of his future life must flash from
his pencils now" (p. 17). It was Spofford's sublimation of eroticism in
a painterly exoticism that helped to provide a literary artist like Emily Dickinson with such volcanic metaphors of the buried life as
"Teneriffe," "Chimborazo," and "Brazil."

The amoral Giorgione Willoughby could not possibly survive in
Protestant America for long. What is most amazing is that she managed to have her say, and that her saying shocked even such young
cosmopolites as Henry James, Jr. In a review of Spofford's collected
tales (*The Amber Gods and Other Stories*) published in the conservative *North American Review* in October of 1863, James came
down on the author's tropical decadence as righteously as the Crom-

wellian North was to come down on the Cavalier South.[14] Recognizing that Spofford's work was full of promise, James yet declared that her "constant contemplation of a diseased side of human nature can scarcely fail to produce an unhealthy state of mind, and thus . . . exert a dangerous influence" (pp. 569–70). Spofford's popularity was undoubtedly due to "the united strength and brilliancy of her descriptions," but James deplored the "low, murky atmosphere" that too often hung over her tales, tales that "almost without exception" had a "morbid and unhealthful tone."

The diseased side of a human nature that most appalled James was the passion of "illicit love" dominating four out of seven of the stories under review, but he could hardly have charged Giorgione Willoughby with practicing such an "unlawful affection." For Yone is not really human at all, and this is the secret of her complete lack of that moral faculty so dear to Americans weaned on the Scottish Common Sense School philosophy. Since she originates in a pre-Adamite world and therefore lacks a soul, Yone is beyond ordinary concepts of law. When Rose describes the origin of amber in that "furious epoch when rioted all monsters and poisons," he notes that both Yone and this mysterious yellow substance are "accidents," throwbacks to a lost world. She replies that amber "harmonizes with me, because I am a symbol of its period. If there had been women then, they would have been like me,—a great creature without a soul" (p. 29).

Once more the name of Hawthorne hovers in the background, but this time Spofford parallels the master rather than developing themes implicit in his earlier work. Hawthorne's *The Marble Faun* was also published in 1860. Its title character, Donatello, is a spontaneous, free, but soulless creature who gains a sorrowful humanness by associating with a potent, beguiling Dark Lady named Miriam. Again, Nina Baym suggests the symbolic resonances of these two emblems of mankind's stifled inwardness:

> Miriam plays much the same role in regard to Donatello that Hester did for Dimmesdale. She is, in fact, much less developed as an independent character, and is much more a functional figure in relation to others, than Hester was. She is another representative of passion, creativity, and spontaneity, also like Zenobia although less flawed. As a woman she stands for the full idea of womanhood that must be ac-

cepted if man is to do her justice and grow to his own fullest
expression. Like Hester in the forest, or Zenobia at the outset of *The Blithedale Romance*, she suggests a richer and
more generous humanity than that permitted under the ster-
ile patriarchy (in the case of a Catholic hierarchy, the ste-
rility is more than metaphorical). And she may also stand for
an alienated part of the masculine psyche—aspects of ten-
derness and passion that the male has repressed and needs to
recover to be a whole person. For although there is a certain
appeal in Donatello as a faun, there is also something con-
temptible about him. The many animal allusions state
plainly that he is not quite human. He is a case of arrested
development, a curiosity. His feelings for Miriam are the
agency by which he is transformed from monstrously over-
grown child to adult. (pp. 235–36)

In England, *The Marble Faun* was published under the title of *The
Transformation*. For Spofford's Yone, however, there was to be no
such transformation or salvation. Spofford creates an emblem of full
and sensual womanhood like Miriam, but joins it to the arrested development of the ego represented by Donatello. Like the untrans-
formed Donatello, Yone is not a human being at all but an elemental, as much a changeling as a vampire, and only this fact of her
nature allows her the freedom to express her complete but transient
voluptuousness. That this theme was a favorite one with Spofford is
proved by the fact that as late as 1911 she published a "flower and
fairy play" entitled *The Fairy Changeling*, which her biographer
calls the "one fair and fragrant result" of her venture into writing poetry for children (p. 177). The changeling was a fairy child who was
substituted for a human child before it was christened, and one of
the tragedies of the fairies is that they are soulless creatures, members of an irredeemable pagan race. Although the changeling is usually ugly as well as peevish, Yone's translation to the tropics and her
mother's death allow her to flourish in an unexpected manner. The
evil seed fructifies and bears strange fruit, but this fruit itself is subject to imminent decay; in spite of her mixed nature, Yone, like
Ligeia, cannot escape the universal decree of death.

This brings us to the famous last sentence of "The Amber Gods"
and those words that so startled Elizabeth Stuart Phelps with their
touch of "something pagan, something pantheistic" that "smote the

young Christian in the face of her faith." In "Story Last" of her tale, subtitled "Astra Castra, Numen Lumen,"[15] Yone is "blasted by disease," yet sees in her mirror "a beauty that every pang has aggravated, heightened, sharpened, to a superb intensity, flushing, rapid, unearthly,—a brilliancy to be dreamed of" (p. 60). Foiled in her design to revel in perpetual possession of her lover, Yone realizes that she is dying and that Rose and Lu are fated to marry after she is gone. The thread holding the amber rosary snaps and "the little cruel gods go tumbling down on the floor" as Yone achieves ultimate freedom in a return to the undifferentiated elements that bore her, in a ghostly merger with her own origins:

> So I passed out of the room, down the staircase. The servants below did not see me, but the hounds crouched and whined. I paused before the great ebony clock; again the fountain broke, and it chimed the half-hour; it was half past one; another quarter, and the next time its ponderous silver hammers woke the house, it would be two. Half past one? Why, then, did not the hands move? Why cling fixed on a point five minutes before the first quarter struck? To and fro, soundless and purposeless, swung the long pendulum. And, ah! What was this thing I had become? I had done with time. Not for me the hands moved on their recurrent circle any more.
> I must have died at ten minutes past one. (pp. 65–66)

In spite of the many echoes of Poe's "Masque of the Red Death," the ending of Spofford's posthumous reverie in "The Amber Gods" was a strikingly original contribution to American fiction. Not only did it inspire Emily Dickinson to dare the technique of describing the moment of death from the dying person's point of view in such poems as "I heard a Fly buzz—when I died," "Because I could not stop for Death," and "I felt a Funeral, in my Brain," but it startled the American public into a confrontation with, if not a tolerance for, the erotic nature of woman. Even the skeptical Henry James could not help falling briefly under Giorgione Willoughby's Gothic spell.[16]

That Spofford hedged her bet by depriving Yone of a soul and punishing her with lingering extinction is counterbalanced by the fact that she also made her an archetypal if anomalous part of the contemporary imaginative firmament. Using the traditional genres of the ghost story and the Gothic romance, Spofford employed these flexible vehicles as her predecessors, from "Monk" Lewis to Hawthorne to Poe, had always employed them: as a means of exploring sexual and psychological dimensions that went far beyond the ordinary pale of genteel respectability. These and her mannered, sentimental style allowed her to have her devil's-food cake and eat it, too. Even so, Yone was too rich a tidbit to be digested whole by her readers, and she was soon banished to the realm of sheer fantasy by a fascinated but appalled public that would repress her overripe substance and remember only the fading shadow of her haunting last words. Like any potent spirit, however, she was destined to return. When in 1873 Walter Pater descanted on the ambiguous beauty of the Mona Lisa in his *Studies in the History of the Renaissance*, and noted how it was "wrought out from within upon the flesh, the deposit, little cell by little cell, of strange thoughts and fantastic reveries and exquisite passions,"[17] Giorgione Willoughby was reborn. Harriet Prescott Spofford's extravagant metaphors and resinous prose were crystallized into an amber revelation by an aestheticism whose time had finally come.

NOTES

1. See Elizabeth K. Halbeisen, *Harriet Prescott Spofford* (Philadelphia: University of Pennsylvania, 1935). The phrase is Higginson's, quoted by Mary Thacher Higginson in *Letters and Journals of T. W. Higginson* (Boston: Houghton Mifflin, 1921), p. 103.

2. *The Letters of Emily Dickinson*, ed. Thomas H. Johnson, 3 vols. (Cambridge, Mass.: Harvard University Press, 1958), 2:404.

3. For the influence of this tale on Dickinson's work and for a recently recovered text of the letter, see my essay "Emily Dickinson's American Grotesque: The Poet as Folk Artist," *Topic 31: Studies in American Literature* 17 (1977): 3–19.

4. Elizabeth Stuart Phelps, "Stories That Stay," *The Century Magazine* n.s. 59 (November 1910) pp. 118–23. I have quoted from p. 119. Phelps was to attempt her own posthumous reverie in a short story called "Sealed Orders," first published in the *Independent* 25 (14 August 1873): 1005–8. This was reprinted in her collection, *Sealed Orders* (Boston: Houghton, Osgood, and Co., 1879), though in *The Gates Ajar* (1868) she had already drawn an imaginative picture of life in the world beyond. Edward Wagenknecht notes that John Greenleaf Whittier told Phelps that *Sealed Orders* was the finest collection of its kind "since Hawthorne's Twice Told Tales." He then amplified the compliment by observing, "Morally and spiritually thine is far better than his." *John Greenleaf Whittier* (New York: Oxford University Press, 1967), p. 119.

5. Lee R. Edwards and Arlyn Diamond, eds., *American Voices, American Women* (New York: Avon Books, 1973), p. 16.

6. Eric W. Carlson, ed. *Introduction to Poe: A Thematic Reader* (Atlanta: Scott, Foresman and Co., 1967), pp. 486–87. Hereafter quotations from Poe will refer to this volume.

7. For a full exploration of the motifs of the Blond Maiden and the Dark Lady, see Leslie Fiedler, *Love and Death in the American Novel* (New York: Delta Publishing Co., 1966).

8. Harriet Prescott Spofford, *The Amber Gods and Other Stories* (Boston: Ticknor and Fields, 1863), pp. 4–5.

9. In his halting English, Van Helsing explains that "the Count's child-thought see nothing; therefore he speaks so free. . . . This criminal has not full man-brain. He is clever and cunning and resourceful; but he be not of man-stature as to brain. He be of child-brain in much." Bram Stoker, *The Annotated Dracula*, ed. Leonard Wolf (New York: Clarkson N. Potter, 1975), p. 299.

10. Herman Melville, *Pierre; or, The Ambiguities* (New York: Grove Press, 1967), p. 489.

11. See especially chap. four, "La Belle Dame Sans Merci," in Mario Praz, *The Romantic Agony* (Cleveland: World Publishing Co., 1965), pp. 189–286.

12. Nina Baym, *The Shape of Hawthorne's Career* (Ithaca: Cornell University Press, 1976), pp. 191–92.

13. David C. Huntington, *The Landscapes of Frederic Edwin Church* (New York: George Braziller, 1966), p. 14.

14. Henry James, review of *The Amber Gods and Other Stories*, *North American Review* 97 (October 1863): 568–70. It is interesting to compare James's high dudgeon here with the Puritan shock and outrage that greeted the publication of Kate Chopin's *The Awakening* almost four decades later (1899). James was to be even more brutal in his lengthy review of Spofford's *Azarian* (1864) in the *North American Review* 100 (January 1865): 268–77, in which he took her to task for "her inveterate bad taste" and urged her "to be *real*, to be true to something." The review is extremely important in that it places Spofford as the leading practitioner of a literary fashion that James calls "the descriptive style," which he traces back to the early poetry of Tennyson. This "Azarian school," as he characterizes it, "is the cheapest writing of the day," and he ridicules its "thick *impasto* of words and images," citing E. B. Browning, George Sand, Gail Hamilton, and H. B. Stowe as other originators and adherents of the mode. The Azarian school was to fall before the exigencies of the Civil War and the triumph of James's own brand of moral realism. The review is reprinted in James, *Notes and Reviews*, ed. Pierre de Chaignon la Rose (Freeport, N.Y.: Books for Libraries Press, 1968), pp. 16–32.

15. This phrase is an unorthodox Latin that would seem to translate as "cut star, numinous light." Significantly, T. W. Higginson used it as a way of further linking the names of Dickinson and Spofford. In *Poems: First Series* (1890), Dickinson's "Departed—to the Judgment" is entitled "Astra Casta," and in *Poems: Third Series* (1896) her "I live with Him—I see His face—" is called "Numen Lumen." Although Higginson actively participated in editing only the first volume along with Mabel Loomis Todd, he was in fact responsible for both titles, for Todd later wrote, "In general I objected to titles in the Latin language, although of course Latin names came naturally to an educated man of that time. But to me, 'Astra Castra,' 'Numen Lumen' and 'Resurgam' sounded stilted when used with the poems of Emily Dickinson." Millicent Todd Bingham, *Ancestor's Brocades: The Literary Début of Emily Dickinson* (New York: Harper and Bros., 1945), p. 58. In an article published in the *Christian Union* on 25 September 1890 Higginson quoted "Departed—to the Judgment," prefacing it with the comment, "Then, approaching the great change from time to eternity at a different angle, she gives two verses of superb concentration, like the following, which might be christened, after the mediaeval motto, ASTRA CASTRA." "An Open Portfolio," reprinted in *The Recognition of Emily Dickinson*, ed. Caesar R. Blake and Carlton F. Wells (Ann Arbor: University of Michigan Press, 1968), p. 8. Whatever the exact medieval source of the motto, Higginson was obviously making an attempt to connect Emily Dickinson's art not only with that of the popular women writers he mentioned in the text—Celia Thaxter, Jean Ingelow, and Helen Hunt Jackson—but with Spofford, whose "Amber Gods" might still be recalled by readers familiar with weird and sensational literature of the 1860s.

16. As Leon Edel points out, the name of the New England family in Henry James's first version of "The Romance of Certain Old Clothes" (1868) was Willoughby, which the author later changed to Wingrave, while in "De Grey: A Romance" (1868) the doomed Margaret is described as "enchanted, baleful, fatal!" *The Ghostly Tales of Henry James* (New Brunswick, N.J.: Rutgers University Press, 1948), pp. 4, 67. The

themes of vampirism, revenge of the blood, the fatal woman, and supernatural return which pervade these early Gothic romances were obviously an inheritance from Spofford and Hawthorne that James was later to transform in his own unique way. There is perhaps a faint and ghostly last reminiscence of Giorgione Willoughby in the character of the trance-medium Verena Tarrant of *The Bostonians* (1885–86). When describing the "fantastic" dress of this "half-bedizened damsel," James takes pains to note that "round her neck, and falling low upon her flat young chest, she had a double chain of amber beads." *The Bostonians*, ed. Alfred Habegger (Indianapolis: Bobbs-Merrill, 1976), p. 56.

17. Pater, quoted by Praz, *The Romantic Agony*, p. 243. The phrase "amber revelation" is from Emily Dickinson's poem "An Ignorance a Sunset," no. 552 in Thomas H. Johnson, ed. *The Complete Poems of Emily Dickinson* (Boston: Little, Brown, 1960). The anonymous author of the biographical sketch of Spofford in Charles Dudley Warner's *Library of the World's Best Literature* (New York: The International Society, 1897), links her name with that of Pater, noting that "Mrs. Spofford, like Pater, combines an almost austere spirituality with the warm sensuousness of the artist, who lives in full and blissful consciousness of color and light and form" (23 : 13805).

JAY MARTIN

Ghostly Rentals, Ghostly Purchases: Haunted Imaginations in James, Twain, and Bellamy

"**D**on't ever do that," the wise maiden aunt, Hetty Maria, cautions a child in Adeline Whitney's *Patience Strong's Outings*, of 1869. "Carry your candle as straight as you can, but never go prowling back into dark closets to look after mischief that you haven't done."[1] During the nineteenth century, many Americans were convinced that it would be unwise and perhaps unchristian to poke into dark corners. They urged their writers, like their children, to be practical and to emphasize the sunny side of life, to be sensible in behavior and idealistic in belief.

Poe, Hawthorne, and Melville had persisted in peering into dark recesses and had suffered for this in popular and critical esteem. Poe's work was called "ill-regulated" and "uncontrolled," "ghostly and unreal." "The prevalent tone" of Hawthorne's *The Marble Faun* (1860), declared one prominent critic, "is sombre and melancholy, and in some measure revolting." The critics agreed that Melville, "embarrassed by . . . spiritual allegories," was lost in "wild imaginings"; his novel *Pierre* (1852) was characterized as a "string of nonsense."

What worried critics and audiences was the propensity of these authors to examine the recesses of the unconscious, the nighttime of the mind that Hawthorne (following Puritanism and Pascal) called the heart, Poe named "the perverse," and Melville called "spirit." But when Mrs. Oliphant criticized Hawthorne for "dissecting . . . 'inner nature,'"[2] she condemned them all.

Before the war, Americans seemed to be convinced Cartesians, defining mind as identical with awareness. Yet in the late sixties many different lines converged to interest Americans in the night life, the other, the supernatural, or the spiritual. Though they repulsed the influences of German *Naturphilosophie*, never according Eduard von Hartmann's *The Philosophy of the Unconscious* (1869) the popularity it gained in Europe; and though they resisted developments in the science of psychology, many Americans were impelled in their own indigenous terms to acknowledge an unconscious mind. The first breach came with contemporary ethical discussions of conscience. Noah Porter, president of Yale, welcomed the idea of the unconscious as a proof of God's indwelling in man and argued "that the soul may act without being conscious of what it does."[3] The unconscious was thus deemed by A. T. Schofield to provide the key to our "highest spirit-life."[4] The rapid growth of modern spiritualism, with its investigations of such mental phenomena as telepathy, also urged the acceptance of psychic powers. Not only the Society for Psychical Research but also several popular books, such as Epes Sargent's *Planchette; or, The Despair of Science* (1869), attacked naïve realism and defended spiritualism. Finally, the idea was accorded a kind of official sanction when Dr. Oliver Wendell Holmes told the Phi Beta Kappa Society at Harvard in 1870, "The automatic, unconscious action of the mind enters largely into all [thought] processes."[5]

The American reader of 1870 was a thoroughgoing materialist who believed in the supernaturalisms of traditional religion and the New Spiritualism. If anything could reconcile these, the concept of the unconscious could. And thus the new mass audience—much larger and quite different from that before the war—was eager to have the writer treat the unconscious in some clear, comfortable fashion.

The largest part of this audience was female, and the writers who first solved the question of how to represent the unconscious in fiction were all women. It was from the writers who elaborately investigated the pietistic conscience and spiritualist practices and powers—women like Charlotte Yonge, Augusta Evans, Grace Greenwood, and Phoebe Cary—and not from prewar male writers, that Henry James, Mark Twain, and Edward Bellamy learned how to treat the unconscious.

The novelist who most fundamentally solved this problem was Elizabeth Stuart Phelps; *The Gates Ajar* (1868) was enormously popular in every region of the country. Phelps (whose mother wrote a book called *Sunny Side*) gave light and comfort to thousands of grieving relatives whose sons and brothers had died in the war by inventing the image of a spirit world exactly parallel to visible creation, a duplicate world in which discarnate but spiritually embodied beings are living happily. Mary Cabot mourns her brother Roy until her aunt, Winifred Forceythe of Lawrence, Kansas, comes with her daughter Faith for a visit. When Mary wonders what heaven will look like, Aunt Winifred drives away her niece's melancholia by speaking about the happiness of discarnate spirits there:

> "Heaven? . . . I think I want some mountains and very many trees. . . . I want a little brook to sit and sing to Faith

by. . . . Flowers, too. . . . I should like, if I had my choice, to
have day-lilies and carnations fresh under my windows all
the time."

"Under your windows?"

"Yes, I hope to have a home of my own."

"Not a house?"

"Something not unlike it. . . . What could be done with
the millions who, from the time of Adam, have been gathering there, unless they lived under the conditions of organized society? Organized society involves homes, not unlike
the homes of this world."

Such a world, according to Aunt Winifred's gospel, is superior to this
world, because spiritualized, but it is coextensive with the world of
experience: the two are only a hair's-breadth apart. The spirit world
is fully aware of the doings in the visible world and spirits visit the
living through the unconscious.

"Then you think, you really think, that Roy remembers
and loves and takes care of me; that he has been listening,
perhaps, and is—why, you don't think he may be *here*?"

"Yes I do. Here close beside you all this time, trying to
speak to you . . . —right here, dear."[6]

The unconscious for Phelps, then, consists of intimations of a superior world in the promptings of God and friendly spirits; it is "other,"
but just a step away, "over there," like the new heaven described by
Swedenborg in *True Christian Religion*—an instrument through
which the spirit world counsels and aids the living. Above all, the
unconscious is understood as a definite place in which, mostly unknown to consciousness, spiritual activity is continuous. With one
stroke Phelps tossed overboard the allegories, symbols, introspec-
tions and transcendental meditations of prewar writers and substituted for these a healthful, eternal spiritual world that stands
behind the conscious world of experience, influences it, and can occasionally break through it.

Once the conventions of Protestant piety were combined with
modern spiritualism and the new psychology of Carl Gustav Carus
and William B. Carpenter, the assertion that the mysteries of the unconscious had been unlocked was but a step away: the unconscious
was the ivory gate through which divine promptings, spiritual visi-

tors, dreams, memories, and prophecies would pass. From having been the center of mystery, only a short time before, the unconscious now became an explanation of mysteries.

Phelps offered too fine a solution for James, Twain, Bellamy, and other postwar writers to miss. Each tended to understand the leading impulse of the unconscious in a slightly different way, but all shared Phelps's belief that the unconscious was spatial, a "great good place"; that its activities were continuous, that its truths were superior to those of experience and its operations much more swift and intricate than those of the reasoning mind, that it determined behavior and that, therefore, the consciousness must do everything possible to establish and maintain a connection with its superficially dark—but really brighter, more angelic—side.

But writers were slow to perceive the desires of the audience and to develop a psychological fiction of the self-haunted self. Phelps herself wrote conventional stories of terror in her next book, *Men, Women, and Ghosts* (1869). James's early story "The Ghostly Rental" (1876), where the "ghost" turns out to be a vengeful daughter, was also conventional. James and his contemporaries needed to learn that the unconscious could not be merely rented, played with in Gothic guise, but must be purchased through allowing the spiritual, the uncanny, the mythical, the ghostlike, the haunted, and the hallucinatory to fracture the consciousness along innumerable planes.

James was slow to treat the unconscious for two reasons. Certainly, he was chiefly preoccupied with the problems of consciousness, and regarded the work of sensibility as a work of reclamation, like the draining of the Zuyder Zee. Second, unlike his father, he scorned Christian piety, and unlike his brother William he dismissed psychical research. In the early satiric tale "Professor Fargo" (1874), after the title character contrasts the "earth life and the summer land" of the spirit, the rationalist Gifford speaks for James: "I speak in the name of science. Science recognizes no such thing as 'spiritual magnetism'; no such thing as mysterious fascination; no such thing as spirit-rappings and ghost-raising."[7]

But by the late eighties, James saw that the consciousness could not be represented apart from the unconscious; he could not do without "ghost-raising" in his own fiction. Influenced then by William's "Census of Hallucinations" and even more by Carpenter's concept of "unconscious cerebration" which he refers to in *The Aspern Papers* (1888),[8] he raised many ghosts. These, to be sure, resided in the unconscious rather than in a Christian heaven, but to represent them—in such tales as "Sir Edmund Orme," "The Private Life," *The Turn of the Screw,* "The Great Good Place," "The Jolly Corner," and *The Sense of the Past*—he borrowed the fictive solution of Elizabeth Phelps. If James had earlier dramatized the consciousness as a circle of light, beginning in the nineties he carried his candle into the jolly corners of the psyche, where the unconscious had all the while been living a separate life. "The Jolly Corner" (1908) is, of course, almost a diagrammatic exhibition of the spatial concept of the unconscious, where the subliminal Spencer Brydon has lived out his mutilated existence (James's spirits have houses and furniture just as Phelps's do). Brilliantly, but precisely in line with the tradition I have been exploring, James turned "The Jolly Corner" inside out in *The Sense of the Past* (1917). Here, Ralph Pendrel exchanges identities with a figure in an eighteenth-century portrait and steps through the picture into the past. Then he is the ghost of the future haunting the past, a real past that is living *pari passu* with the present, like Phelps's heaven. The unconsciousness is the ghost of the consciousness in the world of experience, while the consciousness haunts the spirit world of the unconscious. It is, James wrote in planning the novel, "the double consciousness . . . which makes the thrill and curiosity of the affair, the consciousness of being the other and yet himself also, of being himself and yet the other also."[9] James, it appears, had come around to the side of Professor Fargo, or at least to that of Elizabeth Phelps, by the nineties. *The Gates Ajar* had offered consolation to postwar bereaved. By 1910 James would write a two-part essay titled "Is There a Life after Death?" which concluded a series intended by the editors of *Harper's Bazar* to be "in the nature of a counsel of consolation, addressed to those in immediate bereavement, and containing . . . comfort and hope."[10] James tended to think of the unconscious primarily as memory— past thoughts, actions, cultures. In general Mark Twain tended to think of the unconscious as an ever-present source of instantaneous revelation.

The case for the influence of Elizabeth Phelps on Mark Twain is clear. One of his earliest sketches, "Captain Stormfield Enters Heaven," was intended to be a wholesale satiric slaughter of *The Gates Ajar.* He never could complete this sketch, for even as he projected it, his own imagination was busy exploring the phenomena of the unconscious in terms identical to those employed by Phelps. In his essay "Mental Telegraphy" he recounts how, beginning with a psychic—or unconscious—experience of his own in 1874, he began to keep account "of such experiences . . . as seemed explicable by the theory that minds telegraph thoughts to each other." He spoke of the "intelligent labors of the Psychical Society" and announced his belief that "you can be asleep—at least, wholly unconscious—for a time," and allow the unconscious to break in upon and transform the conscious.[11]

Huckleberry Finn, for instance, has two interior selves: first, the supraunconscious reasoning conscience, which is like a plaguey "yaller dog" (or an ugly dwarf, as Twain described it in "The Recent Carnival of Crime in Connecticut"), and, second, the subunconscious, the intuitive, angelic unconscious that guides Huck to the right conclusions. "I went right along," Huck says, ". . . trusting to Providence to put the right words in my mouth when the time comes; for I'd noticed that Providence always did . . . if I left it alone."[12]

When Mark Twain eventually clarified this idea in "No. 44, The Mysterious Stranger," he saw that what he called Providence was the unconscious and that the unconscious was best understood as the dream self, which lives out its own life separately from the material self but corresponds exactly to it. "You know, of course [Satan explains], that you are not one person, but two. One is your Workaday-Self, and 'tends to business, the other is your Dream Self, and has no responsibilities, and cares only for romance and excursions and adventure." The consciousness, compared to the unconscious, is "as a lightning bug to the lightning."[13] "When my physical body dies," Twain wrote in his notebook, "my dream body will doubtless continue its excursion and activities without change, forever."[14] Such excursions were the subject of the great symbolic works in which he explored the unconscious in spatial terms, as an "over there" that is entered when dreams burst the banal shell of consciousness: "Which Was the Dream?" "The Enchanted Sea Wilderness," "Which Was It?" and "Three Thousand Years among the Microbes."

Edward Bellamy explored the geography of the unconscious in the same material, spatial terms, but with an emphasis precisely opposite James's. He understood unconsciousness as prophecy, the sense of the future. *Looking Backward, 2000–1887* (1888) obviously draws its power from its dreamlike quality. Julian West leaves a nightmarish present (the Workaday-Self, Experience, consciousness) by dreaming of a future Utopian world (the Dream-Self, heaven-on-earth, unconsciousness), only to dream that, like Ralph Pendrel, he is back in the past again. West gets into the future about which he dreams; but then his fears force him to dream that he is back in the present and that his dreams were illusions. Bellamy was bent in all his works on presenting the visionary world of the future that haunts the present. He wished to extirpate memory and create a prophetic unconsciousness that could dream forward. In one of his tales, "The Old Folks' Party," children masquerade as their future selves—"ghosts of the future, instead of ghosts of the past," Bellamy says. And in the remarkable tale, "The Blindman's World," an astronomer falls asleep beside his telescope; his "dream soul" visits Mars and discovers that the creatures on this planet possess extremely weak memories, but are instead endowed with the faculty of foresight.[15] Mars, like his nationalist Utopia, is a spatial location, a place where the dream soul or unconscious is in control and produces marvels. Those who return to the blindman's world of mere consciousness after such visions must be haunted by their own unconscious future.

Phelps's heaven, coextensive with earth; James's spirits, who haunt present or past; Twain's Providence or Dream Self; and Bellamy's forward-looking dream soul stand for the strange voices, activities, intimations, recollections, myths, dreams, fantasies, hopes, magnetisms, and telegraphies that even the most practical American had to admit he sometimes experienced.

I have been giving an account of a dramatic cultural and literary about-face. Pre–Civil War writers who dealt psychologically with man's "inner nature" were coolly received. Writers after the Civil War, contrariwise, began as champions of social realism but were moved more and more by their public toward the exploration of the unconscious. This was true not only of those writers I have named but even of the champion of realism, W. D. Howells, and the realist and social critic Hamlin Garland. In two books, *Questionable Shapes* (1903) and *Between the Dark and the Daylight* (1907), Howells wrote stories about the filmy "shapes that haunt the dusk."[16] He had to admit that by 1903 realism was over and "a whole order of literature has arisen, calling itself psychological, . . . and dealing with life on its mystical side."[17] And almost all of Garland's last works, from *The Tyranny of the Dark* (1906) to *The Mystery of the Buried Crosses*

(1939), concerned psychic phenomena. Even the great naturalistic novelist, Theodore Dreiser, represented the unconscious by the ghostly in *Plays of the Natural and Supernatural* (1916).

These Americans were part of a world-wide literary movement away from naturalism. Ibsen said of *Ghosts* (1881): "The fundamental note shall be the richly flourishing spiritual life among us." His axiom, "It is all ghosts,"[18] might almost sum up the tradition I have been examining. In 1891 Maeterlinck insisted that mystics "alone are the possessors of certainty," and Hauptmann's *The Sunken Bell* of 1896 explored the unconscious autobiographically. This European movement came to a climax in such works of August Strindberg as *A Dream Play* (1901) and *The Ghost Sonata* (1907), deliberate imitations of dreams. Human beings, Strindberg implied, needed to escape the world of appearances (consciousness) and find truth beyond the grave in the world of spirits and the invisible "powers" of the unconscious. So, within a thirty year period writers came to insist that they *must* carry candles into the dark closets of the psyche. The unconscious was no longer regarded as a derangement of awareness but as an instrument in the search for wisdom.

And then the movement ended. Freud's essay of 1915, "The Unconscious," which treated the unconscious as a system of mental acts marks its demise. Keenly aware of the literary movement I have been discussing, Freud later confessed: "The poets and philosophers before me discovered the unconscious."[19] Still, his own application of the scientific method to the unconscious helped to bring this movement to an end and to introduce new forms and metaphors and conditions for psychological fiction.

"Never go prowling back into dark closets," Aunt Hetty Maria cautioned. Unwilling—or unable—to follow her advice, the best American writers between 1870 and 1915 managed to find strange illuminations in the dark.

NOTES

1. Mrs. A. D. T. Whitney, *Patience Strong's Outings* (Boston: Loring, 1869), p. 92.

2. "Modern Novelists—Great and Small," *Blackwood's Magazine* 77 (May 1855): 565.

3. Noah Porter, *The Human Intellect* (1868; rpt. New York: Scribner's, 1885), p. 103.

4. Alfred T. Schofield, *The Unconscious Mind* (New York: Funk and Wagnall, 1907), p. 406.

5. Oliver Wendell Holmes, "Mechanics in Thought and Morals," in *Pages from an Old Volume of Life* (Boston: Houghton Mifflin, 1890), pp. 284–85.

6. Elizabeth Stuart Phelps, *The Gates Ajar*, ed. Helen Sootin Smith (Cambridge, Mass.: Harvard University Press, 1964), pp. 92–94, 66.

7. *The Complete Tales of Henry James*, ed. Leon Edel. 12 vols. (Philadelphia: Lippincott, 1961–64), 3:269, 287.

8. Ibid., 6:380.

9. *The Notebooks of Henry James*, ed. F. O. Matthiessen and Kenneth B. Murdock (New York: Oxford University Press, 1947), p. 364.

10. *Harper's Bazar* 43 (April 1909): 360.

11. Mark Twain, "Mental Telegraphy," *Harper's Monthly* 84 (December 1891): 95, 103.

12. Mark Twain, *Adventures of Huckleberry Finn* (New York: Charles L. Webster, 1885), pp. 292, 278.

13. *Mark Twain's Mysterious Stranger Manuscripts*, ed. William M. Gibson (Berkeley and Los Angeles: University of California Press, 1969), pp. 315, 344.

14. *Mark Twain's Notebooks*, ed. Albert Bigelow Paine (New York: Harper, 1935), p. 351.

15. Edward Bellamy, *The Blindman's World and Other Stories* (New York: Garrett, 1968), pp. 61, 11.

16. *Shapes that Haunt the Dusk* was the title of a volume of psychical tales that Howells edited (New York: Harper, 1907).

17. W. D. Howells, "Editor's Easy Chair," *Harper's Monthly* 107 (June 1903): 149.

18. From Ibsen's working memoranda for *Ghosts*, quoted by William Archer in his introduction to the 1906 edition of his translation (New York: Scribner's, 1906), pp. 195–96.

19. This remark was made on the occasion of Freud's seventieth birthday, and is quoted in Lionel Trilling, "Freud and Literature," *The Liberal Imagination* (1950; rpt. New York: Anchor, 1953), p. 32.

HOWARD KERR

James's Last Early Supernatural Tales: Hawthorne Demagnetized, Poe Depoetized

Henry James's supernatural fiction divides chronologically into two groups of stories separated by an interval of fifteen years: a handful published between 1868 and 1874, and the longer, better-known series running from "Sir Edmund Orme" (1891) through *The Turn of the Screw* (1898) to "The Jolly Corner" (1908) and the unfinished novel, *The Sense of the Past* (1917). Readers and scholars alike have much preferred the later tales, and rightly so. Of the early cluster, James himself thought only "A Romance of Certain Old Clothes" (1868) and "The Last of the Valerii" (1874) worth reprinting, and the latter is more a study in obsession than in the supernatural.

One of James's major problems in these early stories was to establish his own repertoire of supernatural phenomena. Apprentice attempts in the Hawthornesque mode, as their titles suggest, "A Romance of Certain Old Clothes" and "De Grey: A Romance" (1868) are marked by weakly integrated marvels which seem not at all characteristically Jamesian. "Two vengeful ghostly hands" inflict "ten hideous wounds" on the face of a woman who dies opening a forbidden trunk in "Old Clothes,"[1] and if the inadequately explained curse that dooms the male De Greys perhaps echoes the fate of Hawthorne's Pyncheons, the shriek that brings Paul De Grey to his fiancée's side from three miles away resembles nothing so much as the call that in another romance draws Jane Eyre across England to Rochester. Clearly for these mysterious events James looked to a wide range of sensational Gothic conventions, and just as clearly he was uncomfortable with them.

The last two early tales, "Professor Fargo" (1874) and "The Ghostly Rental" (1876), reject such conventions. Taken together, in fact, they constitute a repudiation of much of the supernatural machinery of Hawthorne and Poe, the exemplars who still stood in the way of any new American attempt to mine the occult vein. In both stories literary demystification goes hand in hand with an attack on another legacy from an earlier generation, the mediumistic spiritualism that was once again flourishing in the 1870s. From this matrix of generic and cultural criticism, moreover, emerges a briefly glimpsed supernatural phenomenology of uncanny perception and ghostly presence that anticipates the "inexplicable occurrences" of James's later works.[2]

About James's indebtedness to Hawthorne in "Professor Fargo" there has never been any doubt. The often-cited parallels with *The Blithedale Romance* are obvious and deliberate: voyeuristic narrators; vulnerable young women enslaved by corrupt mesmerists; climactic public exhibitions in which that bondage is broken for Hawthorne's Priscilla by the power of love, but announced and confirmed for James's deaf-mute Miss Gifford when Professor Fargo's "spiritual magnetism" snatches her from her father[3]—an episode also reminiscent of the magnetic ravishment of Alice Pyncheon by Matthew Maule as her father stands by in *The House of the Seven Gables*. Commentators have pointed to the story as a link between Hawthorne's Gothic romance and James's "realistic" *Bostonians* (1886). What needs emphasis here, in the context of James's development as a writer of supernatural fiction, is the extent to which Hawthorne's dependence on mesmerism is rejected in "Professor Fargo."[4]

Abhorrent to Hawthorne personally, the "magnetic miracles" of mesmerism nonetheless appealed to him as metaphors for moral and sexual slavery that were especially suitable for romance because they could be ambiguously presented both as occult "necromancies" and as a genuine force that "modern psychology" might yet "reduce . . . within a system."[5] His male mesmerists dominate trance-maidens with the invading power claimed alike by legendary witches ("the evil eye") and nineteenth-century followers of Mesmer ("magnetism"). One of the maidens, Priscilla, exhibits in addition the spontaneous clairvoyance attributed to the "somnambulists" who were the mesmerists' favorite subjects. Although Hawthorne was skeptical about mesmeric theory and thought the "phenomena" more likely "physical and material" than "spiritual" in origin, that they "really occurred" he seems to have had little doubt.[6] The very language in which their reality is characteristically questioned by his narrators only calls attention to their "marvelous" ambience. In *Hawthorne* (1879), James would criticize exactly that ambience as the "least felicitous" element in *Blithedale*.[7] Here, in "Professor Fargo," he aggressively imposed on Hawthorne's text to strip the evil mesmerist of his supernatural magnetism while preserving a problematical remnant of the maiden's clairvoyance.

Professor Fargo is an itinerant spiritualistic showman, and his sorry performance as "THE INFALLIBLE WAKING MEDIUM AND MAGI-CIAN, CLAIRVOYANT, PROPHET, AND SEER" brands him as a fraud (PF, p. 261). He visits the cemetery of the village in which the tale opens in order, suspects the narrator, "to 'get up' a few names and dates" from the gravestones so as "to treat the townsfolk to messages from their buried relatives" at his evening show (p. 266). (Says the King, his counterpart in *Huckleberry Finn*, "I k'n tell a fortune pretty good, when I've got somebody along to find out the facts for me.")[8] But when Fargo's mediumistic powers are put to the test, only thrice can he hit on the names of the departed, written by members of his audience on slips of paper. Inept even as a charlatan, he lacks what Lafcadio Hearn termed the "Artful Ambidexterity" with which "Professor" Samri Baldwin, one of the most accomplished of American conjurers, executed the "ballot reading" trick in the 1870s.[9]

References to the possibility of visible ghosts indicate that James was aware of spirit "materializations," a spectacular recent addition to séance phenomena that would figure importantly in "The Ghostly Rental." Fargo's spiritualism thus provides a topical introduction to the revision of *Blithedale*'s mesmerism. Although mesmerism was a discredited anachronism by the time James wrote, Fargo's act includes unsuccessful attempts to magnetize the villagers, and he later brags of the power "to exercise a mysterious influence over living organisms. . . . Some folks call it animal magnetism, but I call it spiritual magnetism." He announces that he "can make 'em in love, . . . take 'em out of love again, and make 'em swear they wouldn't marry the loved object" (PF, p. 286), a boast derived directly from a claim for mesmerism that had disgusted *Blithedale*'s narrator: "At the bidding of one of these wizards, the maiden, with her lover's kiss still burning on her lips, would turn from him with icy indifference."[10] Taylor Stoehr sees this as a typically Hawthornesque inversion of the widely held fear that women were sexually vulnerable to the mesmerist's charms.[11]

Just such a conquest becomes Fargo's aim when Colonel Gifford, the quixotic mathematical lecturer who shares his platform, publicly denounces him "in the name of science. Science recognizes no such thing as 'spiritual magnetism.' . . . No intelligent man, woman, or child need fear to be made to do anything against his own will by the supernatural operation of the will of Professor Fargo" (PF, p. 287). Fargo vows to make the colonel acknowledge his power. Already the narrator has seen the professor holding Gifford's deaf-mute daughter "spellbound by an influence best known to himself" (p. 265), in a tryst that the girl has kept secret from her father. At the tale's climax Fargo apparently vindicates his claim. Drawing the girl's attention by fixing her with "his eye," he demands in words to which she is deaf that she "choose . . . between your father and me." With "no will of her own," the "fascinated" girl sinks to her knees before Fargo, then departs with him, evidently a victim of magnetic enchantment (p. 297).

James carefully lays a trail of clues, however, which reveal that Fargo's "influence" over Miss Gifford is no more uncanny than his spiritualistic fakery. From the beginning he has been communicating with her in sign language. Such gestures could double as mesmeric passes, but the manner in which he "brandished his large, plump knuckles before her face" (PF, p. 275), and his recurrently emphasized physicality in general—"the fleshly element in his composition . . . an air of aggressive robustness. . . . the most impudent pair of eyes I ever beheld" (pp. 261–62)—argue that his appeal to the hitherto sheltered girl is frankly sexual. Indeed, he returns from a séance with a young woman of the village "flushed, disheveled, rubbing his hands" (p. 281). As for Miss Gifford's responsiveness in the climactic scene to Fargo's gaze and to words she cannot hear, the narrator has glimpsed another clandestine meeting beforehand, and as the stage is set for the final challenge he notes, "She had evidently been schooled" (p. 297).

Yet her alertness to the professor's wishes may also lie in her own special state of consciousness. If Fargo is devoid of supernatural magnetism, the girl remains a puzzle, "her little imprisoned soundless mind" protected from direct analysis (PF, p. 280). Indeed, she possesses some of the "Sibylline attributes" that James would later fault in Hawthorne's Priscilla.[12] Assisting in her father's mathematical lectures, she is "a little arithmetical fairy" whose "skill at figures is a kind of intuition" (pp. 272, 280). And at least once she appears to demonstrate an altogether spontaneous clairvoyance akin to Priscilla's; "seeming in spite of her deafness to feel" the narrator's presence behind her (pp. 273–74), she turns to look at him. Here is a hint of the psychical consciousness—perceptive rather than, like mesmerism, forcefully attractive—that would distinguish what Martha Banta has called "The Heroine as 'Sensitive'" in James's later works, supernatural and otherwise.[13] Even this touch of preternatural awareness is open to question, however, for the narrator observes that when Fargo enters the room, Miss Gifford does not glance "round at him . . . as she had done at me" (p. 275)—a suggestion either that she conceals her relationship with the magnetist or that neither of them is blessed with unusual powers.

Thus after unsuccessful attempts at Hawthornesque supernatural "romance" in "Old Clothes" and "De Grey," James critically rewrote *Blithedale*'s mesmeric affinities, reducing male magnetism to a combination of humbug and sexual aggressiveness, female susceptibility to a mixture of inexperience, duplicity, and perhaps a trace of clairvoyance. James would go on to explore occult sensitivity as a mode of subliminal consciousness in the heroines of *The Bostonians* and *The Turn of the Screw*, doing so in an ambiguously supernatural context compatible with the "new" psychology and the psychical research pioneered by his brother William and others. But before such possibilities could be fully sounded, it had been necessary to "demagnetize" Hawthorne in "Professor Fargo."

Written in Paris in the spring of 1876, "The Ghostly Rental" is a more sportive attack on Gothic tradition than "Professor Fargo." The narrator, a Harvard divinity student, comes upon an old farmhouse which, despite his "cheerful views of the supernatural," strikes him as "haunted."[14] He witnesses visits to the house by old Captain Diamond, who arrives to meet the ghost of the daughter he thinks he killed with a curse when he caught her with a lover years before. So persistently had she haunted him that he gave up the dwelling, accepting her offer of a "ghostly rental" which ever since he has had to collect in person once each quarter. Striking up a friendship with the captain, the insatiably curious narrator eventually demands "to see what you see" (GR, p. 128). Inside the house, he realizes that "a large definite figure" stands at the top of the stairs, and he becomes "conscious of a feeling to which" he must "apply the vulgar name of fear. . . . I had got what I wanted; I was seeing the ghost" (p. 130). But as a seaside vacation quiets his nerves, he begins to wonder if "the sable phantom" was not in fact "a sham ghost" (p. 132).

His suspicion is proved correct when the dying captain asks him to collect the next rental payment. Again he sees the shape at the top of the stairs, but when the spirit descends to inquire about her father's health in a "perfectly human" voice, he snatches off her veil to discover that the captain's daughter is very much alive—"a beautiful woman, an audacious actress" (GR, p. 137). Insulted, she flings the money at his feet and leaves the room, only to scream and rush back in saying that she has seen her father in his nightshirt: "Oh, heavens, I have seen his ghost. . . . It's the punishment of my long folly!" (p. 138). The revenging haunter has become the haunted. They both depart, the narrator returning to Cambridge to learn that the captain is indeed dead. That night, glimpsing a fire to the northwest, he remembers that Diamond's daughter dropped her candle when frightened by the apparition, and the tale ends bleakly the next day as he finds "the haunted house . . . a mass of charred beams and smoldering ashes" (p. 140).

In several respects this leisurely, rather awkwardly constructed story resembles "Professor Fargo." In both a daughter rebels against an eccentric father with a military title. Both include graveyard scenes tinged with spiritualism: the village plot where Fargo works up his mediumistic act, and the cemetery at Mount Auburn where the divinity student and Diamond discuss "the power of departed spirits to return" (GR, p. 117). The voyeuristic narrators of both are simultaneously curious and skeptical about the supernatural. Moreover, with its "spiritually blighted" New England farmhouse and "tall, impartially drooping elm" (pp. 108, 107), "The Ghostly Rental" seems at first glance reminiscent of Hawthorne.[15] But the "audible eloquence" of this "melancholy mansion" (pp. 108, 110) speaks less of the House of the Seven Gables than it does of "the melancholy House of Usher,"[16] and the object of James's demystification here is not Hawthorne, but rather Poe.

Although Cornelia P. Kelley and Leon Edel refer in passing to Poe's influence on "The Ghostly Rental," the only attempt to demonstrate that influence is a brief discussion in Sidney P. Lind's 1948 dissertation on James's supernatural fiction.[17] To show that James had refreshed his memory of one of the favorite writers of his childhood, Lind points to the April 1876 essay on Baudelaire, with its praise for the Frenchman's careful and precise translation of "all of Poe's prose," and its often quoted opinion that "an enthusiasm for Poe is the mark of a decidedly primitive stage of reflection. Baudelaire thought him a profound philosopher. . . . Poe was much the greater charlatan of the two, as well as the greater genius."[18]

For evidence that James did lay "The Fall of the House of Usher" under obligation, Lind simply offers parallel passages (condensed here) describing the uncanny responses of the two narrators to house and setting. "I know not how it was," says Roderick Usher's friend, "but, with the first glimpse of the building, a sense of insufferable gloom pervaded my spirit. . . . I looked . . . upon the mere house, and the simple landscape features . . . the bleak walls . . . the vacant eye-like windows . . . a few rank sedges . . . a few white trunks of decayed trees . . . with an utter depression of soul" (HU, p. 263). James's divinity student views a similarly desolate scene: "I stopped in front of it gazing hard, I hardly knew why, but with a vague mixture of curiosity and timidity. . . . Behind . . . stretched an [apple] orchard" with "a blighted and exhausted aspect. All the windows of the house had rusty shutters, without slats. . . . There was no sign of life about it; it looked blank, bare and vacant, and yet, as I lingered near it, it seemed to have a familiar meaning—an audible eloquence" (GR, pp. 107–8).

Both narrators try to explain their feelings. Poe's would-be rationalist decides that although "combinations of very simple natural objects . . . have the power of thus affecting us," to analyze "this power lies . . . beyond our depth." His "singular first impression" being reinforced by the reflected image of the house in the waters of the tarn, he has so excited his "imagination as really to believe that about" the place hangs "an atmosphere which [had] no affinity with the air of heaven" (HU, pp. 263, 264). James's equally rationalistic narrator thinks that "the impression made . . . at first sight, by that gray colonial dwelling," offers "proof that induction may sometimes be near akin to divination," for "there [was] nothing on the face of the matter to warrant" his own "very serious induction." He tells himself "with the accent of profound conviction—'The house is simply haunted!'" (GR, p. 108).

If not conclusive, Lind's evidence is certainly suggestive.[19] Yet Burton R. Pollin, the only scholar to mention it in print, dismisses it as "insubstantial and unconvincing." Not until the 1890s, says Pollin, would "Poe's traces in James's creative work . . . become definite."[20] In fact, however, "The Ghostly Rental" bears many more traces of "Usher" than those cited by Lind—more than it would be profitable to list completely. Certainly Poe's famous opening—at the end of "a dull, dark, and soundless day in the autumn of the year, when the clouds hung oppressively low in the heavens, I . . . found myself, as the shades of evening drew on, within view of the melancholy House of Usher" (HU, pp. 262–63)—is reflected in James's account: On "the last day of the year. . . . I . . . found myself before it" as "the light was failing, the sky low and gray. . . . The melancholy mansion stood there" (GR, p. 110). Nor are such echoes confined to the early pages of the tale. Just as Usher's "valet" (in Baudelaire's translation: "*domestique*")[21] "conducted" Poe's narrator through the mansion, "threw open a door and ushered me into the presence of his master" (HU, p. 265), so Diamond's "servant" acts as the divinity student's "conductress. . . . She quickly opened the door and led me in, and I very soon found myself in the presence of my old friend" (GR, p. 133). Usher describes, and James's narrator asks Diamond about, "the nature of his malady" (HU, p. 266; GR, p. 134). Usher's "countenance" is fixed in "stony rigidity" (p. 276), while Diamond lies "rigid," like "some ruggedly carven figure on the lid of a Gothic tomb" (p. 133)—this last a generic allusion equivalent to "the Gothic archway" of the House of Usher (p. 265).

What do these echoes mean? That they were purposeful is shown by James's modification of the "terror" to which Roderick Usher is "a bounden slave." Says Usher, "I *dread* the events of the future. . . . even the most trivial [Baudelaire: "*vulgaire*"][22] incident, which may operate on this intolerable agitation of soul. . . . I feel that the period will sooner or later arrive when I must abandon life and reason together, in some struggle with the grim *phantasm, FEAR*." Poe's narrator is himself overcome by an "astonishment not unmingled with *dread*" when he first sees Madeline Usher (p. 267; emphasis added). These states of fright are combined in James's ghost hunter as he encounters "the sable *phantom*" (GR, p. 131): "I frankly confess that by this time I was conscious of a feeling to which I am in duty bound to apply the *vulgar* name of *fear*. I may *poetize* it and call it *Dread, with a capital letter*; it was at any rate the feeling that makes a man yield ground" (p. 130; emphasis added). Except for *The Turn of the Screw*, "The Ghostly Rental" is the most consistently allusive of James's occult tales, with references to theologians from Plotinus and Augustine to Pascal and William Henry Channing, stories of the marvelous from the Arabian Nights and Bluebeard to the tales of Hoffmann. And by "*poetizing*" his narrator's "fear" as "Dread, with a capital letter," James deliberately gave his game away.

Pun and parallels do more than record an influence. The difference between the tales is the difference between Usher's dead-serious and the divinity student's ironic capitalization of their shared terror. Usher's fear is well grounded; he dies in the grip of "the grim phantasm," and his friend, no longer able to rationalize what he has witnessed, flees the mansion "aghast" (HU, p. 276). But James's narrator is granted second thoughts. His "excitement" subsiding when he has "put thirty miles between" himself and the haunted house, he rightly begins to suspect that "the sable phantom" is "a very clever phantom," perhaps "a sham ghost" (GR, pp. 131, 132).

Throughout "The Ghostly Rental," it is clear, James cheerfully and almost programmatically undermined Poe's Gothic poetics. As a rule, nineteenth-century readers took "Usher" as a supernatural tale, and if James was no exception he simply replaced Madeline, returned from her tomb, with a fraudulent ghost in keeping with the skeptical realism of the 1870s. He may even have presciently read "Usher" in the manner of those recent critics who see it as a psychological hoax, its narrator as deluded in his recital of incredible events.[23] In comparing Baudelaire and Poe, after all, James wrote that the latter "was much the greater charlatan of the two, as well as the greater genius." By allowing the divinity student to recover from his "Dread" and to unveil Diamond's daughter as a fake, James may very well have been unmasking Poe the "charlatan" while parodistically acknowledging his "genius."

In any event, just as James was unwilling to predicate preternatural communication on the basis of Hawthorne's anachronistic magnetism, so he purged Poe's melodramatic effects from the fiction of ghostly presence. Appropriately, "The Ghostly Rental" closes with the House of Usher, which in Poe apocalyptically disintegrates into the waters of the tarn, reduced to "a mass of charred beams and smoldering ashes"—the tarn itself diminished, in James's final word, to "puddles" (GR, p. 140). In his last early supernatural tale, James thoroughly "depoetized" Poe.

We are still left with a second ghost on our hands: what Captain Diamond's daughter thinks is her father's apparition. Terming this sudden reversal of haunter and haunted "the special twist that facile purveyors of the supernatural particularly relish," Martha Banta dismisses it as a "step backward into triteness."[24] The biter-bit twist is rather formulaic. Against the background of the major spiritualistic scandal of the 1870s, however, it can be seen as an instance of poetic if not Poesque justice. The old captain, who reminds the narrator of "a figure out of one of Hoffmann's tales," also resembles "the portraits of Andrew Jackson" (GR, p. 111)—an odd pair of allusions indeed. Yet if mention of Hoffmann points to Poe, as Sidney Lind suggests,[25] Diamond's insistence on "the power of departed spirits to return" (p. 117) could have reminded James's readers of the views of Robert Dale Owen, a venerable relic of the age of Jackson who had himself been deceived, not long before James wrote, by a beautiful false ghost who called him "Father Owen."[26]

After three decades as, successively, utopian socialist, freethinker, legislator, and diplomat, in 1856 Owen had turned to spiritualism. Since then his patient investigations and two relatively sober books on the subject (one of them unfavorably reviewed by the elder Henry James) had made him the leading American spokesman for the movement. A frequent contributor of reminiscence to the *Atlantic Monthly* in the early 1870s, he persuaded W. D. Howells, the magazine's editor, to publish three articles reporting his discovery of "proof of a life to come" in a series of Philadelphia séances at which he had repeatedly witnessed the "materialized spirit" of a young woman named Katie King. Unfortunately for both contributor and editor, in December 1874 Owen learned that Katie was a very human fraud, and he insisted on disclosing her charade to the newspapers before his climactic third article could be withdrawn from the January 1875 *Atlantic*. The fiasco destroyed his reputation and, despite an editorial disclaimer of responsibility for his account, caused no little embarrassment for the magazine, which was roundly condemned by the press for printing such foolishness. Through it all, though, Howells privately expressed respect and sympathy for Owen, whose integrity he would indirectly vindicate in his novel about spiritualism, *The Undiscovered Country* (1880).[27]

James could hardly have avoided knowing about the Katie King episode; the first installment of *Roderick Hudson* appeared in the same issue of the *Atlantic* as Owen's most controversial article, and in *The Bostonians* (1886) he would refer to the exposure of spurious materializations a decade earlier.[28] And whether or not he was aware of Howells's feelings about the affair, it would appear that he took the opportunity in "The Ghostly Rental" to reflect ironically on Owen's downfall. Unable to find incontrovertible evidence of spirit survival in "historical documents, sacred or profane" (many of them theological texts),[29] Owen wrote in the *Atlantic* that he had been brought to an absolute conviction of immortality because, "day after day, for weeks," he had "seen and touched and conversed with [the] materialized spirit" of Katie King.[30] Similarly, for Captain Diamond (whose situation fills the narrator with "curiosity" and "compassion"), "It's not a matter of cold theory—I have not had to pry into old books to learn what to believe. *I know!* With these eyes, I have beheld the departed spirit standing before me as near as you are! . . . You have seen a very honest old man who told you—on his honor—that he had seen a ghost!" (GR, pp. 124, 117). Again, "You have read about the immortality of the soul; you have seen Jonathan Edwards and Dr. Hopkins chopping logic over it, and deciding, chapter by verse, that it is true. But I have seen it with these eyes; I have touched it with these hands!" (p. 125).[31]

When Katie appealed to Owen, with "a look of weary sorrow," for protection from annoying visitors who insisted on touching her and kissing her "pale and beautiful face," he pledged "to protect her . . . as if she were my own daughter." And she allowed him "to see her without her lace veil."[32] Before setting out to collect the rental payment from the ghost, James's narrator is warned by Captain Diamond to "be very respectful—be very polite. . . . If not, I shall know it!" (GR, p. 136). But like the skeptical intruders who sometimes disrupted materialization séances, the divinity student impulsively pulls off the phantom's "long veil" to reveal "a beautiful woman" with "a pale, sorrow-worn face, painted to look paler" (pp. 137, 138). Diamond's daughter is outraged, but anger turns to shame and fright when she sees her father's specter. What better judgment on the false spiritualism that had ruined "Father Owen"—and on the morbidity of the ad hoc familial relationship—than to turn the tables by permitting the haunted to become the haunter, the guilty masquerader to realize that her victim's apparition is "the punishment" for her "long folly" (p. 138)? Rather than a trivial twist, then, the captain's ghost is a more fundamental if less direct attack on occult imposture than is the overt satire of "Professor Fargo."

There is more to Captain Diamond's ghost than topical vengeance. Having demystified both Poe and spiritualism, James set about improving on them with a supernatural experience that would be genuinely problematical. Appearing at about the time of his death, Diamond's spirit is a "crisis apparition" of the sort yet to be so named and reported during the 1880s and 1890s by the British Society for Psychical Research.[33] As such, it is a harbinger of Jamesian ghosts to come. Martha Banta has suggested that Isabel Archer's vision of Ralph Touchett at the moment he is dying in another room may be taken either as a "real" specter or as a subtle rendering of Isabel's understanding of her own ordeal.[34] The more definite ambiguity of a later crisis apparition is clearly tied to the evidentiary problems of the S.P.R. in "The Friends of the Friends" (1896)—originally titled "The Way It Came." The jealous narrator of this tale is impatient with her fiancé's refusal to admit that he has been visited by the spirit rather than, as he would prefer to think, the living person of a woman who has just died. "I should have supposed it more gratifying," says the narrator, "to be the subject of one of those inexplicable occurrences that are chronicled in thrilling books and disputed about at learned meetings."[35] Finally, although they are not crisis apparitions, the much "disputed" ghosts of *The Turn of the Screw* owe a great deal to S.P.R. accounts of such visitants.[36]

Those of us who have argued the case for James's indebtedness to the S.P.R. in the 1890s should note that as early as 1876, when psychical researchers were just beginning to collect their cases, he anticipated such apparitions with the ghost of Captain Diamond. As with its successors, its reality can be inferred from its simultaneity with the captain's death. Yet James carefully makes it perceptible only to the captain's daughter, not to the narrator; unverified, it could originate, as Peter Buitenhuis observes,[37] in the guilty imagination of the daughter, who has just asked whether her father is "dangerously ill" (GR, p. 137). Thus as opposed to the sensational revenant of "A Romance of Certain Old Clothes," to Poe's prematurely buried Madeline Usher, and to the "sham ghost" of the daughter herself, the captain's specter, prefiguring the "inexplicable occurrences" of the later tales, is ambiguous in the best Jamesian sense.

It will not do to regard either "Professor Fargo" or "The Ghostly Rental" as among James's most successful occult fictions. But they do mark a turning point in the canon. Taking leave of his early experiments in the supernatural, he discarded elements of Gothic tradition that he found unsatisfactory, along with the cultural baggage of mesmerism and spiritualism. When he returned to the genre in the "psychical" 1890s, he would be ready to develop more fully the supernatural phenomenology that he evidenced here in demagnetizing Hawthorne and depoetizing Poe.

NOTES

1. *Henry James: Stories of the Supernatural*, ed. Leon Edel (New York: Taplinger, 1970), p. 25.

2. Ibid., p. 419.

3. *The Complete Tales of Henry James*, ed. Leon Edel, vol. 3 (Philadelphia: Lippincott, 1962), p. 286. References to "Professor Fargo" are hereafter cited in the text as PF.

4. See Martha Banta, *Henry James and the Occult: The Great Extension* (Bloomington: Indiana University Press, 1972), pp. 90–94; Howard Kerr, *Mediums, and Spirit-Rappers, and Roaring Radicals: Spiritualism in American Literature, 1850–1900* (Urbana: University of Illinois Press, 1972), pp. 212–13; Maria M. Tatar, *Spellbound: Studies on Mesmerism and Literature* (Princeton: Princeton University Press, 1978), pp. 232–35. None of these distinguish between Fargo's magnetism and Miss Gifford's clairvoyance.

5. Nathaniel Hawthorne, *Love Letters of Nathaniel Hawthorne, 1839–1863* (Washington, D.C.: NCR Microcard Editions, 1972), p. 62; Nathaniel Hawthorne, *The House of the Seven Gables*, ed. William Charvat et al. (Columbus: Ohio State University Press, 1965), p. 26.

6. Hawthorne, *Love Letters*, p. 63.

7. Henry James, *Hawthorne* (Ithaca, N.Y.: Cornell University Press, 1967), p. 108.

8. Mark Twain, *Adventures of Huckleberry Finn* (New York: Charles L. Webster and Co., 1885), p. 162.

9. *Cincinnati Enquirer*, 4 July 1874, p. 8.

10. Nathaniel Hawthorne, *The Blithedale Romance* and *Fanshawe*, ed. William Charvat et al. (Columbus: Ohio State University Press, 1964), p. 198.

11. Taylor Stoehr, *Hawthorne's Mad Scientists: Pseudoscience and Social Science in Nineteenth-Century Life and Letters* (Hamden, Conn.: Shoe String Press, Archon Books, 1978), p. 48.

12. James, *Hawthorne*, p. 108.

13. Banta, *Henry James and the Occult*, pp. 154–63.

14. Edel, ed. *Henry James: Stories of the Supernatural*, p. 108. References to "The Ghostly Rental" are hereafter cited in the text as GR.

15. For remarks about Hawthorne's influence on the tale, see the excellent interpretation by Peter Buitenhuis, *The Grasping Imagination: The American Writings of Henry James* (Toronto: University of Toronto Press, 1970), p. 87. Two other worthwhile treatments of the story are Robert J. Andreach, "Literary Allusion as a Clue to Meaning: James's 'The Ghostly Rental' and Pascal's *Pensées*," *Comparative Literature Studies* 4 (1967): 299–306, and Banta, *Henry James and the Occult*, pp. 106–10.

16. "The Fall of the House of Usher," in *The Complete Poems and Stories of Edgar Allan Poe*, ed. Arthur Hobson Quinn and Edward H. O'Neill (New York: Knopf, 1946), 1:263, hereafter cited in the text as HU.

17. Cornelia P. Kelley, *The Early Development of Henry James*, rev. ed. (Urbana:

University of Illinois Press, 1965), p. 264 (n. 5); Edel, ed. *Henry James: Stories of the Supernatural*, p. 103; Sidney P. Lind, "The Supernatural Tales of Henry James: Conflict and Fantasy," Ph.D. dissertation, New York University, 1948, pp. 92–97.

18. Henry James, *French Poets and Novelists* (New York: Macmillan, 1878), p. 76.

19. Lind also points summarily to "correspondences" between Madeline Usher's return from premature burial to confront her brother and the haunting of Diamond by his daughter, and between the "cataclysmic" collapse of the House of Usher and the fire with which James "more realistically" destroys Diamond's farmhouse ("The Supernatural Tales of Henry James," p. 97).

20. Burton R. Pollin, "Poe and Henry James: A Changing Relationship," *Yearbook of English Studies* 3 (1973): 234. The "relationship" solicits further study.

21. Charles Baudelaire, trans., *Oeuvres en Prose*, by Edgar Allan Poe (Paris: Gallimard, 1951), p. 340. Some of James's verbal borrowings may come from Baudelaire's translation.

22. Baudelaire, *Oeuvres*, p. 343.

23. See G. R. Thompson, *Poe's Fiction: Romantic Irony in the Gothic Tales* (Madison: University of Wisconsin Press, 1973), pp. 87–98, 225–27.

24. Banta, *Henry James and the Occult*, p. 110.

25. Lind, "The Supernatural Tales of Henry James," p. 93.

26. Robert Dale Owen, "Touching Spiritual Visitants from a Higher Life," *Atlantic Monthly* 35 (1875): 65 (n. 1).

27. This account is based on my discussion of the Owen-Howells relationship in *Mediums, and Spirit-Rappers, and Roaring Radicals*, pp. 121–48.

28. Henry James, *The Bostonians*, ed. Alfred Habegger (Indianapolis: Bobbs-Merrill, 1976), p. 146.

29. Robert Dale Owen, "How I Came to Study Spiritual Phenomena," *Atlantic Monthly* 34 (1874): 578.

30. Robert Dale Owen, "Some Results from My Spiritual Studies," *Atlantic Monthly* 34 (1874): 722.

31. Andreach, "Literary Allusion as a Clue to Meaning," pp. 299, 305 (n. 2), suggests that Diamond's words echo Pascal ("Dieu d'Abraham, Dieu d'Isaac, Dieu de Jacob, non des Philosophes et des savants. . . . Père juste, le monde ne t'a point connu, mais je t'ai connu"). I think that they translate Owen more closely.

32. Owen, "Touching Spiritual Visitants," pp. 60, 61.

33. Alan Gauld, *The Founders of Psychical Research* (New York: Schocken Books, 1968), pp. 160–74.

34. Banta, *Henry James and the Occult*, p. 131.

35. Edel, ed., *Henry James: Stories of the Supernatural*, p. 419.

36. For arguments on this point, see Francis X. Roellinger, Jr., "Psychical Research and 'The Turn of the Screw,'" *American Literature* 20 (January 1949): 401–12; Banta, *Henry James and the Occult*, pp. 34–50; Kerr, *Mediums, and Spirit-Rappers, and Roaring Radicals*, pp. 206–11; Ernest Tuveson, "'The Turn of the Screw': A Palimpsest," *Studies in English Literature* 12 (1972): 783–800; E. A. Sheppard, *Henry James and "The Turn of the Screw"* (New York: Oxford University Press, 1974), pp. 116–211; Joseph Backus, "Henry James and Psychical Research," *Journal of the American Society for Psychical Research* 72 (1978): 49–60.

37. Buitenhuis, *The Grasping Imagination*, p. 87.

JOHN W. CROWLEY AND
CHARLES L. CROW

Psychology and the Psychic in W. D. Howells's "A Sleep and a Forgetting"

One tenet of W. D. Howells's realism was the primacy of the commonplace. Early in his career he insisted: "As in literature the true artist will shun the use even of real events if they are of an improbable character, so the sincere observer of man will not desire to look upon his heroic or occasional phases, but will seek him in his habitual moods of vacancy and tiresomeness. To me, at any rate, he is at such times very precious."[1] Howells championed this belief in his criticism, and in his fiction he staked his literary reputation on it.

It was with disquiet, then, that Howells, nearing the age of seventy, realized his loss of interest in what he used to find so precious. From Atlantic City he wrote to Charles Eliot Norton in 1906:

> In all our weeks we have not seen one distinguished figure or striking face, but the decent average has interestingly abounded. It is such an afflux of the ordinary as in earlier life I should have rejoiced in for my poor literature's sake; but now, though I still see all things as before, I no longer make note of them, voluntarily or involuntarily. What interests me in this fact is that it is unexpected. I thought I should wish to keep on gathering material to the end, but I find that I have stored up enough to last my time. I let the most delightful types go by without seeking an impression from them; and I had not supposed that nature would intimate in this way that it was time for me to close up business. From the accumulations of the past I have been writing a long short story, but it is very subjective, almost psychopathic. It is a new field for my ignorance.[2]

Only because of his long-term psychological and literary investment in his earlier beliefs did Howells even momentarily interpret his boredom with the "decent average" as a signal to "close up business." He had been a writer too long for that, and though he feared at times that he was losing his creativity, Howells continued to follow the lead of his imagination, even into paths he had earlier ruled off limits to a realist.

Certainly, Howells's finest work was done before the turn of the century, but in his later years he evinced an imaginative vigor remarkable in a writer half his age. *Literary Friends and Acquaintance* (1900) and *My Mark Twain* (1910) are among the shrewdest and subtlest literary portraits in our literature. *London Films* (1905) and *Certain Delightful English Towns* (1906) are, as Kenneth Lynn asserts, "the most interesting travel books Howells had written since *Venetian Life*, and they have not been surpassed either in descriptive precision or stylistic grace by any other American commentary on Great Britain in this century."[3] From the "accumulations of the past," Howells also produced in this period an autobiography—*Years of My Youth* (1916)—and some of his better novels: *The Kentons* (1902), *New Leaf Mills* (1913), and *The Leatherwood God* (1916). Finally, he accurately observed in his book reviews that realism was evolving into "psychologism," as he called it, and he explored this new field himself in such psychological novels as *The Son of Royal Langbrith* (1904), *Miss Bellard's Inspiration* (1905), and *Fennel and Rue* (1908), as well as in a series of psychic tales, collected in *Questionable Shapes* (1903) and *Between the Dark and the Daylight* (1907).[4]

One of these tales, "A Sleep and a Forgetting," was the "subjective, almost psychopathic" story he described to Norton in 1906. It deserves close examination not only because it is a good story but because it reflects some vital imaginative concerns of Howells's late phase. As he implied to Norton, "A Sleep and a Forgetting" marked a deliberate departure from the commonplace world of his realism into the "borderland between experience and illusion" of romance.[5] Like many of his late tales, this one is both psychological, in its attention to the function of memory, and psychic, in its preoccupation with the conundrum of immortality. Furthermore, the story is autobiographically suggestive in its treatment of a father-daughter relationship.

II

Although Howells spoke of "A Sleep and a Forgetting" as "a new field for my ignorance," he had been assimilating knowledge of psychological theory and psychiatric practice for at least a quarter of a century. This period, among the most revolutionary in the history of

American psychology, took Howells the full distance from the somatic school through the French psychologists whose findings anticipated Freud's. Throughout his life Howells was plagued by neurotic ailments and sometimes by emotional vastations. His personal exposure to formal psychological treatment came, however, not in his own case but in that of his daughter Winifred. The experience of Howells's "black time," the decade of Winny's illness and death, was the genesis of "A Sleep and a Forgetting."

When Winifred suffered her first breakdown at age sixteen (in 1880), she was placed in the care of James Jackson Putnam, the famous neurologist of the Harvard Medical School. Later she was treated by S. Weir Mitchell, whom Howells knew as a writer as well as a psychologist.[6] Both physicians were important members of the somatic school of American psychology, which asserted that mental illness was caused by "lesions" of the nervous system. The treatment both prescribed for Winny—rest and forced feeding—was typical of the somatic approach.[7] Putnam was later to move away from this method and ultimately to accept many of Freud's ideas; Mitchell never did. An often-repeated anecdote has Mitchell flinging his first copy of a work by Freud into his fireplace.

The death of Winifred in 1889 was a tragic illustration for Howells of the shortcomings of the somatic method in diagnosis and treatment. After several years of unsuccessful "cures" at a variety of sanitariums, Winifred had been turned over to Mitchell's care in November 1888. Howells was buoyantly hopeful at first, telling his father that "if you could see Dr. Mitchell, you would see how he differed from all other specialists, and would not have a doubt but she was in the best and wisest and kindest hands in the world." Nonetheless, Mitchell regarded Winny's as "a very difficult case" that was badly complicated by her resisting his hypothesis that her vertigo and other "hypochondriacal illusions" were hysterical, not somatic, symptoms.[8] Through confinement to bed, massage, heavy doses of iron and milk—all standard features of the rest cure—Mitchell hoped to break his patient's will and to fatten her up to health, and within two months, Winifred did gain fifteen pounds, though she continued to be rebellious. Howells went to see her in Philadelphia in February 1889 and found her looking extremely well. Mitchell agreed that it was time to let Winny out of bed and to send her to the country for some fresh air and exercise. On March 2 she died there of heart failure. In a letter to Mitchell a few days later, Howells implied that evidence had been discovered of an organic malady, evidence that brought "the sad satisfaction of knowing that the end which came so suddenly must have come soon at the best, and we are almost happy to be assured that it was not through any error or want of skill." But Howells felt tormented by the thought that "the poor child's pain was all along as great as she fancied, if she was so diseased, as apparently she was" (*SL*, p. 247). Howells seems to have blamed himself rather than the physicians, however. As he told Henry James, "You know perhaps the poor child was not with us when she died; she died homesick and wondering at her separation, in the care of the doctors who fancied they were curing her" (p. 253).

The loss served to intensify Howells's interest in psychological theories. In *The Shadow of a Dream* (1890), for example, his characters discuss a passage from Théodule-Armand Ribot's *Diseases of Personality*. The next year Howells read *The Principles of Psychology*, by his old friend William James, and recognized its importance in a laudatory review.[9] An 1894 letter of Samuel Clemens's suggests how assiduously Howells and his wife kept abreast of new developments in psychology. Elinor Howells, whose own health had collapsed under the strain of Winifred's death, was undergoing "mind cure" treatment, which, she insisted to Clemens, was synonymous with hypnotism. Clemens apparently took hope for his daughter Susy's recovery from Elinor Howells's evident revitalization. He wrote to his wife Livy: "She convinced *me*, before she got through, that she and William James are right—hypnotism & mind-cure are the same thing; no difference between them. Very well; the very source, the very *centre* of hypnotism is *Paris*. Dr. Charcot's pupils & disciples are right there & ready to your hand without fetching poor dear old Susy across the stormy sea. Let Mrs. Mackay . . . tell you whom to go to to learn all you need to learn & how to proceed. *Do*, do it, honey. Don't lose a minute."[10]

The studies of the French psychologists and William James (who drew heavily on their research in *The Principles of Psychology*) overturned the somatic theories by which Winifred had been treated. Summarizing the importance of the French psychologists, Nathan Hale stresses that their discoveries "opened up the whole question of what personality was and what constituted the limits and nature of human consciousness. They established experimentally the existence of the subconscious. They also demonstrated that hypnotic suggestion could induce and cure symptoms. What had seemed the

undeniably physical effects of disease could be regarded as the results of an 'idea' or an 'emotion.'"[11] Especially significant was the
work of Jean Charcot, whose discovery (first announced in 1882)
that symptoms of paralysis could be induced hypnotically discredited the lesion theory of somatic psychology.

III

"A Sleep and a Forgetting" is set at the turn of the century or a few
years after, during the period of upheaval in American psychiatry
caused by these new discoveries. The story explores the relationship
of a psychologically crippled American girl to her father and to the
psychologist who treats her. The triangular relationship begins
when Dr. Matthew Lanfear, vacationing on the Riviera, meets Abner
Gerald and his daughter Nannie. The unusual symptoms of the girl's
mental illness kindle Lanfear's professional curiosity. She saw her
mother killed in an accident several months earlier and, recovering
from shock, manifested a unique form of amnesia. Not only was the
accident erased from her mind, but she retained scarcely any faculty
of memory at all. Events, names, people fade from her mind almost
immediately. Left with Lanfear after their first chance meeting in a
railway station, while her father searches for a porter, she tells the
astonished doctor that she is traveling alone. Yet, paradoxically, the
other forms of normal and intelligent mental activity remain. This
condition persists, in spite of Lanfear's treatment, until the girl witnesses a maniac's attack on her father. She falls into a coma, appears
at its deepest point actually to die, but recovers with her memory restored. The psychologist, now free of professional contraints,
marries the healthy and normal young woman. The ending is shad-
owed, however, by the death of Abner Gerald. Although he recovers
from the madman's attack, his death follows upon Nannie's happy
marriage.

If the story as summarized seems familiar, even hackneyed, it is
because plots based on the psychotherapeutic relationship have become commonplace both in serious modern fiction and, often in a
debased form, in bestsellers, movies, and television melodramas.
The neurotic character and his psychiatrist (in the various roles of
confessor, lover, sleuth, seducer, or charlatan) have become such
stock figures that they figure satirically in recent fiction.

When Howells wrote "A Sleep and a Forgetting," the psychotherapeutic relationship was not a shopworn plot device; he was, in
fact, pioneering a new fictional territory. While psychologists had
appeared in American fiction before, most notably in S. Weir Mitchell's stories, Howells's tale, written in the year of the American lectures of Pierre Janet (the formulator of the theory of psychic trauma)
and three years before Freud's famous appearance at Clark University, comes much closer to the modern spirit. Strong undercurrents
of doubt run through the work, including doubt about the definitions of health and disease. And in a way dimly predictive of *Tender
Is the Night*—perhaps the greatest American novel in the psychotherapeutic tradition—the buried motives of the characters often
run counter to their roles and professed intentions.

Howells's psychiatrist-hero, Matthew Lanfear, reflects the uncertainties of a profession in transition. Like many psychiatrists now,
he has specialized in the neuroses of the rich. Lanfear is visiting the
Riviera at the beginning of the story in part to find a suitable place
for a wealthy neurasthenic woman to recuperate. His treatment of
Nannie consists of little more than mild exercise and therapeutic
conversation, prescriptions which would have been unexceptional
in the somatic method. Yet he can say of dreams, "A good third of
our lives here is passed in sleep. I'm not always sure that we are right
in treating the mental—for certainly they are mental—experiences
of that time as altogether trivial, or insignificant." [12] His statement
seems pathetically naïve after Freud, but it is a clear departure from
the somatic insistence on the meaninglessness of dream phenomena. Similarly, Lanfear understands that the cause of Nannie's amnesia was the mental impact of seeing her mother's death, and he
believes that "there's a kind of psychopathic logic— If she lost her
memory through one great shock, she might find it through another" (p. 58). Lanfear thus voices an understanding of trauma theory, as developed by Pierre Janet, in accordance with which Nannie's
amnesia does end.

Lanfear, however, does little to bring about the girl's recovery, and
he is hampered not only by the limited state of his science but by
two emotional crosscurrents: he clearly loves the girl, and in some
ways he does not want her to get well. Like Fitzgerald's Dick Diver,
he is torn between the roles of lover and physician.

Both Lanfear and Gerald have reasons to prefer Nannie ill to Nannie well. The central paradox of the story is created by the attractive-

ness of her condition, which combines intact personality with loss of long-term memory.[13] Nannie Gerald is the ultimate evolution of the innocent American girl abroad who had intrigued readers for decades. Like Daisy Miller, she sweeps through a complex social environment oblivious to the misunderstandings she creates. Men, unable to understand her behavior, project their own expectations upon her. A young Englishman attempts to court her and leaves heartbroken at her inadvertent indifference; an Italian officer misinterprets her greeting as coquettishness and stalks her as fair game for seduction. Unlike other innocents abroad, however, Nannie does not raise questions about the nature of American as contrasted to European society. By focusing on the medical rather than social causes of her behavior, Howells explores the nature of innocence itself, divorced from its relation to experience and from cultural influences.

Miss Gerald's innocence responds with an aesthetic purity impossible for the memory-clogged mind of a normal person. When she plays the piano, as her father reports, "it is like composing the music for herself; she does not seem to remember the pieces, she seems to improvise them" (pp. 16–17). Each piece of music, like all experience, is responded to freshly, as if for the first time. In contrast, Lanfear has the complicated reactions engendered by personal and cultural memory. He is saddened when he reflects on the landscape around San Remo because he recalls its history: "You know the pirates used to come sailing over the peaceful sea yonder from Africa, to harry these coasts, and carry off as many as they could capture into slavery in Tunis and Algiers. It was a long, dumb kind of misery that scarcely made an echo in history, but it haunted my fancy yesterday, and I saw these valleys full of the flight and the pursuit which used to fill them, up to the walls of the villages, perched on the heights where men could have built only for safety. Then, I got to thinking of other things—" (p. 51). Lanfear's train of melancholy associations is the conditioned response of a man of genteel nineteenth-century education. As Henry Nash Smith notes of an analogous landscape description in Mark Twain's *Innocents Abroad*: "Exploiting associations in this fashion was a heritage from eighteenth-century Scottish literary theorists, especially Lord Kames, Hugh Blair, and Archibald Alison. The notion that a writer could endow a landscape with aesthetic value by evoking images of past events connected with it in his mind had been a commonplace of

American criticism for fifty years or more."[14] Lanfear's associationist response contrasts with Nannie's responsiveness to the beauty of
the landscape itself, an aesthetic reaction that denies associationist
aesthetics even as her condition denies associationist psychology.
"How strange it is," Nannie says to Lanfear on one such occasion,
"that you see things for what they are like, and not for what they
are!" (p. 27).

It is not surprising, then, that Lanfear and Gerald share a fascination for Nannie's paradoxically beautiful illness. Gerald knows that
she is spared the pain of her mother's death by her amnesia. Moreover, her invalidism re-creates the dependency and simplicity of
childhood that every parent sees pass with regret and recalls with
nostalgia. Nannie senses her father's mixed feelings and revealingly
asks Lanfear, "Then why doesn't papa want me to remember things?"
(p. 28). Lanfear, too, catches himself about to say that "he would not
have her so" when she expresses a hope of recovering her memory
and being "like other people" (p. 51). Of course he would not, when
he finds in her a perpetually unfallen Eve, "a nature knowing itself
from moment to moment as if newly created" (p. 39).

IV

Nannie's psychological illness, so far as it may be regarded, paradoxically, as psychic health, raises questions that are ultimately epistemological. By drawing the title of "A Sleep and a Forgetting" from
Wordsworth's ode, and by alluding to it in the story, Howells asks
whether it is possible to believe that an innocent child can have intimations of immortality, and thus whether it is possible to believe in
immortality itself.

> Our birth is but a sleep and a forgetting:
> The Soul that rises with us, our life's Star,
>   Hath had elsewhere its setting,
>   And cometh from afar:
>   And not in utter nakedness,
> But trailing clouds of glory do we come
>   From God, who is our home.[15]

Early in the story Howells dramatizes a conversation between
Nannie and Lanfear that reflects his own ambivalence about immor-

tality. "But don't you sometimes—sometimes . . . have a feeling as if what you were doing, or saying, or seeing, had all happened before, just as it is now?" she asks him. When he replies that such an experience is a psychological commonplace, she persists:

> "But don't you—don't you have hints of things, of ideas, as if you had known them, in some previous existence—"
> She stopped, and Lanfear recognized, with a kind of impatience, the experience which young people make much of when they have it, and sometimes pretend to when they have merely heard of it. But there could be no pose or pretence in her. He smilingly suggested:
> "'For something is, or something seems,
> Like glimpses of forgotten dreams.'
> These weird impressions are no more than that, probably."
> "Ah, I don't believe it," the girl said. "They are too real for that. They come too often, and they make me feel as if they would come more fully, some time. If there was a life before this—do you believe there was?—they may be things that happened there. Or they may be things that will happen in a life after this. You believe in *that*, don't you?"
> "In a life after this, or their happening in it?"
> "Well, both."
> Lanfear evaded her, partly. "They could be premonitions, prophecies, of a future life, as easily as fragmentary records of a past life. I suppose we do not begin to be immortal merely after death." (pp. 23–24)

Lanfear, the man of science, is clearly discomfited when the discussion ranges beyond the realm of the psychological into the realm of the psychic. He would prefer to explain Nannie's intimations of immortality as "floating illusions" associated with her amnesia (p. 24). What she takes to be glimpses of forgotten dreams or premonitions of a future life are really, he supposes, normal human memories crowding upon the edge of her consciousness, appearing and disappearing in tantalizing flashes.

For Lanfear, Nannie's condition makes her less than fully human; it also makes her more than human: "When he saw in her the persistence of an exquisite personality independent of the means by which he realized his own continuous identity, he sometimes felt as if in the presence of some angel so long freed from earthly allegiance that it had left all record behind" (p. 39). Half-child, half-angel, Nannie can remain neither. She recovers, suffers the human pain of remembering, and becomes the *woman* that Lanfear marries. Like Wordsworth, Howells suggests that the tragic cost of maturation is the loss of a divine and divining light that fades into the light of common day. But Howells also suggests that the light of childhood innocence may be an illusion, a phenomenon that seems psychic only because a psychological explanation has yet to be found.

A better gloss than Wordsworth's ode on Howells's attitudes in "A Sleep and a Forgetting" is Maurice Maeterlinck's essay, "Of Immortality," which Howells read while he was writing the story.[16] On 24 January 1906, he thanked Frederick Duneka, editor at Harper Brothers, for reminding him of Maeterlinck's paper, and he added, "It is a great and consoling effort, and it quite jumps with the motive I am working out in a story."[17] Howells's shock of recognition is understandable, since Maeterlinck's ideas are almost identical to his own. In brief, Maeterlinck argues that because memory is the core of human identity, no person can easily believe, or even desire, an immortality that would not preserve "the mnemonic ego." Our earthly consciousness prevents us from conceiving of "an enlarged and transformed consciousness," just as "our imperfect eye prevents us from conceiving any other light than that which goes from infra-red to ultra-violet, whereas it is certain that those probably prodigious lights would dazzle on every side, in the darkest night, a pupil differently shaped from ours" (p. 136). Maeterlinck sees "no other means of escaping from one's consciousness than to deny it, to look upon it as an organic disease of the terrestrial intelligence—a disease which we must endeavor to cure by an action which must appear to us an action of violent and wilful madness, but which, on the other side of our appearances, is probably an action of health" (p. 136). (This inversion of the definitions of health and disease perfectly elucidates the paradoxical attractiveness of Nannie Gerald's illness.) By opening our imaginations to the chance of a different kind of consciousness, which Maeterlinck thinks may be analogous to detached aesthetic experience, we can posit "an existence much more spacious, lofty, perfect, durable, and secure than that which is offered to us by our actual consciousness. Admitting this possibility—and there are few as probable—the problem of our immortality is, in principle, solved" (p. 137).

In essence, Maeterlinck urges something very much like William

James's "will to believe."[18] Just as Howells found himself in agreement with James's psychology, so he also shared James's questing for religious faith and his fascination with psychic phenomena. "A Sleep and a Forgetting" owes as much to the Society for Psychical Research (James was a founder of the American branch) as it does to *The Principles of Psychology*. Through the character of Lanfear, Howells expresses his own grasp of psychological theory and his agnosticism about immortality. But, as in his other late tales, he does not foreclose psychic possibilities; he deliberately allows an air of mystery to surround Nannie Gerald. The theory of trauma may explain to some degree both the onset and the remission of Nannie's amnesia, but it does not definitively account for her psychic intuitions.

Similarly, her unconscious memory of an earlier outing may explain how Nannie manages to find the way back to the Berigo road after she and Lanfear get lost, but it cannot account for her uncanny behavior during their later visits to the ruins of Possana, a town leveled by an earthquake in 1887. With feelings of intense melancholy, Lanfear has explored the ruins on the previous day, and, although she was not with him on that occasion, Nannie has somehow divined his private mood. "Why were you so sad?" she asks him abruptly (p. 50). This is only the first of several instances in which Nannie seems to enter the thoughts and feelings of others. As they pause in a ruined church, symbolic of the romantic, disordered beauty of Nannie's mind, they speak of a madman lurking on the trail to the nearby village. His sanity was destroyed by the tragedy of the earthquake, just as her mind was affected by her own disaster. Nannie asserts her psychic kinship with him as she earlier has with Lanfear and as she later does with a peasant girl orphaned by the quake. She reflects, "How strange it must all have seemed to them, here where they lived so safely always! They thought such a dreadful thing could happen to others, but not to them. That is the way!" (p. 53). Lanfear senses that she may be "on the verge of the knowledge so long kept from her" (p. 53). He notices, too, that Nannie speaks "of the earthquake as if she had been reading or hearing of it; but he doubted if, with her broken memory, this could be so. It was rather as if she was exploring his own mind in the way of which he had more than once been sensible, and making use of his memory" (pp. 53–54). And when they lose their path in the labyrinthine ruins, she finds it, though he has been there before and she has not, apparently by tapping the memory that has slipped below the level of his recall. "In some mystical sort the effect was hers, but the means was his" (p. 54).

This "mystical" perception of hers is never explained in the story, but Howells surely intended it to be recognized as mental telepathy of the sort studied by the Society for Psychical Research. He also uses Nannie's telepathic powers to raise the same kinds of questions and hopes about immortality raised by Frederic Myers and other psychical researchers.[19] That is, Howells perceived a gap of mystery between the state of psychological knowledge and the psychic phenomena represented by Nannie's telepathy and her intimations of immortality; in this crevice between the rational and the mystical Howells's own will to believe took root. As Lanfear reflects Howells's rational side, Nannie Gerald reflects his susceptibility to psychic phenomena, especially with regard to Winifred.

Winifred's death devastated Howells, compelling him to reconsider his religious beliefs, or, more accurately, his lack of them. That no afterlife would exist to compensate Winifred for her suffering was an almost unbearable thought. Perhaps encouraged by William James's experiences with the psychic Leonora Piper, Howells approached the American branch of the Society for Psychical Research in 1891 and arranged to attend a séance at a farmhouse. But the séance and a later "sort of ghost-story swap" with members of the society left him skeptical of ever making contact with Winifred.[20] He did, however, continue to take hope from dream visions of her, even though he recognized that such dreams might be delusory. "It may be that this is our anguish compelling the echo of love out of the darkness where nothing is," he admitted in 1895, "but it may be that there is something there, which answers to our throe with pity and with longing like our own. Again, no one knows, but in a matter impossible of definite solution, I will not refuse the comfort which belief can give. Unbelief can be no gain in it, and belief no loss."[21]

Five years later, in a quasi-autobiographical verse-drama, Howells depicted the parents of a dead girl, witnessing on the day of her funeral what the Society for Psychical Research might have called a veridical phantasm. The mother and father become suddenly and mutually aware of their lost child:

THE MOTHER: How natural she is! How strong and bright,
And all that sick look gone! It must be true

That it is she, but how shall we be sure
After it passes? Where is it you see her?
Where is it that you hear her speak?
   THE FATHER: Within.
Within my brain, my heart, my life, my love!
   THE MOTHER: Yes, that is where I see and hear her too.
And oh, I feel her! This is her dear hand
In mine! How warm and soft it is once more,
After that sickness! Yes, we have her back,
Dearest, we have our child again! [22]

Although Howells probably did not experience any such waking vision, his imagining it may be regarded as a kind of wish-fulfillment. Haunted by grief for Winifred and guilt about his impotence in the face of her pain and death, Howells yearned for the consolation of knowing that she lived on, that her agony had not been so meaningless or so cosmically unjust as he sometimes felt.

V

Howells's anguish over Winifred's death sheds light on the puzzling ending of "A Sleep and a Forgetting." The logic of the plot does not seem to require Abner Gerald to die; in fact, he has every reason to feel rejuvenated. His daughter has recovered her memory without the suffering he feared she might incur; almost like Sleeping Beauty, she has awakened to marry her Prince Charming. And yet, without apparent cause, he dies within months of the wedding. "He gave his life that I might have mine!" Nannie laments (p. 61), and, despite Lanfear's rejection of this view, she is right, at least figuratively.

On one level the ending suggests a purgation of Howells's personal tragedy. Like Howells, stocky, kindly Gerald is helpless in his attempts to care for his daughter.[23] Nannie literally dies in her coma (her pulse stops), then revives. Her recovery is exactly the return from a psychological illness that Howells had wished for Winifred. But she, of course, had not recovered, and Howells's killing off Gerald may be seen as a symbolic act of atonement, a fantasy in which Winifred is brought to life again by his own sacrifice.

On another level, however, the autobiographical implications are more complicated and disturbing. Like Lanfear, Abner Gerald vacillates throughout the story between hoping for Nannie's recovery and hoping against it. While she lies in her coma, he paces the floor, terrified by the prospect of her being shocked into health. "If I could die myself, and save her from living through it—" he says, and then checks himself; "I don't know what I'm saying! But if—but if—if she could somehow be kept from it a little longer!" (p. 58). In fact, Gerald's apparent illogic makes perfect psychological sense, as he himself begins to perceive a few moments later. In "a husky undertone, and brokenly, incoherently," he asks Lanfear: "Do you think I am to blame for wishing her never to know it, though without it she must remain deprived of one whole side of life? Do you think my wishing that could have had anything to do with keeping her—" (p. 58).

Gerald never completes his thought because its implications are too shocking for him to admit fully. Unconsciously, Gerald has wished to keep Nannie imprisoned in a state of incestuous, infantile attachment to him, to prevent her (again, like Sleeping Beauty) from waking into psychological and sexual maturity.[24] With her telepathic sensitivity to others, Nannie has intuited and obeyed his wish. Indeed, her recovery is triggered only when her belief that he has been killed breaks her father's spell: Her first words after she comes out of the coma are, "My father! Where is he? . . . I thought you were dead" (p. 59). Gerald dies because he no longer has a purpose in living; he has been replaced by Lanfear, who, after Gerald's death, begins to call Nannie "by the pet name which her father always used" (p. 61).

Of course, Gerald never becomes fully conscious of his motivations or of their effect on Nannie. But so far as Howells *is* conscious of Gerald's subliminal possessiveness, killing him off may be a symbolic act of suicide, inspired by guilt for whatever wishes he may have harbored that Winifred would never recover.[25]

VI

It would be a mistake, however, to reduce "A Sleep and a Forgetting" to an autobiographical psychodrama. These dark undercurrents, so pervasive in Howells's late work, serve rather to qualify his more conscious and more hopeful emphasis on the power of love. Gerald's unconscious selfishness is balanced by his conscious devotion to his daughter. And if he fears what he will lose in her recovery, he regrets as well what *she* will lose—precisely that perfect childish innocence that not only allows her intimations of immortality, but leaves her love for other mortals untainted by the selfishness of normal human nature.

Early in the story, Nannie sees her father sitting on a bench, observing the "northern consumptives" and peasant girls and "wrinkled grandmothers" who pass by. She says to Lanfear: "When he sits there among those sick people and poor people, then he knows they are in the world" (p. 22). "Yes," he replies, "we might help them oftener if we could remember that their misery was going on all the time, like some great natural process, day or dark, heat or cold, which seems to stop when we stop thinking of it. Nothing, for us, at least, exists unless it is recalled to us" (p. 23). Only a nature like Nannie's in her illness, incapable of remembering pain, is capable of untiring compassion for the misery of others.[26] Such love is possible for normal persons only for brief moments when they overcome their forgetfulness, the self-protective amnesia that allows them to put out of mind what would be too burdensome to remember always.

In "Father and Mother," Howells has the father assert that the spirit of their daughter may be recalled, not by will, "which is a part of us, / And filled full of ourselves," but through love, "which is a part of some life else, and filled / With something not ourselves, but better, purer."[27] Like Wordsworth, Howells implies that the celestial light that fades into the light of common day may be partly recoverable in those acts of perfect love that release humans from the prison of self-consciousness:

> Though nothing can bring back the hour
> Of splendour in the grass, of glory in the flower;
> We will grieve not, rather find
> Strength in what remains behind;
> In the primal sympathy
> Which having been must ever be;
> In the soothing thoughts that spring
> Out of human suffering.

This "primal sympathy" lay at the heart of Howells's realistic vision even when, as in the writing of "A Sleep and a Forgetting," he felt himself to be far removed from the "decent average."

NOTES

1. W. D. Howells, *Their Wedding Journey*, ed. John K. Reeves (Bloomington: Indiana University Press, 1968), p. 55.

2. Letter of 11 March 1906; MS quoted by permission of the Houghton Library and William White Howells for the heirs of the Howells estate. No republication may be made without the same permissions.

3. Kenneth Lynn, *William Dean Howells: An American Life* (New York: Harcourt Brace Jovanovich, 1971), p. 320.

4. On these psychic tales see Charles L. Crow, "Howells and William James: 'A Case of Metaphantasmia' Solved," *American Quarterly* 27 (1975): 169–77; John W. Crowley, "Howells' *Questionable Shapes*: From Psychologism to Psychic Romance," *ESQ* 21 (1975): 169–78.

5. This phrase is taken from Howells's introduction to an anthology of psychic tales he edited: *Shapes that Haunt the Dusk* (New York: Harper, 1907), p. v.

6. On Putnam and Winifred, see Lynn, *William Dean Howells*, p. 252; on Mitchell and Winifred, see ibid., pp. 297–98, and Edwin H. Cady, *The Realist at War: The Mature Years of William Dean Howells 1885–1920* (Syracuse: Syracuse University Press, 1958), pp. 97–98.

7. For an account of the somatic school, see Nathan G. Hale, Jr., *Freud and the Americans: The Beginnings of Psychoanalysis in the United States, 1876–1917* (New York: Oxford University Press, 1971), pp. 47–97.

8. W. D. Howells, *Selected Letters*, vol. 3, *1882–1891*, ed. Robert C. Leitz III et al. (Boston: Twayne, 1980), p. 235n. Further quotations are documented in the text as *SL*.

9. W. D. Howells, *The Shadow of a Dream*, ed. Martha Banta (Bloomington: Indiana University Press, 1970), pp. 32–33; *Harper's Monthly* 83 (July 1891): 314–18.

10. *Mark Twain–Howells Letters: The Correspondence of Samuel L. Clemens and William Dean Howells 1872–1910*, ed. Henry Nash Smith and William M. Gibson (Cambridge, Mass.: Harvard University Press, Belknap Press, 1960), 2:659.

11. Hale, *Freud and the Americans*, p. 125.

12. W. D. Howells, "A Sleep and a Forgetting," in *Between the Dark and the Daylight* (New York: Harper, 1907), p. 24. Subsequent references are documented in the text.

13. Howells's etiology of Nannie Gerald's condition is apparently a medical impossibility. Although Howells claimed to have known of such a case, it could not have arisen, as he believed, from purely psychological causes. Amnesia induced by trauma might block memories of a certain period or all memory before a certain point; but, as S. Weir Mitchell told Howells after reading "A Sleep and a Forgetting," "I never saw a case of loss of all memorial records of the past in which there was a disorder of memory as to immediately recent events—my cases lost all memory but were as keenly reminiscent of the new things as anyone" (letter of 19 November 1907, quoted by per-

mission of the Charles Patterson Van Pelt Library, University of Pennsylvania). Severe anterograde amnesia for ongoing events (the type suffered by Nannie Gerald) has been found only in cases where irreversible damage to a specific region of the brain, not trauma, is involved.

There is, for instance, the extraordinary case of H.M., a man who in 1953 underwent surgical removal of his hippocampus as a last-resort remedy for epilepsy, and who subsequently was found to be incapable of remembering anything new for more than fifteen minutes, but whose "perceptual and intellectual capacities remain intact, as manifested by normal or superior performance on a fairly wide range of experimental tasks." H.M. does remember remote events that antedate his surgery. See Brenda Milner, Suzanne Corkin, and H.-L. Teuber, "Further Analysis of the Hippocampal Amnesic Syndrome: 14-Year Follow-Up Study of H.M.," *Neuropsychologia* 6 (1968): 215. We are grateful to Dr. Colin Blakemore for calling our attention to Dr. Milner's study of H.M.

Aside from the actual case he claimed to have observed, Howells may have had another source for his conception of Miss Gerald's serenely innocent character. In *Literary Friends and Acquaintance* (1900; rpt. Bloomington: Indiana University Press, 1968), Howells had written of Ralph Waldo Emerson in his later years of failing memory, when "from moment to moment the record inscribed upon his mind was erased." Howells recalled that Emerson's "great soul" had seemed to work "so independently of memory as we conceive it" that one could not help wondering "if, after all, our personal continuity, our identity hereafter, was necessarily trammeled up with our enduring knowledge of what happens here." Emerson's "remembrance absolutely ceased with an event, and yet his character, his personality, his identity fully persisted" (pp. 114−15).

14. Henry Nash Smith, *Mark Twain: The Development of a Writer* (Cambridge, Mass.: Harvard University Press, 1963), p. 26.

15. "Ode: Intimations of Immortality from Recollections of Early Childhood," *The Poetical Works of William Wordsworth*, ed. E. de Selincourt and Helen Darbishire, rev. ed. (Oxford: Clarendon Press, 1958), 4:281.

16. Maurice Maeterlinck, "Of Immortality," *Harper's Monthly* 112 (December 1905): 131−37.

17. Letter in the collection of George Arms; MS quoted by his permission and that of William White Howells for the heirs of the Howells estate. No republication may be made without the same permissions. On 28 January 1906 Howells elaborated to his sister on his intentions in "A Sleep and a Forgetting": "I am writing a short story about a girl who had actually lost her memory but keeps her personality and mind perfectly otherwise. I knew such a case once, and it interests me to work it out in its bearings on the question of the persistence of the individuality in another life independently of memory." Quoted in Arnold B. Fox, "Spiritualism and the 'Supernatural' in William Dean Howells," *Journal of the American Society for Psychical Research* 53 (1959): 129.

18. "Now, I wish to make you feel . . . that we have a right to believe the physical order to be only a partial order; that we have a right to supplement it by an unseen spiritual order which we assume on trust, if only thereby life may seem to us better worth living again." William James, "Is Life Worth Living?" *The Will to Believe and Other Essays in Popular Philosophy* (London: Longmans, Green, 1897), p. 52.

19. The most complete treatment of the subject is in F. W. H. Myers, *Human Personality and Its Survival of Bodily Death* (London: Longmans, Green, 1903).

20. Cady, *The Realist at War*, p. 243.

21. W. D. Howells, "True, I Talk of Dreams," *Harper's Monthly* 90 (May 1895): 844.

22. W. D. Howells, "Father and Mother: A Mystery," *Harper's Monthly* 100 (May 1900): 872–73. This verse-drama, heavily revised and retitled "The Father," was combined with two others like it and published in *The Mother and the Father* (New York: Harper, 1909).

23. A biographical reading of the story is supported by Howells's letter to S. Weir Mitchell of 21 November 1907: "'A Sleep and a Forgetting' was founded with almost no fundamental change on a case I knew intimately in the Adirondacks eighteen years ago." (Quoted by permission of the Houghton Library and William White Howells for the heirs of the Howells estate; no republication may be made without the same permissions.) The case he knew intimately "eighteen years ago" must have come to his attention in 1889, the year of Winifred's death.

24. On the psychological themes of the Sleeping Beauty story, see Bruno Bettelheim, *The Uses of Enchantment: The Meaning and Importance of Fairy Tales* (New York: Knopf, 1976), pp. 225–36.

25. For another view of Howells's psychological ambivalence toward Winifred's illness, see Gail Thain Parker, "William Dean Howells: Realism and Feminism," *Uses of Literature*, Harvard English Studies No. 4, ed. Monroe Engel (Cambridge, Mass.: Harvard University Press, 1973), pp. 133–61. The incestuous overtones in Abner Gerald's relationship to his daughter are strongly prefigured in the relationships of Dr. Boynton to Egeria in *The Undiscovered Country* (1880) and of Squire Gaylord to Marcia in *A Modern Instance* (1882), the novels that bracket the period of Winifred's first psychic collapse.

26. As the amnesiac H.M. has said, "Every day is alone in itself, whatever enjoyment I've had, and whatever sorrow I've had." Quoted in Colin Blakemore, "The Unsolved Marvel of Memory," *New York Times Magazine* (6 February 1977), p. 42. Blakemore characterizes H.M. as a child of the moment, "trapped, interminably, in the naïveté of infancy."

27. Howells, "Father and Mother," p. 872.

ALAN GRIBBEN

"When Other Amusements Fail":
Mark Twain and the Occult

One Sunday morning in 1969 the literary editor of the Mark Twain Papers, a manuscript archive and publishing project in Berkeley, California, picked up the telephone receiver and found himself speaking to an insistent gentleman from South Carolina who had previously written to ask for reproductions of Mark Twain's fingerprints. Now the man desperately implored the editor to send them, or some other means of positive identification. The reason? He held political, religious, and philosophical views so close to those expressed in Twain's writings that he had become convinced he was the reincarnation of that author—and he urgently sought fingerprint records to certify this fact.[1]

Whatever the telephone caller eventually concluded, the editor was less astonished or dismayed than might be supposed. After all, a husband and wife in Missouri had been corresponding with him about their progress in communicating with Mark Twain by means of their Ouija board. Indeed, people have been reporting posthumous contact with him periodically ever since his first message from beyond the grave, *Jap Herron: A Novel Written from the Ouija Board* (1917). The title character of that literary effort was named Jasper Herron; he lived in Happy Hollow. Two patient scribes, Emily Grant Hutchings and Lola V. Hays, copied down twenty-six chapters, letter by letter, as Twain purportedly dictated them during the course of many séances. Unfortunately, the settings, characters, and prose style of this tedious novel do not bear any resemblance to those of Mark Twain's earthly writings.

More recently a medium in Independence, Missouri, Mildred Burris Swanson, received messages filled with fatherly advice, and published them as *God Bless U, Daughter* (1968). Another woman living in a New York City townhouse began witnessing omens and other-worldly presences; the resulting book—Jan Bryant Bartell's *Spindrift: Spray from a Psychic Sea* (1974)—centered on the deceased author so noticeably that a sympathetic reviewer noted, "She was obsessed with Twain. At times her own writing took on the satirical, unwholesome humor of Twain."[2] Obviously Mark Twain's presence is missed in the twentieth century. As the popularity of Hal Holbrook's re-creation of the elderly author's public performances reminds us, Americans did not want this national icon to perish; in fact, the nation grieved at his passing as though a former president had died. If science someday contrives a method to bring a few human beings back to life many years after their presumed deaths, he will inevitably be one of the candidates for early reanimation.

Yet Mark Twain's celebrity and the affection he inspired only partially explain why people who dabble in the magic arts believe that his spirit will be receptive to their efforts at reestablishing communication, or why, next to Edgar Allan Poe, he is the major nineteenth-century American writer most readily associated with spiritualism, reincarnation, and the entire realm of occult sciences. The fact is, his literary works, correspondence, newspaper interviews, notebooks, and marginalia provide generous evidence that his imagination was recurrently drawn toward supernatural phenomena. Consequently, when Albert Bigelow Paine published in 1912 his lengthy biography of Samuel L. Clemens, a book in whose inception, format, and documentation Clemens had collaborated eagerly, Paine appropriately titled an entire chapter "Matters Psychic and Otherwise."[3] There Clemens's authorized biographer described the lifelong fascination that Clemens displayed with dream-portents, dematerialization (citing the incident in which a billiard ball mysteriously vanished and then reappeared on the table while Clemens and Paine were playing), mental telepathy, clairvoyance, and fortunetelling. Mentioning one fortuneteller's prediction that Clemens "would probably live to a great age and die in a foreign land—a prophecy which did not comfort him," Paine observed that "Clemens was always having his fortune told, in one way or another, being superstitious, . . . though at times professing little faith in these prognostics."

Paine was correct as usual, stressing the duality of his subject's behavior. From an early age, Clemens had enjoyed mysteries, rituals, and marvels, longing for proof of paranormal powers. While he privately experimented again and again with the skills of those who claimed extrasensory abilities, publicly he scoffed at most practitioners and their gullible clients. This pattern of behavior was already established by 1861, when as a young Mississippi River pilot he visited the fortunetelling parlor of Madame Caprell in New Orleans. He was amazed when she promptly announced, "You gain your livelihood on the water," then correctly assigned his father's death ("the turning-point in your life") to the year 1847, and identi-

fied his brother Orion's chief character-defect ("he is too visionary—
is always flying off on a new hobby"), but he nevertheless could not
refrain from teasing the "right smart little woman"—at least his ver-
batim transcript of Madame Caprell's revelations quotes several
wisecracks he supposedly interjected. His concluding comment in
the letter he wrote to Orion shortly thereafter indicates Clemens's
tendency to doubt and hope simultaneously: "Paid her $2 and left—
under the decided impression that going to the fortune-teller's was
just as good as going to the opera . . . —*ergo*, I will disguise myself
and go again, one of these days, when other amusements fail" (*MTB*,
pp. 157–59).

There is no existing evidence that Clemens carried out this sportive intention before the outbreak of the Civil War ended his idyllic
piloting career, but he perpetrated similar testing schemes on unsuspecting spiritualist mediums, phrenologists, and palm-readers
throughout the five ensuing decades. At the same time, his fictional
works featured caricatures of various mountebanks who prey on humankind's inquisitiveness about superhuman feats. In these ways,
Clemens's private trials and published pronouncements epitomize a
generation of American writers who teetered anxiously between the
absolute certainties of the eighteenth century and the fixed sus-
picions of the twentieth; between the ghost tales of rural commu-
nities and the businesslike cupidity of urban charlatans; between
pre–Civil War credulity and postwar investigative journalism; between a yearning for faiths that comfort and an intellectual commitment to reigning empiricism. Although Clemens subscribed to the
tenets of an age increasingly dominated by skeptical and materialist
thinking, his ambivalence can be gauged by the prevalence in his
works of ghost stories, folk beliefs, and elements of Gothic terror,
however ironically handled, and by his endorsements in print of certain palmists, clairvoyants, and other occultists.

Since Clemens's interest in supernatural activity presumably took
root in the church and Sunday School readings and sermons of his
childhood in the 1840s, the evolution of his religious beliefs—from
conventional Christian orthodoxy toward skepticism regarding biblical miracles, the divinity of Christ, and even the revealed nature of
God and His laws—marks him as a casebook representative of the
Gilded Age that produced Robert G. Ingersoll, a professional agnostic who attracted enormous crowds wherever he lectured or debated
fundamentalist ministers. In the preface of Clemens's copy of a book

by the devout Lew Wallace, *The First Christmas, from "Ben-Hur"* (1902), Clemens poked fun at Wallace's earnest account of his own conversion after listening to Ingersoll denounce theological falsehoods during a railroad journey: "Ah—the finger of God in it. How nice," Clemens noted at one point. Farther on, he added: "In this fairy tale we have a curiously grotesque situation: God, ambushed in a Pullman sleeper, surreptitiously & unfairly betraying an unsuspecting good & honest infidel into converting Lew Wallace. To what trivial uses may we come at last."[4] However, as Paul A. Carter testifies in *The Spiritual Crisis of the Gilded Age*, "the weakening or outright rejection of traditional religion did not necessarily carry with it a corresponding rejection of supernaturalism in literature."[5] In the most imaginative passages in his fiction, Clemens tended to forsake the technological age—the age that ensured that the book he was writing would be printed on a steam press and delivered to consumers by an efficient railroad system—and set his stories ever more remotely in history and location—antebellum Hannibal, Tudor England, Arthurian England, medieval Austria. For the inhabitants of these islands in time, reality includes witches, demons, haunts, oracles, sorcerers, Satan. The tension behind Clemens's admiration for scientific rationalism and industrial technology that many critics have discerned in *A Connecticut Yankee in King Arthur's Court* (1889) is latent in many of Clemens's other works, which implicitly escape his own era by sampling the quality of life in other historical periods and countries.

Significant to any discussion of Clemens's views about supernatural influences is an understanding of his intense wish to be ranked by later ages as the intrepid discoverer of major new truths. The writer who so admired Henry M. Stanley hoped himself to match Stanley's African exploits by a spectacular intellectual or commercial success. Even Clemens's all but incredible bankruptcy in the cause of his unreliable typesetting machine can be comprehended in light of this overwhelming fantasy; he wanted to achieve in the field of publishing what his subsequent financial advisor, Henry H. Rogers, had gained in Wall Street and petroleum marketing—recognition as a farsighted prophet, a shrewd analyst, a dauntless player of hunches. This is the reason that, during the middle decades of Twain's literary career, the detective became a paramount figure in much of his fiction. Though Simon Wheeler's efforts to imitate Allan Pinkerton's agents seem as ludicrous as the burlesque of Sherlock Holmes in "A Double-Barrelled Detective Story," the central achievement that these characters seek in comic futility is what Pudd'nhead Wilson masters—a startling verity arrived at by brilliant deductive sleuthing. The first author to make substantial use of fingerprint analysis,[6] Twain performed in his *Pudd'nhead Wilson* novel what he strove less effectively to accomplish in real life.

In another connection, an associate of his remembered that Clemens became convinced that Queen Elizabeth actually had been a man and spent many hours researching history books for corroborative proof. As far as Clemens was concerned, no long-held and cherished belief should be sacrosanct; indeed, the widespread acceptance of a seemingly innocuous belief bred in him the uncontrollable urge to disprove it, to bare its falsehood with a lightning-stroke of ingenious reasoning. James Fenimore Cooper's idealized Indians were frauds; their creator deserved flaying by the real-life fiends who depredated white settlements and enslaved the women. The widely admired Bret Harte was guilty of "apprentice-art" and "artificialities," not to mention (and Clemens often did) moral character flaws. Jane Austen, George Eliot, Henry James, and other novelists venerated by leading literary critics were actually unreadable. "I dragged through three chapters" of *Daniel Deronda*, Clemens informed W. D. Howells in 1885, "losing flesh all the time, & then was honest enough to quit."[7] Newspaper editor Whitelaw Reid was a vile, reprehensible villain, despite his ostensible respectability. From the texts of Shakespeare's plays it is possible to demonstrate that he could not possibly have been their author. The founder of Christian Science, Mary Baker Eddy, plagiarized her major book and misled her followers.

The essential element in these and other crusades that Clemens undertook for weeks or months at a time is his willingness to flaunt his maverick contentions in the face of accepted public opinion. As a result, he was capable of investigating occult phenomena by the modern, experimental approaches of scientific inquiry, volunteering to be a subject at virtually every opportunity. Ridiculing previous mistaken claims, Clemens nonetheless harbored a hope that the cynicism of a dawning twentieth century was wrong in *this* particular case; in such an event he stood ready to endorse unequivocally whatever occult art could withstand his rational scrutiny. Such an astonishing discovery would substantiate his unflagging conviction that the majority of our safest assumptions are utterly erroneous, waiting merely for the penetrating vision of an original thinker, the iconoclast who will prove their mendacity and toss them into the dustbin of human foibles. All of us, then, reside in this Hadleyburg of complacent illusions. For these reasons, Clemens was capable of vacillating about pseudosciences like palmistry and phrenology, disparaging them in certain contexts, lauding them in others; he is consistent only in his unquenchable need to ferret out hidden truths that contradict prevailing notions.

There were limits to his open-mindedness, however. Witchcraft always seemed to him an absurd chimera of fevered imaginations, and his own fiction resisted the supernatural ambiguity of Hawthorne's tales like "Young Goodman Brown." When Twain read Cotton Mather's *Wonders of the Invisible World*, he marveled that Mather's opinions were not mocked when the book first appeared in 1693.[8] "The wise man of one age is the idiot of the next," he noted sadly in his copy of *Magnalia Christi Americana*.[9] Robert Calef, author of *More Wonders of the Invisible World* (1700), a work critical of Cotton Mather, "really deserves a monument," he declared.[10] He termed Calef's account of the Salem witchcraft trials "a dreadful history," writing the word "drunk" beside testimonies that supported the charges. He would portray witch hunters' fears as baseless in chapters 4 and 7 of "The Chronicle of Young Satan," a manuscript written between 1897 and 1900.[11] He also pointed the finger of scorn at the trials and tortures of suspected witch women in "Bible Teaching and Religious Practice" (1890), "The Esquimau Maiden's Romance" (1893), "The Secret History of Eddypus" (written 1901–1902), "Three Thousand Years among the Microbes" (written in 1905), and "No. 44, The Mysterious Stranger" (written 1902–1908). Readers best remember Twain's association of witches with fearful black slaves. In chapter 2 of *Huckleberry Finn* (1885), Miss Watson's Jim "said the witches bewitched him and put him in a trance, and rode him all over the State, and then set him under the trees again and hung his hat on a limb to show who done it." Near the conclusion of the novel, in chapter 34, Tom Sawyer and Huck Finn easily manipulate a credulous slave on Silas Phelps's plantation who "had a good-natured, chuckle-headed face, and his wool was all tied up in little bunches with thread. That was to keep witches off. He said the witches was pestering him awful, these nights, and making him see all kinds of strange things, and hear all kinds of strange words and noises." The slave pleads with the boys not to reveal his beliefs: "Please to don't tell nobody 'bout it sah, er ole Mars Silas he'll scole me; 'kase he say dey *ain't* no witches." Even the superstitious Huck and Tom are amused.

The marginal notations in Clemens's copy of Samuel P. Fowler's *Salem Witchcraft* (1865) make a suggestive parallel; Clemens comments that the testimonies about supposed witchcraft are as sensible as those supporting biblical events. He was ever fascinated (if unconvinced) by new claims of Christian miracles. For instance, he owned and annotated a copy of Mary Francis Cusack's *Three Visits to Knock* (1898), an account of visions of the Virgin Mary, Saint Joseph, and Saint John allegedly seen at Knock, a tiny village in County Mayo, Ireland.[12] In the second volume of his copy of Andrew D. White's *A History of the Warfare of Science with Theology in Christendom* (1901), he averred that religion and science "*are* enemies, & ought forever to remain so" (p. 410, MTP). Hank Morgan's remarks in *A Connecticut Yankee* (1889) resemble Twain's views as they appear in his other writings, favoring the prerogative of science in all matters where a conflict with religious authority exists. Chapter 23 of that romance significantly links Christian faith and magical incantations in opposition to rational thinking and progressive technology: modern pumps and pipes restore the flow of miraculous waters in the Valley of Holiness, and the Yankee reinstitutes bathing as a practical use of the well. He accomplishes this plumbing feat on the heels of Merlin's failure to cast an efficacious spell, even though Merlin invoked "the powerfulest enchantment known to the princes of the occult arts in the lands of the East."

On several topics related to Christian dogma, Clemens remained dubious but noncommittal. He was suspicious of, but intrigued by, the possibility of life beyond death. In "The Story of Mamie Grant, the Child-Missionary," which Twain entered in Notebook 11 in July 1868, he lampooned Elizabeth Stuart Phelps's *The Gates Ajar* (1868), a popular novel. But Livy Clemens evidently shared a literal concept of paradisiacal eternity similar to the heaven discussed in *The Gates Ajar*; in her diary for 12 July 1885 she notes that she "cannot help wondering" if a longtime friend of her father and mother "will see father and tell him all about us."[13] And as Paul A. Carter observed about the reasoning of Clemens's contemporaries, "Personal immortality might . . . turn out to be not a mysterious disclosure of God's grace, to be accepted on faith, but a hitherto unrecognized natural phenomenon, to be measured like any other. Even in the matter-of-fact nineteenth century not all occult beliefs had turned out upon

careful examination to be superstitions."[14] Still, Mark Twain labored for many years on the manuscript that eventually appeared
in print in 1909 as *Extracts from Captain Stormfield's Visit to
Heaven*, an amusing satire on harp-and-halo visions of the Christian
hereafter.[15]

If conventional notions about the afterlife struck Clemens as a
doubtful probability, the claims for spiritualistic communication
fascinated him immensely, though he scoffed at fanatical adherents.
Howard Kerr documents Clemens's sophisticated familiarity with
spirit-rappings and séances, whose demonstrations he began to
investigate as a newspaper reporter in 1865, and whose inconclusive results became his subject matter in good-humored newspaper
sketches in San Francisco. Franklin Walker summarized Twain's
1866 series of articles on psychic mediums by noting that "he neither scoffed nor believed," although he "joked of their experiences."[16]
In the caustic chapter 48 of *Life on the Mississippi* (1883), the episode
of supposed poltergeists at the Phelps farm in *Adventures of Huckleberry Finn* (1885), Colonel Sellers's "materialization" scheme in *The
American Claimant* (1892), and the comic séance in the "Schoolhouse Hill" version of *The Mysterious Stranger* (written 1898),
Twain continued this joshing. Kerr testifies to Twain's consistent
"vexation and amusement at the fraudulent and inane mediums,
vapid spirits, and credulous believers he encountered," concluding
that in his writings Twain never introduced "spiritualism for serious
occult effect."[17] Truly, none of Twain's fiction would ever commemorate the suggestiveness of the unconscious mind to the extent that
O. Henry does in "The Furnished Room," the tale in which a sweet
odor of mignonette haunts the rented chamber once inhabited in
New York City by a suicide victim. In a letter of 24 January 1880,
moreover, Clemens congratulated William Dean Howells for his
ability in the novel *The Undiscovered Country* "to jabber the nau-
seating professional slang of spiritism."[18]

And yet, as Hamlin Hill points out, Samuel and Livy Clemens experimented pathetically with several spiritualists in 1900 and 1901
in attempts to reestablish mind-to-mind contact with their daughter
Susy.[19] Clemens wrote to Livy in 1902 or 1903 about Isaac K. Funk's
"furnishing some spiritualism of a most unaccountable & interesting character," and his library would contain a presentation copy of
Funk's *The Psychic Riddle* (1907).[20] After Susy's death the Clem-
enses came to know F. W. H. Myers of the *Journal of the Society for*

Psychical Research; Myers's *Human Personality and Its Survival of Bodily Death* (1903) is mentioned in an autobiographical dictation of 1907.[21] In 1896 Clemens had written a notebook entry in London: "Been reading Apparitions [*sic*] of the Living—Gladstone suddenly appears—is *solid*—talks, & disappears. Emperor William, Barnum, P. of Wales, &c."[22] As John S. Tuckey has discovered, Clemens was referring to *Phantasms of the Living* (1886), a work by Myers, Edmund Gurney, and Frank Podmore that drew on the proceedings of the Society for Psychical Research to evaluate cases of apparitions, materializations, dematerializations, clairvoyance, telepathy, precognition, and dreams. Mark Twain conceded in "Mental Telegraphy," a sketch he published in 1891, that "ever since the English Society for Psychical Research began its investigations of ghost stories, haunted houses, and apparitions of the living and the dead, I have read their pamphlets with avidity as fast as they arrived." In fact, he belonged to the Society from 1884 until 1902, recording its London address in Notebook 26 in October 1886.[23] Equally significative, Clemens's copy of T. W. Doane's *Bible Myths*, a book he signed in 1908, contains a note he jotted about Daniel Dunglas Home, the Scottish spiritualist who grew up in the United States from the age of nine and became the most famous nineteenth-century medium in Britain and Europe: "The Cheneys [a Hartford family] often saw Home rise & fly at his ease when they were all boys together. Later, Dickens, Huxley & others saw Home do this."[24]

A similar attitude of wishful interest (balanced by mistrustfulness concerning the motives of those who practice professionally) is discernible in Clemens's relations with phrenology, the faddish nineteenth-century method of predicting character traits primarily on the basis of the contours of the subject's skull. Here Clemens was even more "scientific" in his modes of experimentation. From avowed credulity in 1855 at the age of nineteen, Clemens turned toward remorseless ridicule of this pseudoscience and its practitioners in *Huckleberry Finn* and other writings, presumably aware that its prestige and credibility were declining rapidly. However, Twain himself employed its jargon in several of his literary works, including *Innocents Abroad* (1869), in which the narrator acknowledges that "a very liberal amount of space was given to the organ which enables me to *make* promises," but avers that he "had rather have one faculty nobly developed than two faculties of mere ordinary capacity."

More significant than these occasional and self-conscious refer-

ences to its terminology is the documented fact that Clemens repeatedly submitted his head to phrenological examinations as late as
the final decade of his life, as though its gradual rejection by the
masses merely imbued its doctrines with renewed appeal. We should
remember, of course, that Clemens and others who tentatively accepted the basic tenets of phrenology in the nineteenth century
thought that they were benefiting from anatomical research into the
nature of the brain and its functions; they had little reason to associate this method of character diagnosis with the occult arts, though
the antics of traveling charlatans like the Duke in *Huckleberry Finn*
ultimately brought the field into disrepute. Today the few practicing
phrenologists are more apt to operate in tenement slums and carnival sideshows than in professional offices. Since 1970, when a self-
proclaimed occultist named Sybil Leek embraced the theories of
phrenology and reissued a nineteenth-century Fowler & Wells hand-
book on the subject,[25] this pseudoscience has become associated
with palm-reading and fortunetelling by tarot cards. While phrenology proved to be mistaken in its fundamental premise—that the
skull infallibly reflects one's character—its ostensibly rational theory resembled other occult arts only in its determination to depart
from conventional ways of gaining knowledge and its emphasis on
the special powers of its professional examiners, who discerned messages hidden from the laymen.[26]

Curiously, Clemens had fewer qualms about subscribing to the
truly occult fortunetelling devices of palmistry. In chapter 11 of
Pudd'nhead Wilson (1894) the unappreciated David Wilson examines the hands of the twin named Luigi. (Wilson is rather out of practice, since the townspeople of Dawson's Landing have chaffed him
so much that he has "stopped to let the talk die down.") His method-
ical procedures—tracing life lines, heart lines, head lines—are described in considerable detail. "He mapped out Luigi's character and
disposition, his tastes, aversions, proclivities, ambitions, and eccen-
tricities. . . . The chart was artistically drawn and was correct." Wilson even discloses the fact that someone once prophesied Luigi
would kill a man, and that the prediction came true. An astonished
Tom Driscoll exclaims: "Why, a man's own hand is his deadliest enemy! . . . [It] is treacherously ready to expose him to any black-
magic stranger that comes along." Driscoll refuses to allow Wilson
to read the secrets of his own palm, yet consents to Wilson's seemingly harmless suggestion that he be fingerprinted. Part of Twain's

purpose in writing this passage was to set the stage for Wilson's subsequent revelation of Tom Driscoll's crime and his true identity, to make readers of the novel conscious of ways that our own bodies can offer testimony against us. At the same time, though, Twain's endorsement of palmistry is absolutely unequivocal in tone.

Another reference to palmistry is less enthusiastic. In an undated manuscript titled "Palm Readings" (MTP), Twain reports that seven British palmists were unable to deduce his occupation as a humorist from prints of his palm that the editor W. T. Snead submitted for their examination. Later Twain repeated this experiment in New York City, again with disappointing results.[27] The same pattern of public dubiety and private experimentation prevailed here as in Clemens's attitudes toward phrenology. In 1895, however, the bankrupt, sixty-year-old Clemens gained a modicum of hope from the prognostics of Louis Hamon, the palmist who practiced in New York City under the name of Cheiro. Two years later Cheiro repeated his prophecies when he examined Clemens's palms in London. As Clemens's fortunes began to recover, he joked in a letter to Henry H. Rogers written on 3 January 1899: "Do you believe Cheiro can come on me for commission?" He flattered Rogers, the business advisor who directed the recouping of his finances: "We have about $52,000 on hand. . . . That is good news, and shows that Cheiro can work his prophecy-mill very well when you stand behind him and turn the crank." But he confided to William Dean Howells on 26 December 1902: "I have been persecuted by superstitions born of Cheiro's prediction of 7 years ago—repeated in London 4 years ago: 'In your 68th year you will become—rather suddenly—very rich.'" When Clemens signed his lucrative publishing contract with Harper and Brothers on 22 October 1903, an agreement assuring him of wealth for years to come, he reflected on the Cheiro prophecy of 1895 when he had been $94,000 in debt: "I am superstitious. I kept the prediction in mind and often thought of it. When at last it came true, Oct. 22, / 03, there was but a month and 9 days to spare."[28]

Mental telepathy—which Mark Twain preferred to term "mental telegraphy" or "phrenography"—was another supernatural phenomenon that gained his belief. The 1891 essay titled "Mental Telegraphy" cites numerous instances of duplicate thoughts too similar to have resulted from mere coincidences; "Mental Telegraphy Again" (1895) contributes additional case histories. Satan has telepathic powers in *The Mysterious Stranger*. Even more telling, perhaps, is the fact that Twain published no criticisms of people who reported occurrences of simultaneous ideas.

A number of experiences peripherally related to supernatural powers also gained Twain's credence. His dream that foretold Henry Clemens's death disturbed the surviving brother for years after Henry's steamboat exploded in 1858. Possibly this ghastly omen—a vision of Henry lying in a coffin, white and red flowers on his chest—lay behind a fragmentary story, "Clairvoyant," which Twain began during the 1880s and in which a young man named John H. Day was to be gifted and cursed with the ability to foresee local events and even, if he wished, to prevent them.[29] Such capabilities adumbrate Satan's prophetic powers in "The Chronicle of Young Satan" (written 1897–1900). However the case may be, Howard G. Baetzhold has traced Twain's recurrent dreams of a "platonic sweetheart" to a real-life sweetheart of 1858, Laura Wright.[30] Indeed, the compelling illusion of actuality that invests certain dreams led Twain to ponder the question of whether our worldly selves are simply part of some vast dream, an occult theme he pursued in "No. 44, The Mysterious Stranger" (written in 1902–1908), various autobiographical dictations in 1906 and 1907, "Which Was the Dream," "The Great Dark," and other late pieces.

In the nineteenth century, hypnotism seemed more like a black art than it does today. Clemens repeatedly told the story about the mesmerist who came to Hannibal around 1850 and gave a public performance of his methods. A youthful printer, Urban E. Hicks, allowed himself to be hypnotized; not to be outdone, young Sam Clemens (perhaps remembering his habit of sleepwalking) pretended to be put under a spell, then executed astounding feats at the instructions of the mesmerist.[31] Analyzing this episode, Susan Kuhlmann speculates that in the first few moments Clemens "fears that the showman will expose him as a fake. But he soon realizes that one con man will not betray another when their 'games' are mutually profitable."[32] Despite his play-acting, his versions of the anecdote neither endorse nor refute the powers of the hypnotist; Clemens merely stresses his own Tom Sawyer–like hunger for the villagers' admiration. During the last decade of Clemens's life, however, he undertook an urgent investigation of hypnosis as possible therapy for Jean Clemens's increasingly severe epileptic seizures. His library contained John D. Quackenbos's *Hypnotic Therapeutics in Theory and Practice* (1908), marked with ink where Quackenbos concludes pessimistically that the chances of curing epilepsy with hypnosis are remote if "the mental faculties are seriously impaired as the result of organic brain conditions" (MTP). He also possessed a copy of Saint-Germain's *Practical Hypnotism: Theories and Experiments* (1901).[33]

Additionally, Mark Twain's writings contain numerous usages of occult materials where his belief or disbelief is less at issue, instances where he utilized literary traditions of the supernatural to achieve desired atmospheric effects of suspense, surprise, or even comedy. Until "A Ghost Story" (1870) degenerates into a burlesque interview with the spirit of the Cardiff Giant, Twain deftly employs elements belonging to the Gothic tales of terror in anticipating a spectral apparition: the narrator inhabits an otherwise deserted building, rain and wind and creaking shutters set the scene, a dismal moan awakens the perplexed narrator from his sleep. In chapter 53 of *Life on the Mississippi* (1883), Twain would remark that "it seems incredible that people believed in ghosts so short a time ago. But they did." He had demonstrated this inclination in chapter 3 of that book by relating (in a passage pilfered from *Huckleberry Finn*, the manuscript of which was then in progress) an effective ghost tale told by the raftsman called Ed—Dick Allbright's encounters with the haunted barrel that floats on the waters of the Mississippi, pursuing Allbright for an act of infanticide. Twain could make an audience almost believe in haunting visitations again whenever he told them his variant of a black folk tale about ghostly vengeance, "The Golden Arm." With its wailing refrain, "Who—got—my—golden—arm?" and its shouted last line, "*You've* got it!" this became one of his favorite stories for oral delivery.[34]

Examples abound of Twain's fondness for the macabre. He was particularly fascinated by mental struggles against impending insanity, yet he hardly can be said to have equaled the vivid intensity of, for example, Charlotte Perkins Gilman's "The Yellow Wall-Paper" (1892). A never-completed manuscript begun in 1875 portrays the plight of a bridegroom accidentally sealed in a dungeon and forced to employ the few items at hand for his entertainment and education as years pass.[35] Twain recurrently depicts the plight of vessels drifting lifelessly within an inescapable vacuum: a Poe-like chapter discarded from his manuscript for *Life on the Mississippi* describes a region of the stratosphere occupied only by hovering balloons and the mummified corpses of their passengers; "The Enchanted Sea-

Wilderness," written in 1896, portrays a similar nightmare vision of a becalmed ocean. In *A Tramp Abroad* (1880), he invented several mock-legends set among the crumbling castles he viewed while traveling. One story recounts a case of insanity brought on by a practical joke, a theme he also rehearsed in chapter 53 of *Life on the Mississippi*, where a prankster dressed as a ghost unintentionally sends a woman into confinement in an insane asylum—and in "Doughface," a brief sketch written between 1897 and 1902, in which "a beautiful young lady" wearing a false-face frightens "a superstitious old maid" so badly that she goes mad. "The Californian's Tale" (1893) hinges on the narrator's failure to recognize signs of merciful insanity in the prospector's feverish delusion that his young wife will soon arrive home safely.

Twain passingly sketched a tale of premature burial in "Villagers of 1840–3," a sheaf of Hannibal recollections he set down in 1897; there he wrote about a young Kentucky lawyer who was accidentally shut inside his mother's burial vault on the day of his intended wedding.[36] Besides having affinities with several of Edgar Allan Poe's tales, this claustrophobic notation is reminiscent of another literary work with which Twain was familiar: Thomas Haynes Bayly's "The Mistletoe Bough," a poem about a young bride to be who hides in a large chest during a family game of hide-and-seek, and thereby disappears for half a century. Chapter 31 of *Life on the Mississippi* includes the tale he subtitled "A Dying Man's Confession," a situation resembling Poe's "The Cask of Amontillado." A man discovers his enemy, still alive, mistakenly laid out for burial in a Bavarian mortuary; relishing this ghoulish revenge, the narrator pulls up a chair, sips brandy to ward off the chill of the dead-house, and nonchalantly reads a newspaper while his weakened adversary pleads in vain for assistance.

Comic rather than ghoulish, but still reaching into the depths of the unconscious mind, is Twain's "Recent Carnival of Crime in Connecticut" (1876), wherein the narrator meets, converses with, and dispatches his detested twin, his conscience. Small wonder that a writer like Twain, intrigued by the concept of double identities, referred several times in Notebooks 40 and 47 (MTP) to Stevenson's *Dr. Jekyll and Mr. Hyde*. Here again, however, Twain's fiction never achieved the explorations of double consciousness attained in Poe's "William Wilson," Henry James's "The Jolly Corner," or Joseph Conrad's "The Secret Sharer." Monster creations likewise drew his interest. Beginning in 1883, he often alluded to Mary Shelley's *Franken-stein*; a character named Hollister in his "Little Bessie" (written in 1908–1909) argues that God's creation of the cat that tortures a mouse is "just the case of Frankenstein and his Monster over again. . . . Frankenstein was horrified and . . . said, *I* made him, without asking his consent, and it makes me responsible for every crime he commits."[37] But in contriving his fictional situations, Twain's imagination stopped short of the ingenuity W. W. Jacobs displays in a story like "The Monkey's Paw," in which the White family is destroyed by the offer of three wishes from a lucky talisman; they soon understand why they were warned that a previous owner's "third was for death." Twain's experiment with a wish-granting theme takes the form of a grim fable, "The Five Boons of Life" (1902).[38] In it, as in the Jacobs story, death comes to be welcomed, but Clemens's treatment of the theme is antiseptic.

In other instances he relied on supernatural formulas as more than stage props of stern parables of Gothic horror. The Connecticut Yankee begins his narrative by asking, "You know about transmigration of souls; do you know about transposition of epochs—and bodies?" Until we see Will Rogers (1931) or Bing Crosby (1949) wake up near Camelot in the film versions, we sometimes overlook the extent to which we accept an occult premise of time-travel in order to enjoy this work. *A Connecticut Yankee* also depends on the many supernatural characters and events that Twain found in Malory's *Le Morte d'Arthur*, and whereas Twain's fiction generally depicts sorcerers, wizards, and magicians as impotent, in chapter 44 of this romance the aged Merlin succeeds (before being electrocuted) in casting a spell that keeps the Yankee asleep until his own century arrives. Another literary character, Joan of Arc, true to his historical sources, hears mysterious voices and obeys unearthly communications. Mark Twain borrowed such literary materials less self-consciously than most of his contemporaries, and in spite of his own bias in favor of rationalism and his advocacy of scientific progress.

An overview of Twain's relationship with the occult reminds us that his search for humorous materials often brought to his attention the enthusiastic claims of cults of the supernatural. At one point or another he ridiculed virtually every occult fad that flourished during his lifetime, even those he occasionally professed to believe in himself. Just as often, however, he assumed a noncommittal stance. Privately, it seems, he maintained a relatively tolerant attitude toward most students of occult phenomena, and he experimented with practitioners of these arts during every decade of his life, suspiciously but hopefully testing the powers of fortunetellers and character-readers. He relied noticeably on elements associated with black magic and the Gothic tradition of horror in creating his own fiction, but he seldom if ever matched the chilling masterstrokes in Kipling (the werewolf-tale, "The Mark of the Beast," and the tantalizingly apparitional " 'They' " are superior to any suspense Twain ever created) or in the better works of Hawthorne, Dickens, Stevenson, or Hardy. Twain's line of vision was habitually focused on the perceivable details of our visible world, and so in savoring the consummate passages of *Huckleberry Finn* and his other writings we readers willingly forgive whatever deficiencies may become apparent when he is compared to the finest literary craftsmen in the subgenre of supernatural fiction. Though Twain's works are representative of various occult themes, his enormous talents chiefly lay in other directions.

In all likelihood, as a matter of fact, dedicated psychics probably read his remarks too selectively; he seldom admitted to uncritical acceptance of any dogma, whether it was conventional Christianity or otherworldly occultism. He summed up his dubiousness about supernatural sources of knowledge—at the same time admitting his abiding half-belief—during a London interview with a reporter for the *New York Herald* on 18 June 1907. Clemens was unflustered when the conversation turned awkwardly to the subject of funerals. One of the newspapermen who was present inquired whether the elderly Clemens ever contemplated his own death. "All the clairvoyants and palmists I have consulted tell me I am going to die," quipped the celebrated author, "but I may add they would have impressed me more had they named the date."

NOTES

1. During the eight years (1967–74) in which I was a research editor for the publications of the Mark Twain Papers in Berkeley, I grew accustomed to receiving requests nearly as strange from idolators across the nation.

2. Leona Rasmussen Phillips and Jill M. Phillips, *The Occult: Hauntings, Witchcraft, Dreams and All Other Avenues of Paranormal Phenomena—An Annotated Bibliography* (New York: Gordon Press, 1977), p. 16.

3. Chap. 260 of Albert Bigelow Paine, *Mark Twain: A Biography* (New York: Harper and Brothers, 1912), pp. 1405–10, hereafter cited as *MTB*. On pp. 542–43 Paine mentions that "psychic theories and phenomena always attracted Mark Twain. In thought-transference, especially, he had a frank interest. . . . He was always having these vehement interests—rages we may call them."

4. Humanities Research Center, University of Texas at Austin. Clemens's marginalia appear on pp. vi and vii.

5. Paul A. Carter, *The Spiritual Crisis of the Gilded Age* (DeKalb: Northern Illinois University Press, 1971), p. 78.

6. See Anne P. Wigger, "The Source of Fingerprint Material in Mark Twain's *Pudd'nhead Wilson and Those Extraordinary Twains*," *American Literature* 28 (January 1957): 517–20, a note that establishes Clemens's familiarity with Sir Francis Galton's *Finger Prints* (1892). Previously Clemens somehow learned enough about this method of identification to include in chap. 31 of *Life on the Mississippi* (1883) a character who solves a murder case by collecting thumbprints of various suspects.

7. Letter of 21 July 1885, *Mark Twain–Howells Letters: The Correspondence of Samuel L. Clemens and William Dean Howells 1872–1910*, ed. Henry Nash Smith and William M. Gibson (Cambridge, Mass.: Harvard University Press, Belknap Press, 1960), p. 533.

8. Collected in Samuel P. Fowler's *Salem Witchcraft* (Boston: William Veazie, 1865). The volume is part of the Mark Twain Project (formerly the Mark Twain Papers), Bancroft Library, University of California at Berkeley, a collection hereafter cited as MTP. I am grateful to its editor, Robert H. Hirst, for access to these materials.

9. Special Collections, Case Western Reserve University Libraries, Cleveland, Ohio.

10. Marginalia in Fowler's *Salem Witchcraft*, p. 450, MTP.

11. *Mark Twain's Mysterious Stranger Manuscripts*, ed. William M. Gibson (Berkeley and Los Angeles: University of California Press, 1969), pp. 78–80, 133. See also Gibson's remarks on p. 21.

12. Antenne-Dorrance Collection, Rice Lake, Wisconsin.

13. Olivia L. Clemens Diary, DV161, MTP.

14. Carter, *Spiritual Crisis*, pp. 95–96.

15. Robert A. Rees has disputed the common assumption that Twain was parody-

ing Phelps's novel; see "*Captain Stormfield's Visit to Heaven* and *The Gates Ajar*," *English Language Notes* 7 (March 1970): 197–202.

16. Franklin Walker, *San Francisco's Literary Frontier* (Seattle: University of Washington Press, 1939, 1969), pp. 203–4.

17. Howard Kerr, *Mediums, and Spirit-Rappers, and Roaring Radicals: Spiritualism in American Literature, 1850–1900* (Urbana: University of Illinois Press, 1972), pp. 155–89, esp. p. 188.

18. *Mark Twain–Howells Letters*, p. 288.

19. Hamlin Hill, *Mark Twain: God's Fool* (New York: Harper and Row, 1973), pp. 33–34.

20. Alan Gribben, *Mark Twain's Library: A Reconstruction*, 2 vols. (Boston: G. K. Hall and Co., 1980), p. 249.

21. *Mark Twain in Eruption*, ed. Bernard DeVoto (New York: Harper and Brothers, 1940), pp. 339–42.

22. Notebook 39, TS p. 36, MTP. See John S. Tuckey, *Mark Twain and Little Satan* (West Lafayette: Purdue University Studies, 1963), p. 26.

23. *Mark Twain's Notebooks and Journals*, ed. Frederick Anderson et al. (Berkeley and Los Angeles: University of California Press, 1979), 3:260–61.

24. Marginalia on p. 267; volume in the Mark Twain Library, Redding, Connecticut.

25. Sybil Leek, *Phrenology* (New York: Collier Books, 1970. Also distributed the same year by Macmillan). Leek's publications include books on astrology (among others, *The Astrological Cookbook*, 1968), spell-casting, witchcraft, ESP, numerology, fortunetelling, telepathy, herbalism, faith-healing, and reincarnation.

26. I have elaborated on these distinctions in "Mark Twain, Phrenology and the 'Temperaments': A Study of Pseudoscientific Influence," *American Quarterly* 24 (March 1972): 45–68.

27. A reproduction of Clemens's palm print appears in Milton Meltzer's *Mark Twain Himself: A Pictorial Biography* (Hannibal, Mo.: Becky Thatcher Book Shop, 1960), p. 151. In March 1894 W. T. Stead published uncredited photographs of Clemens's palms in *Borderland*, a popular quarterly of psychical research. See Joseph O. Baylen, "Mark Twain, W. T. Stead and 'The Tell-Tale Hands,'" *American Quarterly* 16 (Winter 1964): 606–12.

28. Notebook 35, TS p. 10, MTP; *Mark Twain's Correspondence with Henry Huttleston Rogers*, ed. Lewis Leary (Berkeley and Los Angeles: University of California Press, 1969), pp. 378, 385, 395; *Mark Twain–Howells Letters*, p. 757; Notebook 36, TS p. 15, MTP.

29. *Mark Twain's Hannibal, Huck and Tom*, ed. Walter Blair (Berkeley and Los Angeles: University of California Press, 1969), pp. 58–66.

30. Howard G. Baetzhold, "Found: Mark Twain's 'Lost Sweetheart,'" *American Literature* 44 (November 1972): 414–29.

31. Clemens recounted this incident in Notebook 41 (1897), TS pp. 56, 58, MTP and Notebook 45 (1902); he also recalled his pretended trance in an autobiographical dictation (*Mark Twain in Eruption*, pp. 118–25).

32. Susan Kuhlmann, *Knave, Fool, and Genius: The Confidence Man as He Appears in Nineteenth-Century American Fiction* (Chapel Hill: University of North Carolina Press, 1973), p. 51. On pp. 87–90 Kuhlmann also discusses Clemens's responses to spiritualism.

33. Gribben, *Mark Twain's Library*, pp. 565–66, 598.

34. Twain incorporates a version of "The Golden Arm" in his instructive essay, "How to Tell a Story" (1895); another variant appears in *Mark Twain Speaking*, ed. Paul Fatout (Iowa City: University of Iowa Press, 1976), pp. 155–56.

35. "The Mysterious Chamber," DV56, MTP.

36. *Mark Twain's Hannibal*, p. 38.

37. *Mark Twain's Fables of Man*, ed. John S. Tuckey (Berkeley and Los Angeles: University of California Press, 1972), p. 38.

38. In *What Is Man? and Other Philosophical Writings*, ed. Paul Baender (Berkeley and Los Angeles: University of California Press, 1973), pp. 98–100.

CHARLES N. WATSON, JR.

Jack London: Up from Spiritualism

Though all his life Jack London denied that he believed in the supernatural, he found himself compelled repeatedly to fend off the overtures of spiritualists who had mistaken him for a fellow believer. His reply to one such person, in early 1915, was polite but firmly discouraging. "When I tell you that I am hopelessly a realist and a materialist," he wrote, "believing that when I die I am dead and shall be forever dead, you will understand how unable I am to join with you in the prosecution of your most interesting researches. . . . I was born amongst spiritualists and lived my childhood and boyhood life amongst spiritualists. The result of this close contact was to make an unbeliever out of me."[1] After London's death in 1916 his widow, Charmian, was similarly beset by well-meaning believers assuring her that Jack's spirit survived and, according to some, was sending messages from beyond the grave. Charmian was as blunt as her husband, however, in spurning any such consolation. "Don't EVER, in any impressions you give of Jack London," she replied to one correspondent, "make the mistake of thinking he believed in occultism."[2] As late as 1930 she suggested to Upton Sinclair that if he had made "as thoroughgoing a study of modern and olden spiritualist-mediums' general methods as did Jack himself," he would take a more skeptical view of "messages" from the dead.[3]

Yet the inquiries of these spiritualists, if overeager, were not entirely groundless, for like so many of London's most insistent pronouncements, his declarations of skepticism conceal as much as they reveal. London was a man of complex, sometimes confused, emotional and intellectual stances—a man seldom able to embrace one position without also entertaining its opposite. Such ambivalence, rooted in his early childhood as well as in the intellectual uncertainties of the era, inevitably emerged in his fiction, especially in his stories of the occult. These stories are rarely among his best; indeed, he often dismissed them as potboilers. Yet behind the mask of his indifference or contempt lay a continuing fascination with nonrational experience. Though he had no patience with the cruder varieties of nineteenth-century spiritualism, he often hedged his rejection of occultism and actively explored such alternative psychic phenomena as mystical transcendence, creative inspiration, and subconscious motivation.

II

When London's mother, Flora Wellman, was eight years old and living in Massillon, Ohio, in 1851, she must have been aware of the controversial case of Abby Warner, whose spirit-rappings prompted the congregation of St. Timothy's Episcopal Church to sue her for having "willfully and in malice prepense disturbed a Christian assembly in the solemn act of worship."[4] Sometime thereafter Flora herself became interested in the occult and eventually gravitated to San Francisco, where in 1874 she was living with a "professor" of astrology named William Henry Chaney, holding séances, and lecturing on spiritualism. The next year she became pregnant, creating a minor public scandal when she unsuccessfully attempted suicide and was then deserted by Chaney. Her child was born out of wedlock on 12 January 1876, but later in the same year she married a middle-aged widower, John London, who gave the future writer his name.

Although Jack London did not learn the full story of his birth until he was in his early twenties, he experienced its effects throughout his childhood. He always recalled with gratitude the kindness of his stepfather, but he felt his mother's emotional rejection. In an understandable act of psychological displacement, he remembered his youth as a time of hunger, especially for meat, although contemporary accounts reveal that there was plenty of meat on the table. This longing for emotional nurture, however, was counterbalanced by an opposite impulse: an early revulsion from his mother's hysterical fits and terrifying séances. Indian "controls" were apparently in vogue at this time, and Flora's favorite, a chieftain named Plume, made a habit of punctuating his messages with "unexpected yells and gibberish."[5] It is not hard to see how London could have emerged from such a childhood with a deep ambivalence toward his mother and the forms of irrationality she represented. All his adult life he loathed feminine hysteria, scorned the supernatural, and embraced scientific rationalism with a confidence that at times bordered on complacency. When in 1904 his friend Cloudesley Johns sent him a clipping on telepathy, he replied loftily: "Please do not forget that I am fairly scientific, & that I have a fair knowledge of fakes and fakirs."[6]

Yet even as he insisted on his immunity to the nonrational in all its forms, his deeply emotional nature asserted itself in his volatile personal life and intermittently in his fiction, from early apprentice work to later ideas for stories he never lived to write. Especially in his early years, he seems to have considered his stories of the occult mere finger-exercises and hack work, and in commenting on them he invariably insisted on his disbelief in their supernatural events. Yet what is remarkable is the consistency with which, in the clash between believer and skeptic, the last word goes to the believer. Characteristically, London portrayed the skeptic as something of a fool and the believer as a possessor of esoteric wisdom. Two of these stories date from London's earliest apprentice period, between his return from his tramp journey to the East in the fall of 1894 and his departure for the Klondike in the summer of 1897. Each deals with two young friends, sophomoric know-it-alls who pompously proclaim their disbelief in the supernatural to a man who proposes to put their disbelief to the test.

In "A Ghostly Chess Game," the more skeptical of the two friends, Pythias, denounces séances as frauds: "Rapping, table-tipping, slate-writing and other physical manifestations," he adds, "are just as bad, being but little better bosh than clairvoyance, clairaudience, impersonation and trance-mediumship."[7] Pythias thus dismisses at a sweep the entire panoply of the spiritualist movement, while the more temperate Damon contents himself with rejecting the "very idea" of ghosts as "absurd." The language of these denunciations may at first seem to express London's own reaction against the spiritualism of his mother. Yet throughout the story the pomposities of the unbelievers are set against the seemingly plausible supernatural beliefs of their more knowing friend, George, whose wish that they may experience "a speedy conversion through the most horrible of proofs" is fulfilled in the ensuing action. Complacently proposing to test themselves by spending the night in a reputedly haunted mansion, the two find themselves uncannily reenacting a murder committed by the former resident. Though George comes to the rescue just in time to prevent Damon from strangling Pythias, the skeptics have presumably been cured of their disbelief.

In a later version of the same motif, "The Mahatma's Little Joke," the skeptical friends are Jack and Charley, who begin by discussing whether apparently supernatural phenomena will ultimately be explained scientifically. The argument is resolved for them by the Mahatma of the title, a middle-aged savant whose face combines "the brooding wisdom of the sphinx and the mysterious solemnity of a Monte Cristo."[8] After all, the Mahatma argues, a hundred years ago "telegraphy was beyond practical conception; and thus, to day the disintegration and reintegration of form by psychic impulses, is beyond both yours and the popular conception. . . . Do you take upon yourself the infinite knowledge necessary to declare that such is infinitely impossible? Surely you would not be so egotistical. On this point, then, your only consistent attitude must be that of agnosticism—you do not know but would like to know." Once again London portrays dogmatic disbelief as arrant conceit. The Mahatma, moreover, like George in the earlier story, vanquishes the boys' doubts by performing a demonstration, translating the "astral form" of each into the body of the other, thereby allowing the two shy fellows to propose to each other's sisters "by proxy."

Both of these stories are amateurish and quite preposterous, and neither should be taken as clear evidence against London's often-repeated skepticism. To a degree, they merely exploit the popular taste for supernatural fantasy without committing the author to the slightest belief in the occult. Still, the Mahatma's advice to Jack and Charley is eminently reasonable. Surely, as he argues, it *is* "egotistical" to declare "infinitely impossible" those phenomena beyond the reach of present scientific knowledge. The Mahatma's definition of an enlightened agnosticism, in fact, differs little from the Spencerian attitude that London recommended to Cloudesley Johns in 1899. "Remember," he wrote, "the infidel that positively asserts that there is no God, no first cause, is just as imbecile a creature as the deist that asserts positively that there is a God, a first cause," and he goes on to remind Johns of the "adamantine line" that Spencer had drawn between "the knowable and the unknowable."[9]

After he returned from the Klondike in 1898 and began his second period of apprenticeship, London continued to toy with ideas for occult fiction. Twice he made notes for further revisions of "A Ghostly Chess Game," and in the same notebook the conflict between belief and disbelief was embodied in a plan for a story involving the "materializing" of a baby, who would then be "stolen by a skeptic." Another story, to be titled "The Dust of the Dead," was conceived thus: "Rose, planted in ashes of dead husband who might have been a clever botanist; also, woman might have been deceived, or some unknown psychic force played a part." The characterization of the dead husband as a scientist, as well as London's irresolution over whether the woman was "deceived" or was the victim of "some unknown psychic force," suggests that this tale, too, might have taken an ambivalent view of the supernatural. Less equivocal was a plan for a play intended to dramatize the fraudulence of séances: "Fake mediumship plays big part. Either detectives, or villains, or both, are the mediums. Place on the stage both parts of the seance. What the public sees and what is done by the fake mediums and which the public does not see."[10] But while this scenario obviously reflects more directly London's rebellion against his mother, three of his later stories suggest that even as he issued his periodic disclaimers of belief, he never rested easy in his skepticism.

III

The first such story, "Planchette," was written in the spring of 1905, at a critical juncture in London's life. After nearly two years he was beginning to emerge from what he called his "long sickness," the period of depression following his separation from his first wife and the early months of his love affair with Charmian Kittredge. For the better part of 1904 and early 1905 his relationship with Charmian had deteriorated, but in the spring their love revived as they visited Charmian's aunt and uncle at Glen Ellen, rode over the wooded hills, and made excited plans to buy a nearby ranch, all the while looking forward to the time when London's divorce would become final and they could marry. On 28 May, however, Charmian experienced a momentary scare when her horse fell down a ditch with Jack in the saddle, and she recorded in her diary her relief that he was "unhurt, thank God."[11] But though London broke no bones, the near miss tripped a wire in his imagination, uncovering a source of buried guilt—perhaps over his desertion of his first wife and their two daughters, perhaps over the secret of his birth, which he may not yet have revealed to Charmian. Whatever the cause, a day or two later he began a long story that re-created the circumstances of his accident, endowing them with a convincing aura of the occult.

The tale opens with a horseback ride during which Chris Dunbar tells the woman he loves, Lute Story, that he cannot marry her and cannot tell her why. Shortly afterward, Chris mounts Lute's horse, who suddenly bolts through the trees, stopping only after Chris has been badly gashed and bruised. For a moment the two wonder whimsically whether the horse was a victim of "obsession" or an "evil spirit," but they "laughed together at the idea, for both were twentieth-century products, healthy-minded and normal, with souls that delighted in the butterfly-chase of ideals but that halted before the brink where superstition begins." [12] Nevertheless, the next afternoon Chris's own horse suddenly rears and falls backward into a rocky stream twelve feet below while Chris miraculously frees his feet from the stirrups and leaps clear. Back at the home of Lute's aunt and uncle, they try to forget these weird accidents amid the flurry of excitement over the planchette [13] that has been produced for a session of spirit-writing. When Chris, jocular and skeptical, agrees to put the board to a test, he finds it scrawling: "BEWARE! BEWARE! BEWARE! Chris Dunbar, I intend to destroy you. I have already made two attempts upon your life, and failed. I shall yet succeed" (p. 240).

Chris continues to view the whole matter as a joke, but Lute is moved by the memory of the two horseback accidents and by the discovery that the handwriting of the message resembles that of her long-dead father. Though conscious of a "vague and nameless fear at this toying with the supernatural" (p. 246), she decides to try the planchette herself and promptly receives a message from her dead mother. "What if there be something in it?" she wonders aloud. "I am not so sure. Science may be too dogmatic in its denial of the unseen. The forces of the unseen, of the spirit, may well be too subtle, too sublimated, for science to lay hold of, and recognize, and formulate. Don't you see, Chris, that there is rationality in the very doubt?" (p. 252). Chris, however, will go no further than the agnosticism of a scientific rationalist: "We are playing with the subjective forces of our own being, with phenomena which science has not yet explained, that is all. Psychology is so young a science. The subconscious mind has just been discovered, one might say. It is all mystery as yet; the laws of it are yet to be formulated. This is simply unexplained phenomena. But that is no reason that we should immediately account for it by labelling it spiritism" (pp. 257–58). Chris thus states what the rational side of London's mind persistently believed.

Yet as the story moves quickly to a climax, its action refutes such rationalism in the most telling way: by making Chris pay for it with his life. As he and Lute tempt fate by taking a final ride, they ascend to the rim of a canyon, where they exult in their love and experience a moment of ecstatic communion with the rhythms of natural life.

To their wonder-struck vision, the stream below is like a Platonic idea, "a-breath with movement, ever falling and ever remaining, changing its substance but never its form, an aërial waterway as immaterial as gauze and as permanent as the hills" (p. 268). As their exultation reaches a climax, the imagery becomes simultaneously erotic and spiritual:

> All things tended to key them to an exquisite pitch—the movement of their bodies, at one with the moving bodies of the animals beneath them; the gently stimulated blood caressing the flesh through and through with the soft vigors of health; the warm air fanning their faces, flowing over the skin with balmy and tonic touch, permeating them and bathing them, subtly, with faint, sensuous delight; and the beauty of the world, more subtly still, flowing upon them and bathing them in the delight that is of the spirit and is personal and holy, that is inexpressible yet communicable by the flash of an eye and the dissolving of the veils of the soul. (pp. 268–69)

This moment of revelation, expressed in the language of religious mysticism, is entirely characteristic of the side of London's imagination that transcends his theoretical rationalism. In the next instant, moreover, it is validated by the fulfillment of the planchette's prophecy as Chris's horse plunges without warning into the canyon below. This time Chris does not leap clear.

"Planchette" may thus serve as a paradigm of London's double vision. It presents a character who is very much like London and who holds the skeptical views that London always professed. Yet the story as a whole constitutes a critique of those views, implying that a dogmatic materialism must give place, if not to open credulity, then at least to a suspension of disbelief consistent with the present state of scientific ignorance.[14] In addition, the story offers two sources of nonrational experience. One of them is the sense of ineffable joy that Chris and Lute feel in their moment of mystical communion with nature. But another and darker source appears in Lute's "instinctive fear," expressive of "man's inheritance from the wild and howling ages when his hairy, apelike prototype was afraid of the dark" (p. 246). This is more than the familiar naturalistic insistence that, beneath the veneer of civilization, human beings harbor atavistic impulses. The key to its further dimension lies in Lute's remark that the whole experience, while it may be "delusion and unreal," is nevertheless "very real . . . as a nightmare is real" (p. 253). On the one hand, such an experience moves in the direction of Jung's theory of the collective unconscious, an inherited racial memory with its shadowy archetypes. Yet because it also involves Chris's unrevealed source of personal guilt, it touches those facets of the subconscious mind that had recently been explored by Freud.

IV

A second story of occult experience, "The Eternity of Forms," written in the fall of 1910,[15] deals with the materialization of a ghost. Less successful artistically than "Planchette," it reads like a second-rate Poe arabesque, with a fantastic plot involving a probable fratricide and all the complications of a mind disordered by guilt. Yet at the center of the tale, as at the center of "Planchette," lies a conflict between belief and disbelief; and once again a skeptic is forced to pay dearly for his dogmatic rationalism. The story takes the form of extracts from a journal kept by an old man named Sedley Crayden in the last months of his life, while his sanity and health deteriorate following the mysterious death of his brother, James. Psychologically, the journal serves as a forum for Sedley's desperate effort to convince himself that he did not, in a fit of passion during a philosophical argument, murder his brother. Philosophically, it constitutes his final attempt to convince himself that his own rationalistic side of that argument was correct. But as the tale progresses and the evidence of the supernatural accumulates, his mind disintegrates along with his argument.

The focus of the brothers' conflict soon becomes clear. James, the idealist, believed in the "eternity of forms," while according to Sedley, "Form is mutable. This is the last word of positive science. The dead do not come back" (p. 67). Sedley is thus another of London's complacent dogmatists, who "laughed at the unseen world" while believing that "chemistry and physics explained everything" (p. 71). Even at this early stage, however, Sedley's desperate tone reveals that his "positive science" is beginning to weaken under attack. "It is not true that I have recanted," he cries. "I still believe that I live in a mechanical universe" (p. 68). What prompts this outburst is the repeated materialization of the dead brother in the chair he occupied when alive. Like Chris Dunbar in "Planchette," Sedley adopts every rational expedient to explain away this ghost, but under such continuous pressure his certitudes begin to crumble. At this point Sedley falls back on an explanation that, while not inconsistent with his rationalism, nevertheless ventures into little-understood areas of man's psychic and spiritual life. For a time he relishes his new sensations, which he can disarm by labeling them "hallucinations." He has wanted to "experience such phenomena" all his life. But having reached such a point, he takes a step beyond it and links the hallucinations to the less scientifically manageable phenomenon of "imagination." Initially he is content to speculate tentatively: "What is imagination? It can make something where there is nothing" (pp. 68–69). Though he quickly dismisses the notion, he later returns to it more receptively: "My brother was right. There is an unseen world. . . . Call it a thought, an idea, anything you will, still it is there. . . . Thoughts are entities. We create with every act of thinking. I have created this phantom that sits in my chair and uses my ink" (p. 82). From here it is but a short step to that characteristically romantic theory of creativity in which the human imagination assumes godlike powers. If a mere man can create a new entity, Sedley speculates, "then is not the hypothesis of a Creator made substantial?" And since he himself has exercised such powers, he is "unlike other men. I am a god. I have created" (pp. 83–84).

The story then moves to its ironic ending, in which Sedley at last succeeds in banishing the ghost by displacing him—by occupying the chair and never moving from it until he dies. He has convinced himself that his rationalism, though "severely tried for a time," has passed the test, and that the ghost "never was." Yet he takes no chances: "I do not leave my chair. I am afraid to leave the chair" (p. 86). The ending thus leaves in suspension the protagonist's theoretical rationalism and practical credulity, although the story as a whole clearly dramatizes the inadequacy of his scientific dogmatism while affirming the facet of nonrational experience that London himself most fully embraced: the power of the creative imagination.

V

This continuing interest in occult fiction came to a climax in the novel *The Star Rover* (1915), which initially grew out of London's longstanding interest in prison conditions and his more recent friendship with Edward Morrell, who, during five years of torture and solitary confinement in San Quentin, claimed to have mastered a process of self-hypnosis that allowed his spirit to escape his body. London insisted that he never believed in such spirit-roving, and to the editor of *Cosmopolitan* he described the new book somewhat cynically as one which, though "pseudo-scientific and pseudo-philosophic," nevertheless contained "good accessible stuff to the Christian Science [and] New Thought folks."[16] Yet he characteristically underestimated his emotional involvement in Morrell's story. He saw in it the vehicle for a fantasy of escape, in which the protagonist, an imprisoned science professor named Darrell Standing, learns to suppress his scientific rationalism and to abandon his present body, freeing himself to reexperience in spirit his former selves and lives.

In this story, too, the believer has a skeptical foil, a prisoner named Jake Oppenheimer, whose disbelief prevents him from joining Standing in his spiritual excursions. Oppenheimer speaks for that side of himself that London liked to think was the whole—the rationalist immune to the nonsense of the spiritualists, an "earthman" devoted to the "irrefragable fact."[17] Oppenheimer's account of his youthful apostasy links him even more clearly with London:

> My mother believed in spirits. When I was a kid she was always seeing them and talking with them and getting advice from them. But she never came across with any goods from them. The spirits couldn't tell her where the old man could nail a job or find a gold mine or mark an eight-spot in Chinese lottery. Not on your life. The bunk they told her was that the old man's uncle had had a goitre, or that the old man's grandfather had died of galloping consumption, or that we were going to move house inside four months, which last was dead easy, seeing as we moved on an average of six times a year. (p. 161)

Yet behind this appealingly commonsensical rationalism lies a naïve literal-mindedness reminiscent of Huck Finn's consternation when the prayers he learns from Miss Watson fail to produce a set of fishhooks.

Oppenheimer's skepticism is not, in any case, given much weight. At times he even begins to look rather foolish as he racks his brain for some means of explaining away Standing's spiritual feats, which are endowed with a powerful aura of quasi-scientific plausibility and narrative verisimilitude. Standing's experiences, like those in the earlier stories, provide a bridge from nineteenth-century mesmerism to the methods of the new psychoanalysis. By self-hypnosis, Standing says, "I became able to put my conscious mind to sleep and to awaken and loose my subconscious mind. But the latter was an undisciplined and lawless thing. It wandered through all nightmarish madness, without coherence, without continuity of scene, event, or person" (p. 46). Eventually he learns to discipline these impulses and to master the art of the "little death," attaining a "passivity" that is "almost dream-like," and yet "positive almost to a pitch of exaltation" (p. 77). Experiencing an expansion of space and time, he declares, "I trod interstellar space, exalted by the knowledge that I was bound on vast adventure, where, at the end, I would find all the cosmic formulae and have made clear to me the ultimate secret of the universe" (p. 80).

VI

A "pitch of exaltation." A "vast adventure." These are the touchstones of London's most vital creative life. For all his loudly proclaimed scientific rationalism, he was also a deeply intuitive artist who believed (as he put it in *Martin Eden*) in the "mystery of beauty," in an "impassioned realism, shot through with human aspiration and faith."[18] Again and again he embraces in his fiction those moments of ecstatic experience that are not precisely supernatural but do embody the sense of wonder and mystery that transcends the limits of an unimaginative materialism. In *The Call of the Wild*, Buck comes to know the "ecstasy that marks the summit of life," which entails, paradoxically, "a complete forgetfulness that one is alive." Significantly, the same sensation comes to "the artist," who is "caught up and out of himself in a sheet of flame";[19] and there would seem only the thinnest of lines between an inspired artist, "caught up and out of himself," and a Darrell Standing, whose spirit abandons his body in the ecstasy of the "little death." Such an experience belongs also to that arch-rationalist Wolf Larsen, in *The Sea-Wolf*, who in a climactic moment is filled with a "strange uplift," feels as if "all time were echoing through [him]," can see "clear and far," and can "almost believe in God."[20]

In his last years, London's mind grew still more receptive to the possibility that heaven and earth contained more than nineteenth-century positivism had dreamt of. He read William James's *The Will to Believe* (1897) and *The Varieties of Religious Experience* (1902), and also Henry Holt's *On the Cosmic Relations* (1915), in which he marked and annotated numerous passages on telepathy, the evidence for and against "spiritism," and the way time and space are annihilated in dreams.[21] But nothing since his early reading of Herbert Spencer so moved him as his initial encounter with a translation of Carl Jung's *Psychology of the Unconscious* (1916), which seemed to him the long-sought key to those facets of the human imagination that had eluded rational formulation. He had begun reading Freud with considerable interest sometime after 1912, but his reading of Jung led him to exclaim to his wife, "I tell you I am standing on the edge of a world so new, so terrible, so wonderful, that I am almost afraid to look over into it."[22] Sometime during these years he made notes for a "Future Story Metaphysical," which, though it remained unwritten, reveals something of the direction of his mind: "The isolation of the death spirit—new forces, radium, telepathy, etc.—not so very much known. . . . Work in the confuting of the materialists, etc. Striking testimony of one man who almost died."[23]

It would be misleading to end with the implication that London rejected his scientific rationalism and became a convert to some sort of spiritual beliefs, as if he had come home to mother at last. One can go no further than to suggest that the conflict between belief and doubt continued throughout his life, providing him with an important source of imaginative power. In response to a correspondent who expressed her delight in the spiritual consolations of *The Star Rover*, he replied with almost bewildering candor: "I do not believe in the continuation of the spirit after the body is dead. . . . What I wrote in THE STAR ROVER was merely the argument of my opponents on this question of immortality. I tried to state their side for them—myself not believing in one word that I wrote."[24] Certainly London is telling the truth here—up to a point. But he may also be overstating his position, indulging his penchant for bluntly delivering unorthodox opinions calculated to shock more conventional minds. Against that letter should be measured another minor yet revealing incident. According to his wife, early in 1913 his distress at the death of a young woman "for once made his philosophy waver. 'I did something last night I never did before,' he confessed. 'I concentrated every thought and actually tried to call that girl back. . . . Of course,' he smiled half-foolishly, 'there was no answer.'"[25] London never abandoned his lifelong rationalism. Yet he loved new experience, new knowledge, too well ever to fence himself off from any part of it. Though he continued to hope and believe that science held the key to all mysteries, he was never completely sure.

NOTES

1. Jack London to John E. Purdon, 26 January 1915, in *Letters from Jack London,* ed. King Hendricks and Irving Shepard (New York: Odyssey, 1965), p. 444.

2. Charmian London to Louise Griffiths, 20 December 1916, carbon copy in the Jack London Collection at the Henry E. Huntington Library, JL 9896. I am grateful to the Huntington Library and to I. Milo Shepard, executor of the Jack London estate, for permission to quote this and subsequent passages from the Londons' unpublished papers.

3. Charmian London to Upton Sinclair, 21 December 1930, Huntington Library, JL 10566.

4. Quoted in Joan London, *Jack London and His Times: An Unconventional Biography* (1939; rpt. Seattle: University of Washington Press, 1968), p. 5.

5. Joan London, *Jack London and His Times,* p. 30. Franklin Walker and Andrew Sinclair, the only later biographers who had access to London's papers, accepted Joan London's account of her father's early years. See Sinclair's *Jack: A Biography of Jack London* (New York: Harper and Row, 1977) and the typescript of the early chapters of Walker's uncompleted biography in the Walker Collection, Huntington Library, HM 45284.

6. Jack London to Cloudesley Johns, 8 October 1904, Huntington Library, JL 12188. Andrew Sinclair sums up London's rebellion thus: "He could feel no gratitude in the face of such a denial by his presumed father, such a false start from his true mother. He began to go against every influence they might have had on him. For their worlds of spiritualism and astrology, mysticism, and nonsense, he substituted his own positivism and rationalism" (*Jack,* p. 37).

7. "A Ghostly Chess Game" was originally entitled "Who Believes in Ghosts!" when London published it in the Oakland *High School Aegis* 10 (21 October 1895): 1–4. Sometime after his return from the Klondike in 1898, he revised this rather Biercean story and gave it its new title. The revised version was apparently never published, and the passages quoted here are from the typescript in the Huntington Library, JL 705.

8. "The Mahatma's Little Joke," typescript in Huntington Library, JL 908. I am grateful to Howard Kerr for pointing out to me the resemblance between this story and John Kendrick Bangs's "A Psychical Prank," in *The Water Ghost and Others* (New York: Harper, 1894). Both stories deal with the Theosophical notion of "astral forms," as well as with jokes involving proposals of marriage. London was reading some of Bangs's stories in late 1899 (see *Letters from Jack London,* p. 62), and it is possible that he had come across "A Psychical Prank" a few years earlier.

9. Jack London to Cloudesley Johns, 12 June 1899, Huntington Library, JL 12101.

10. These notes, and those cited earlier in the same paragraph, are in the Huntington Library, JL 1004, JL 652.

11. MS diary for 1905 in Huntington Library, JL 218. On a few of his MSS, London

date-stamped occasional pages, thus giving a precise indication of the chronology of composition. "Planchette" is one such MS (Huntington Library, JL 1062).

12. Jack London, *Moon-Face and Other Stories* (New York: Macmillan, 1906), p. 217. The story appeared originally in *Cosmopolitan* 41 (June, July, August 1906): 157–65, 259–66, 378–86.

13. A planchette was a triangular board fitted with wheels and a pencil. When a hand was placed on it, the board was supposed to move at the dictation of a spirit, thus recording messages from beyond the grave. For a brief account of its place in the history of nineteenth-century spiritualism, see Howard Kerr, *Mediums, and Spirit-Rappers, and Roaring Radicals: Spiritualism in American Literature, 1850–1900* (Urbana: University of Illinois Press, 1972), pp. 109–10.

14. Andrew Sinclair makes an apt comment on the biographical significance of "Planchette": "Evidently Jack had not wholly outgrown his mother's belief in evil spirits" (*Jack*, p. 120).

15. The last leaf of the MS in the Huntington Library (JL 644) is dated 2 October 1910. The story first appeared in *Red Book Magazine* 16 (March 1911): 866–73, and was reprinted in *The Turtles of Tasman* (New York: Macmillan, 1916). Page references in the text are to the latter publication.

16. Jack London to Roland Phillips, 26 March 1914, in *Letters from Jack London*, p. 418.

17. Jack London, *The Star Rover* (New York: Macmillan, 1915), p. 162.

18. Jack London, *Martin Eden* (New York: Macmillan, 1909), pp. 197, 232.

19. Jack London, *The Call of the Wild* (New York: Macmillan, 1903), p. 91. Sam S. Baskett, in a paper read at the 1978 meeting of the Modern Language Association, "Calls of the Wild and Jack London's Esthetic Suppositions," has usefully focused on this passage as an expression of London's artistic impulses.

20. Jack London, *The Sea-Wolf*, ed. Matthew J. Bruccoli (Boston: Houghton, Mifflin, 1964), p. 54.

21. I am grateful to David Mike Hamilton for allowing me to read the MS of his bibliography of the annotated books in London's library.

22. Charmian London, *The Book of Jack London* (New York: Century, 1921), 2:323. Hamilton's bibliography provides evidence of London's reading of Freud between 1912 and 1916.

23. MS notes, Huntington Library, JL 812.

24. Jack London to Emma Kelly, 29 April 1915, Huntington Library, JL 12261.

25. Charmian London, *Book of Jack London*, 2:252. Another writer who should be given credit for recognizing this double vision in London's character and fiction is his friend Edward Biron Payne, whose book *The Soul of Jack London* (London: Rider, 1926) has usually been dismissed as a curiosity because, in the last half of it, Payne tentatively accepted the testimony of a young woman who claimed to have received from London's spirit a recantation of his materialist views. In the first half of his book, however, Payne argues quite effectively for the idea that London was never so purely the scientific rationalist as he liked to think. A "real war," Payne says, "was going on in Jack London's nature" between his "science" and his "spiritual instincts," the latter being unacknowledged but present as "something felt" (pp. 61, 68). More recently, Earle Labor has suggested that London's Northland fiction is dominated by "an instinctive mysticism, not a logical positivism" (*Jack London* [New York: Twayne, 1974], p. 61).

CRUCE STARK

The Color of "the Damned Thing": The Occult as the Suprasensational

During the first half of the nineteenth century, Americans who thought about such things could responsibly hope that a correspondence existed between themselves and nature. In 1836 Emerson could assert that "particular natural facts are symbols of particular spiritual facts," that "nature is the symbol of spirit." The primary residence of that spirit, it went without saying, was within the collective soul of humanity.[1] As the century progressed, however, such suggestions of a linkage between the internal and the external lost credibility. And if, with the loss, the mysteries of the outside world had become more exciting, they were becoming more threatening as well. The possibility, even the likelihood, was increasing that humankind would have to adjust to a universe whose values were more egalitarian than merely anthropocentric. The basic categories by which people had organized their experience were being undermined, and at least some of the most concerned commentators were far from sure that more workable constructs were in the offing.

Such a shift in perspective affected many areas of late nineteenth- and early twentieth-century American culture, and, as is evident in the fictional treatment of the occult, spiritualism was among them. But my concern in this essay is not so much with spiritualism itself as with the way in which some of its variants reflected a more broadly based attitude toward the place of humanity within nature. Not all of my sources are directly related to the occult; some, for that matter, have little to do with fiction. But it is with the future of fiction that I am most concerned. Although some of my sources may seem peripheral to the mainstreams of literary development, all reflect a climate of opinion which contributed to imaginative literature's increased concern with psychological conflicts and developments. If the external world had no intention of adjusting itself to human limitations, then perhaps fiction's probings should be inward, toward what *could* be known from within the confines of human perception.

There are many reasons for the sense of displacement apparent in much late nineteenth-century thought, but among them must be included the impact of scientific discovery. The effects of Darwin's evolutionary findings are well known, but the physical sciences were not far behind the biological in their disruptive influence. The world was being revealed as a much more complicated affair than those of Emerson's generation could have dreamed, causing people of many persuasions to begin seeking means of reconciling their positions with—or, if possible, substantiating them by—the new findings in physics.

Among these, paradoxically, were the spiritualists.[2] Despite their customary optimism, their efforts to bring the supernatural into the finite merely indicate that humanity could no longer pretend to be at home in its universe. Their attempts to reduce spiritualistic forces to a scientific model reveal a growing sense of vulnerability engendered by a world that is indifferent to human convenience. The balance of power had shifted. No longer could humanity believe nature's purposes to be its own, certainly not to be the reflection of its collective soul. External forces were now in control.

William James, although no spiritualist himself, presents the most complete study of the possibilities of defining spiritualism within a psychophysiological framework, and he is, of course, among the most optimistically tough-minded. But even he admitted that "when all is said and done, we are in the end absolutely dependent on the universe."[3] What that universe might contain was growing increasingly uncertain. Yet it was just that uncertainty that offered hope to many. Why might there not be, among the forces impinging on us, something spiritual?

Frederic Hedge, at one time a major spokesman for transcendentalism, attempted in 1881 to explain orthodox science's self-satisfied neglect of spiritualism. "The aversion of science to this class of phenomena," he wrote, "is due to the prevalent assumption of supernatural origin. Call them supernatural and you shut them out from the field of scientific inquiry, whose limits are the bounds of nature." Such terminology, Hedge insisted, was misleading. "With what there may be outside of nature, we have nothing to do in this connection. If nature means anything, it means all of finite being." The question at issue, Hedge suggested, is whether the occult (specifically, the existence of ghosts), is "part of that all, subject to nature's method and rule." His conclusion was tentative. Spirits do, in fact, exist; but their realm is "that unseen world where science cannot reach."[4]

Ambrose Bierce had a more definitive answer. In "The Damned

Thing" (1893) he departed from his more customary solipsistic confines to speak of the destructive forces beyond human consciousness. In the story, Hugh Morgan has been physically obliterated by an invisible force. For weeks Morgan had known that this "damned thing" had been pursuing him, and he had written in his diary an interpretation of his antagonist's invisibility:

> I have the solution of the mystery; it came to me last night —suddenly, as by revelation. How simple—how terribly simple!
> There are sounds that we cannot hear. At either end of the scale are notes that stir no chord of that imperfect instrument, the human ear. They are too high or too grave. . . . As with sounds, so with colors. At each end of the solar spectrum the chemist can detect the presence of what are known as "actinic" rays. They represent colors—integral colors in the composition of light—which we are unable to discern. The human eye is an imperfect instrument; its range is but a few octaves of the "chromatic scale." I am not mad; there are colors that we cannot see.
> And, God help me! the Damned Thing is of such a color![5]

Hugh Morgan has, not too happily, provided an answer to Hedge's question. Unseen forces do exist in the world of finite nature, and there is no need to label them supernatural; it is enough that they are suprasensational.

During the second half of the nineteenth century, many of those sympathetic to spiritualistic possibilities felt that science itself was increasingly providing substantiation for their position. Most attempts to define the occult within a scientific framework relied, whether consciously or not, on the researches into sensational response conducted by two German scientists, G. T. Fechner and E. H. Weber. According to their studies, some stimuli are too faint for sensation. "In other words," William James summarized, "a certain finite amount of outward stimulus is required to produce any sensation of its presence at all." Fechner called such a condition "the law of the *threshold*," James continued; "something must be stepped over before the object can gain entrance to the mind."[6] Within limits, our senses respond in direct proportion to the increase of outward stimulus. At a certain level, however, disproportionate outward force must be exerted to cause the expected increase in sensory reaction. Finally, a level is reached beyond which our senses do not respond at all, regardless of any increases in stimulus.

According to this model, human beings are, at least in one aspect, sensation-receiving machines; and although our receptory apparatus is competent to select and organize outward stimuli within the narrow range necessary for physical survival within our environment, it does not necessarily tell us very much about the nature of that environment. People, in other words, have little access to the possible world existing beyond their sensations. James's experiences with multiple personalities, with trance states, with "all these new facts that are gradually coming to light about our organization," had led him to believe that "some infernality in the body *prevents* really existing parts of the mind from coming to their effective rights at all, suppresses them, and blots them out from participation in this world's experiences, although they are *there* all the time."[7] Even though our minds might have unthought-of potentialities, we are trapped within the confines of our senses. Far from being in control of our universe, we may be unaware even of its basic attributes. "Why *may* we not be in the universe," James asked, "as our dogs and cats are in our drawingrooms and libraries?"[8]

Few writers in the late nineteenth and early twentieth centuries were so acutely aware of how inadequate the senses are for understanding our world as Henry Adams. In a famous section of *The Education of Henry Adams*, Adams, already in London on business, receives a message that his sister in Italy has been thrown from a cab and injured. He rushes to Bagni di Lucca to find her dying horribly yet courageously of lockjaw, and his reactions move from disbelief to horror. "The first serious consciousness of Nature's gesture—her attitude towards life—took form then as a phantasm, a nightmare, an insanity of force. For the first time, the stage-scenery of the senses collapsed; the human mind felt itself stripped naked, vibrating in a void of shapeless energies, with resistless mass, colliding, crushing, wasting, and destroying what these same energies had created and labored from eternity to perfect."[9]

Adams must, in some way, attempt to restore "the stage-scenery of the senses." After his sister's death he journeys northward with friends and stops on the shores of Lake Geneva "to recover his balance in a new world." The ordered, external world, whose reality he earlier had no reason to doubt, now seems to "reproduce the distorted nightmare of his personal horror." But even if the nightmare be real, the psyche cannot for long withstand such disorder, and, seemingly with conscious purpose, Adams reimposes order. "For the first time in his life, Mont Blanc for a moment looked to him what it was—a chaos of anarchic and purposeless forces—and he needed days of repose to see it clothe itself again with the illusions of his senses, the white purity of its snows, the splendor of its light, and the infinity of its heavenly peace. Nature was kind; Lake Geneva was beautiful beyond itself, and the Alps put on charms real as terrors" (p. 289). Order is a function not so much of the objects perceived as of the perceiver himself. "Unity is vision; it must have been part of the process of learning to see" (p. 398). The human consciousness demanded order; nature, in its multiplicity, provided the raw material for it. But such constructions did nothing to alter the chaos Adams had seen when he first looked out upon Mont Blanc.

Even at their most accurate, Adams maintains, our senses are unreliable, suggesting more about our internal state than about the outlines of external nature. But it is not only man's need for order, "the illusions of his senses," that separates him from an accurate determination of nature. Even before we have the opportunity to misinterpret, our physiological limitations make distortions inevitable. Sardonically delighted with his depiction of a regressive evolution, Adams's persona in *Mont-Saint-Michel and Chartres* explains that "primitive man seems to have had a natural colour-sense, instinctive like the scent of a dog. Society has no right to feel it as a moral reproach to be told that it has reached an age when it can no longer depend, as in childhood, on its taste, or smell, or sight, or hearing, or memory; the fact seems likely enough, and in no way sinful; yet society always denies it, and is invariably angry about it; and, therefore, one had better not say it."[10]

Far from being the center about which external reality revolved, far from being the end for whose enlightenment nature existed, humanity is simply a receptor for some, by no means even most, of nature's signals. The scientist Karl Pearson, according to Adams, told his students "that they must put up with a fraction of the universe, and a very small fraction at that—the circle reached by the senses, where sequence could be taken for granted—much as the deep-sea fish takes for granted the circle of light which he generates. 'Order and reason, beauty and benevolence, are characteristics and conceptions which we find solely associated with the mind of man'" (*Education*, p. 450).

Beyond our senses, in that part of nature's experience we are unequipped to share, is a world totally foreign to our needs. Pearson, again according to Adams, insisted that

> these conceptions must stop: "Into the chaos beyond sense-impressions we cannot scientifically project them." We cannot even infer them: "In the chaos behind sensations, in the 'beyond' of sense-impressions, we cannot infer necessity, order or routine, for these are concepts formed by the mind of man on this side of sense-impressions"; but we must infer chaos: "Briefly chaos is all that science can logically assert of the supersensuous." The kinetic theory of gas is an assertion of ultimate chaos. In plain words, Chaos was the law of nature; Order was the dream of man. (*Education*, p. 451)

The world of the suprasensational is one not only uninterested in human needs but also disdainful even of human measurements. Mankind had "translated himself into a new universe which had no common scale of measurement with the old. He had entered a super-sensual world, in which he could measure nothing except by chance collisions of movements imperceptible to his senses, perhaps even imperceptible to his instruments" (pp. 381–82). Science and, in effect, humanity are "adrift on a sensual raft in the midst of a super-sensual chaos" (p. 452). And the forces of that chaos, the waves and rays and particles, all unavailable to our perception, are "occult, su-persensual, irrational" (p. 383). Mystery is no longer relegated to the supernatural. The occult now is uncomfortably closer, very much in the natural world, only beyond our senses.

Research into X-rays, radio waves, and other movements beyond our normal sensory reception emphasized the limitations of the accustomed range of human experience. Sir William Crookes in his 1898 presidential address to the British Association for the Advancement of Science pointed out that "Roentgen has familiarised us with an order of vibrations of extreme minuteness compared with the smallest waves with which we have hitherto been acquainted, and of dimensions comparable with the distances between the centres of the atoms of which the material universe is built up; and there is no reason to suppose that we have reached the limit of frequency."[11] Addresses before such august societies might seem beyond the usual literary scope of most spiritualists, but Crookes was a special case. In 1898 he was president not only of the British Association for the

Advancement of Science but also of the British Society for Psychical Research, and spiritualists saw in his research, which at least to him suggested "something like continuity between . . . unexamined forces and laws already known" (p. 30), a substantiation of their paranormal experiences.[12]

Isaac K. Funk, cofounder of Funk and Wagnalls, could wait no longer than the preface of his *The Widow's Mite and Other Psychic Phenomena* to enlist Crookes's authority. The British scientist "opens up a line of startling speculation in his provisional explanation of telepathy," Funk wrote, and "if this speculation turns out to be true, worlds upon worlds of astounding proportions open to science." According to Funk's understanding of Crookes's findings, "The differences between sound, electricity, light, x-rays, and radium are only the differences in the frequency of vibrations of waves." So, Funk concluded, "if an ear were sufficiently sensitive it could *hear* color, hear the beauty of a picture."[13]

In an appendix, Funk reproduced a table of the ranges of vibrations per second, from sound at the low end to radium at the high. "It may be," Funk commented, "that the x-waves and the radium-waves are only at the threshold of the wonders of the unseen universe." The conclusion for any spiritualist was obvious. "May it not be that thought waves, waves by which spirits communicate, be continuous with the waves that begin with sound, light and radium, and that the spirit body . . . be but continuous with the physical bodies which we have in this world, raised to an indescribable number of vibrations?" (p. 519). Crookes himself, although his response was less enthusiastic than Funk's, did not disagree. "It seems to me," Funk quoted the scientist, "that in these rays we may have a possible mode of transmitting intelligence, which with a few reasonable postulates, may supply a key to much that is obscure in psychical research." If occult phenomena are considered from such a perspective, Crookes concluded, "no physical laws are violated, neither is it necessary to invoke what is commonly called the supernatural" (Funk, pp. 519–20).

Frederic Myers, longtime friend of William James and one of the founders of the British Society for Psychical Research, used a similar model. In his 1890 essay "What Psychical Research Has Accomplished," James explained that "ordinary consciousness Mr. Myers likens to the visible part of the solar spectrum; the total consciousness is like that spectrum prolonged by the inclusion of the ultra-red and ultra-violet rays. In the psychic spectrum the 'ultra' parts may embrace a far wider range, both of physiological and of psychical activity, than is open to our ordinary consciousness and memory" (*Psychical Research*, pp. 38–39).

Funk's conversations with the spirit world seemed to support such hypotheses. A control, the spirit who serves as the link to the medium, once explained to him that "there are emanations that come from some persons which strike the medium like shots from a gun, and even I, experienced as I am, find it difficult to keep my balance in earth conditions while these adverse waves strike me." But such experiences should not seem strange, the control continued, "in an age when it is known that waves of the electric ocean go around the world in a second or two, and that there are waves of substances like radium that travel hundreds of thousands of miles in a second and have amazing potency. Foolish mortals, when will you learn that the potency of the coarse and clumsy forces of the physical world are as nothing compared with that of psychic forces?" (Funk, pp. 105–6).

Just as a radio receiver must be attuned to the proper frequency, so only exceptional receptors can experience these psychic forces. During another of Funk's psychic interviews, the control explained that such discoveries as those of X-rays and radio waves "were not given you until earth conditions were right for them."

> When these conditions have ripened, then they are impinged on some brain fitted to receive them. The only credit that is thus due to that brain is that it was ready to receive the invention. The receiver of the wireless message can claim only one credit, and that is that it was attuned to the transmitter; otherwise the waves would have passed by unheeded. A brain when attuned to the spiritual message will receive that message, and only that brain and others thus attuned can receive it. To all other brains there is absolute silence. Were the earth world ready, what it has received in the way of inventions are as nothing to what would be given it. (p. 201)

The control continued that it was not he who was responsible for the trivialities of the messages received by those at the séance. It was the fault of the earthbound, who simply were not yet tuned into the more profound bandwidths. "You ask," the control responded, "why we do not tell you more. We tell you all that you can receive. Why does not the receiver get messages for which it is not attuned? Waves may be passing in all directions, and weighted with most important information, but the receiver, not attuned to them, responds not at all" (p. 201).[14]

A medium from Denver, having heard of the publisher's psychic experiences, explained his communication with the spirit world in terms surprisingly similar to those of Funk's control. "There are two elements inseparable from success in thought transference on all mental planes," he wrote from Colorado.

> First, the transmitter and receiver must be in harmony with scientific laws governing through vibration.
>
> Secondly, the spirit or inner consciousness liberates a series of thought-waves generated through electromagnetism by chemical affinity within the human brain, the reservoir of dynamic force. This power becomes the transmitter and stimulates nerve currents to receive and convey to the perceptive faculties, or receiver, the ideas conveyed. Thought-waves may be thus continued through unlimited space should sensitive minds be acted upon as receivers, thus renewing dynamic force to repeat the process of thought transmission. (Funk, p. 183)

There were, however, messages received by those normally restricted to more commonplace communications. For instance, a mother and her daughters, seated in their English living room, heard the cries of their son and brother who was on the verge of drowning in the Indies east of Java. "In this case," Funk explained, "it will be observed that a number of persons heard the voice at the same time."

> If thought transference be the correct explanation of it, it would seem that this thought must have been impressed upon the different minds by something objective. Of course it is not the physical voice that is carried, but it is possible that intense psychic or mental excitement may make waves on something we may call psychic ether or thought ether, and that these waves enter the minds of all who are in harmony with the transmitting soul in some such way as we

may imagine the waves produced by the transmitter of the
wireless telegraph report themselves to the instruments attuned in harmony with the transmitter, be they one or a
thousand. (p. 316)

At isolated moments of crisis, Funk believed, it is possible for persons normally limited to the conventional receptory bandwidth to
expand their sensitivities. Such abilities are latent in everyone,
awaiting development. "Is it hard to believe," Funk wrote, "that
these rudimentary faculties are growing for the next stage of evolutionary development, in harmony with the environment of our objective or subjective nature, or both; and that when developed they
will make us citizens of the universe—both the inner and outer—as
our present physical senses have made us citizens of this planet?
This is man's history, a slow adjustment of himself to his environment" (p. 10). Our next stage of evolution, then, would be psychical,
not physical.

Others were not so optimistic. In fact, the populist Ignatius Donnelly saw such attempts to justify spiritual matters scientifically as
an indication of the decadence of American society. In his 1890 best-
seller, *Caesar's Column*, Donnelly had his innocent African traveler
attend a "Twentieth-Century Sermon," in which the minister presents a close parallel to Funk's scientific model of spiritualism. The
clergy's role in Donnelly's anti-Utopia consists of spreading entertaining information to spiritually unconcerned parishioners. On this
particular Sunday the pastor describes a newly invented machine
that, through "telephonic communication," can reach the spirit
world, which "our senses had hitherto not been able to perceive."
The preacher goes on to announce that "the field in this direction
had just been opened, and it was difficult to tell how far the diversity
of multiplicity of creation extended."

He said it was remarkable that our ancestors had not fore-
seen these revelations, for they knew that there were sound-
waves both above and below the register of our hearing; and
light-waves of which our eyes were able to take no cog-
nizance; and therefore it followed, *a priori*, that nature
might possess an infinite number of forms of life which our
senses were not fitted to perceive. . . . All that we knew of
Nature taught us that she was tireless in the prodigality of

her creative force, and boundless in the diversity of her workmanship; and we now knew that what the ancients called *spirit* was simply an attenuated condition of matter.[15]

Donnelly had only disgust for such "free thinking." Any new speculation that led to the possibility that "what the ancients called spirit was simply an attenuated condition of matter" could, Donnelly felt, only intensify the nation's disintegration. If, as he had proclaimed in the preamble to the First National Convention of the People's Party in 1892, the nation was on "the verge of moral, political, and material ruin," then questioning the nature of the world beyond our senses, the world that could not be verified empirically, would surely hasten the collapse.[16]

There were, of course, reactions that fell somewhere between Funk's conviction and Donnelly's disdain. Funk had written to William James, asking for his interpretation of a particular psychic episode the publisher had experienced. James's reply demonstrated both the openness and the skepticism that characterized his excursions into psychical research. "The hypothesis of spirit communication," he responded, "is undoubtedly a possible one and simpler than any other, provided one supposes the spirits in question to have been tremendously inhibited in their communications. This is a necessary inference from the gaps and guesses which the facts they reported exhibited" (Funk, p. 179). James, in other words, would not dismiss the possibilities of spirit communication even though he was unimpressed with much of the evidence he encountered.

In fact, he was refreshingly open to unorthodox ideas—sometimes, in the opinion of his more conservative colleagues, embarrassingly so.[17] "I think," Walter Lippmann wrote after James's death in 1910, "he would have listened with an open mind to the devil's account of heaven, and I'm sure he would have heard him out on hell."[18] James listened, not credulously but respectfully, to persons usually dismissed by the world of science as mere quacks. He found little of substance in the table knockings and the Ouija boards, and most of the mediums he and his fellow researchers investigated proved fraudulent. But there was always just enough tantalizing credibility, just enough of the experience left unexplained, to warrant continuing the search.

Mediumship, for instance, was a "phenomenon of human life" that the psychologists "do not even attempt to connect with any of the other facts of nature." But anyone familiar with mediumism knew that "there is method in it; it must have a context of some sort and belong to a region where other things must be found also. It cries aloud for serious investigation" (*Psychical Research*, p. 239).

The concept of a threshold is at the core of James's hypotheses of psychical experience. Although he objected strenuously to the quantitative conclusions Fechner and Weber derived from their researches, he agreed thoroughly with their assumption concerning sensory thresholds.[19] James, however, was far more interested in the thresholds between the conscious and the subconscious, or subliminal, than in the graphing of degrees of sensation. In his letter to Funk, James referred to "the many recent proofs that our 'subconscious self' may often know what our conscious self is ignorant of" (Funk, p. 178). Experiments with hypnotism had demonstrated "the simultaneous existence of two different strata of consciousness, ignorant of each other, in the same person" (*Psychical Research*, p. 34).

The two selves are not, however, totally separate. The subconscious, on occasion, may intrude on the conscious. When such "incursions" take place, "the subject does not guess the source," and so they "take for him the form of unaccountable impulses to act, or inhibitions of action, of obsessive ideas, or even of hallucinations of sight or hearing" (*Varieties of Religious Experience*, p. 229). The important phrase, at least for James's ventures into psychical research, was "the subject does not guess the source," for James was not sure that he knew either. The incursions came from the subliminal regions, of course, but the question remained, How did they get there?[20] James had little doubt that "we all have potentially a 'subliminal self,' which may make at any time irruption into our ordinary lives. At its lowest, it is only the depository of our forgotten memories; at its highest, we do not know what it is at all" (*Psychical Research*, pp. 42–43). Within that "not knowing" resided the possibility that the mediums and the mystics might be right.

"My subliminal," James wrote, "has my ordinary consciousness for one of its environments, but has it additional environments on the remoter side?" (*Psychical Research*, p. 228). If the aspect of the subliminal self that allows us to encounter our forgotten memories is but the most familiar edge of a subconscious continuum stretching into ever more uncharted areas, James saw no reason to set limits to its outer edge. If the senses were activated by material stimuli, why might not the extremities of the subconscious be receptive to forces of a higher level? "Just as our primary wide-awake consciousness throws open our senses to the touch of things material, so it is logically conceivable that *if there be* higher spiritual agencies that can directly touch us, the psychological condition of their doing so *might be* our possession of a subconscious region which alone should yield access to them." Should spiritual forces exist, "they may get access to us only through the subliminal door" (*Varieties of Religious Experience*, pp. 237–38).

When James hypothesized the means by which such an access might occur, he relied on the same threshold model by which Fechner explained sense impression. According to science, James stated in *Human Immortality*, our inner life is merely "a function of that famous material, the so-called 'gray matter' of our cerebral convolutions."[21] All brain activity, according to this view, is a result of a previous influence on our sensory system. When external forces achieve sufficient strength to break through our sensory threshold, the brain produces "sensations and mental images, and out of the sensations and images the higher forms of thought and knowledge in their turn are framed" (pp. 25–26). The brain, therefore, produces the experiences making up our inner lives.

Such an explanation of the mental process assumes, of course, a prior impression on our senses. But there are "mysterious phenomena"—"religious conversions, providential leadings in answer to prayer, instantaneous healings, premonitions, apparitions at time of death, clairvoyant visions or impressions, and the whole range of mediumistic capacities, to say nothing of still more exceptional and incomprehensible things"—in which it is difficult to understand how this sense action occurs (*Immortality*, pp. 26–27). For such experiences, the production theory of the brain seems inapplicable.

But, James insisted, the production theory is not the only available option. The brain may have a transmissive function as well. If, as the experience of many seems to imply, there does occur "a power from without, quite different from the ordinary action of the sense or of the sense-led mind," then "all such experiences, quite paradoxical and meaningless on the production-theory, fall naturally into place" on a transmission theory. According to such a theory, inner experiences do not need to be mentally produced. "They exist ready-made in the transcendental world." To provide for their communication, "we need only suppose the continuity of our consciousness with a mother sea, to allow for exceptional waves occasionally pouring over the dam."

The dam, of course, is very much there. According to the transmission theory, the brain not only channels suprasensory forces into our consciousness but it also creates a barrier which they must overcome. There is, in other words, a threshold for spiritual as well as sensory response, and just as the sensory threshold fluctuates, so the height of the spiritual may vary according to the circumstances or the individual. But whatever the case, the transmission of suprasensory forces requires only "an abnormal lowering of the brain-threshold to let them through." James's explanation of the process stopped here. "The causes of these odd lowerings of the brain's threshold," he conceded, "still remain a mystery on any terms."[22]

James had, within a psycho-physiological framework, provided for the possibility of spiritual forces transcending human senses. But he was aware, as many were not, that postulating a theory of the suprasensational occult suggested more about our limitations within nature than about nature's patterns themselves. Human beings could no longer dream of subjugating external reality either philosophically or imaginatively, for they could not so much as perceive all its terms. James responded to such a circumstance with a blend of skepticism, curiosity, and delight. But regardless of a writer's reaction to the suprasensational, whether it be Bierce's horror or Donnelly's disdain, Adams's pessimism or Funk's confidence, the hypothesis implied that forces which humanity had once assumed were outside of nature might be more at home there than humanity itself.

The senses were inadequate to describe the world; consequently, many serious thinkers and writers turned back toward themselves. "The only form of thing that we directly encounter," James wrote, "the only experience that we concretely have, is our own personal life" (*Psychical Research*, p. 47). If our perceptions are not necessarily an accurate reflection of an external world, they may be a mirror of an inner one. What we see, in other words, may not be able to tell us precisely *where* we are in an indeterminate world, but the way we order that world and react to it may tell us a great deal about *who* we are.

Even so minor a writer as Ambrose Bierce demonstrates the increased concern with the way psychological realities shape our responses, whether empirically appropriate or not, to external conditions. "The Damned Thing" is atypical of Bierce's tales of terror. More often, Bierce's characters are destroyed not by an inexplicable external force but by uncontrollable terrors from within, many times triggered by misinterpretations of their physical situation. In "One of the Missing," Jerome Searing dies because he thinks he has been shot by a gun he does not know is unloaded. In "The Man and the Snake," Harker Brayton is driven mad and then destroyed by a confrontation with a snake that, unknown to him, is stuffed. And in Bierce's most famous story, "An Occurrence at Owl Creek Bridge," most of the narrative is actually a projection of Peyton Farquhar's imagination, telling us nothing of external conditions but a great deal about his desperate needs.

Henry James is, of course, a far greater analyst of psychological states. He offers perhaps the clearest example of the lessened concern with interpreting external conditions, the increased emphasis on examining the internal. In his most famous ghost story, *The Turn of the Screw*, James has almost perversely made sure that, on the basis of the text, we will probably never satisfactorily determine whether Quint and Miss Jessel are empirically present, whether they are truly supernatural beings or merely projections of the governess's troubled psyche. But whatever the case, the governess's response to them lays bare her own moral and psychological limitations. The supernatural ambiguities of the story provide the context, but James's psychological probings form the thematic core.

Henry James has, in a sense, forced the reader into the same relation to external reality as many late nineteenth- and early twentieth-century writers found themselves. The external world surrounding them was mysterious and unapproachable. The human psyche might be just as mysterious, but at least it offered a more intimate encounter. So those with insight and imagination became concerned, as they almost always eventually do, with the mysteries within. Although many of them would have been unsympathetic to much of Josiah Royce's thought, they almost certainly would have shared his conviction that, when confronted by concerns that really mattered, "my nearest friends are occult enough for me."[23]

NOTES

1. *Nature*, in *The Complete Works of Ralph Waldo Emerson* (Boston: Houghton Mifflin, 1903), 1:25.

2. See Trevor H. Hall, *The Spiritualists* (London: Gerald Duckworth and Co., 1962), pp. xi–xii.

3. William James, *The Varieties of Religious Experience* (New York: Modern Library, 1929), p. 51.

4. Frederic Hedge, "Ghost-Seeing," *North American Review* 133 (1881): 287, 301.

5. *The Collected Writings of Ambrose Bierce* (New York: Citadel Press, 1946), pp. 526–27.

6. William James, *Psychology: Briefer Course* (New York: Collier Books, 1962), p. 29.

7. William James to Alice James, 6 July 1891, in *William James on Psychical Research*, ed. Gardner Murphy and Robert O. Ballou (London: Chatto and Windus, 1961), p. 260.

8. William James to Charles A. Strong, 9 April 1907, ibid., p. 277.

9. Henry Adams, *The Education of Henry Adams* (New York: Modern Library, 1931), p. 288.

10. Henry Adams, *Mont-Saint-Michel and Chartres* (Boston: Houghton Mifflin, 1936), p. 151.

11. William Crookes, "Address by the President," *Report of the British Association for the Advancement of Science: 1898* (London: John Murray, 1899), p. 31.

12. For background on Crookes's relation to psychical research, see Hall, *Spiritualists*, chaps. 5–6.

13. Isaac K. Funk, *The Widow's Mite and Other Psychic Phenomena* (New York: Funk and Wagnalls, 1904), p. vii.

14. Although beyond the scope of this essay, Rudyard Kipling's "Wireless," in *The Works of Rudyard Kipling* (New York: Charles Scribner's Sons, 1909), 22: 239–68, offers an interesting parallel. The narrator is watching a young experimenter set up a primitive wireless radio in the back room of his uncle's pharmacy so that he can receive a message from Poole, a nearby town. A consumptive clerk is sleeping deeply in the outer room, partly because of a cocktail the narrator has concocted from the pharmaceutical wares near at hand, partly because of his precarious physical condition. The experimenter is disturbed because, while he is not receiving any messages from Poole, he *is* receiving messages from two battleships off the Isle of Wight who are unsuccessfully trying to communicate with each other. The narrator has returned to the outer room when the clerk suddenly awakes and begins writing, as though in a trance, Keats's "Eve of St. Agnes." Afterward the narrator proves to his satisfaction that the clerk has not only never read the poem but also has never heard of John Keats. The implication, of course, is that just as the radio waves—the "Hertzian waves" in

the story—can be sent through the air, so can waves of a more ethereal sort be transmitted by less mundane sources.

At the conclusion of the story, the clerk snaps out of his spell, about which he recalls nothing, and the narrator asks the experimenter why he is receiving the battleships' messages. The young man answers, "God knows—and Science will know tomorrow. Perhaps the induction is faulty; perhaps the receivers aren't tuned to receive just the number of vibrations per second that the transmitter sends. Only a word here and there. Just enough to tantalise." After receiving a final message from the ships, the experimenter comments, "It's quite pathetic. Have you ever seen a spiritualistic seance? It reminds me of that sometimes—odds and ends of messages coming out of nowhere—a word here and there—no good at all." He is answered by the clerk: "But mediums are all imposters. . . . They only do it for the money they can make. I've seen them" (p. 268).

15. Ignatius Donnelly, *Caesar's Column* (Cambridge, Mass.: Harvard University Press, 1960), pp. 181–82.

16. Walter B. Rideout, preface to *Caesar's Column*, p. xi.

17. For examples of such criticism of James, see Ralph Barton Perry, *The Thought and Character of William James* (Boston: Little, Brown, 1935), 2: 99–100, 153.

18. Walter Lippmann, "An Open Mind: William James," *Everybody's Magazine* 23 (1910): 800.

19. See Perry, *Thought and Character*, 2: 3–4; and William James, *The Principles of Psychology* (New York: Dover Publications, 1950), 1: 533–49.

20. James did not discount the possibility that "states of mystical intuition may be only very sudden and great extensions of the ordinary 'field of consciousness.'" "A Suggestion about Mysticism," in *Essays in Philosophy* (Cambridge, Mass.: Harvard University Press, 1978), p. 157.

21. William James, *The Will to Believe* and *Human Immortality* (New York: Dover Publications, 1956), p. 7.

22. James, *Immortality*, pp. 26–27; see also "A Suggestion about Mysticism," p. 158. The difference between the climate of opinion at the turn of the century and that at the middle of the twentieth century is apparent in the way Thomas Pynchon treats something very similar to the threshold theory in *Gravity's Rainbow* (New York: Bantam Books, 1974). Pointsman, a behavioral psychologist and therefore, from Pynchon's point of view, decidedly unsympathetic, is discussing possible reasons for a young soldier's continually becoming sexually aroused at the precise locations where V-2 rockets will fall soon afterward. "Think of it," Pointsman insists. "He's out there, and he can *feel them coming*, days in advance. But it's a reflex. A reflex to something that's in the air *right now*. Something we're too coarsely put together to sense—but *Slothrop can*" (p. 56). Such a solution, for Pynchon, is not only wrongheaded but irresponsible, for it attempts to force an irrational occurrence, a mysterious event, into a mechanical model. Pointsman, in essence, is saying that the stimulus, even though it is beyond our normal experience, is nevertheless an extension of our commonplace reality and so is in no way mysterious. The threshold hypothesis, then, which reflected human vulnerability at the turn of the century, now can be used as a defensive rationalization to defuse the mysterious.

23. Quoted in Beatrice H. Zedler, "Royce and James on Psychical Research," *Transactions of the Charles S. Peirce Society* (Fall 1974), p. 247. Zedler's essay provides a helpful summary of James's assumptions concerning psychical research.

The Contributors

CHARLES L. CROW is associate professor of English at Bowling Green State University. He is the author of *Janet Lewis*, a study of the twentieth-century poet and novelist, and of articles on Frank Norris and W. D. Howells.

JOHN W. CROWLEY, professor of English at Syracuse University, is the author of *George Cabot Lodge* and the editor of *George Cabot Lodge: Selected Fiction and Verse*. He has published numerous essays on W. D. Howells and other American writers, and is writing a psychoanalytic study of Howells and his fiction.

ALAN GRIBBEN is associate professor of English at the University of Texas at Austin. The author of many essays on Mark Twain, he has also published a two-volume annotated catalogue titled *Mark Twain's Library: A Reconstruction*.

CAROLYN L. KARCHER is assistant professor of English at Temple University. She is the author of *Shadow over the Promised Land: Slavery, Race, and Violence in Melville's America*.

J. GERALD KENNEDY, associate professor of English at Louisiana State University, has published articles on Malamud, Barthes, and Walker Percy. He is the author of numerous essays on Poe and has constructed the biography of another nineteenth-century magazinist in *The Astonished Traveler: William Darby, Frontier Geographer and Man of Letters*.

HOWARD KERR is associate professor of English at the University of Illinois, Chicago. He is the author of *Mediums, and Spirit-Rappers, and Roaring Radicals: Spiritualism in American Literature, 1850–1900*, and with Charles L. Crow has edited a forthcoming volume titled *The Occult in America*.

JAY MARTIN, Leo S. Bing Professor of Literature at the University of Southern California, is the author of *Conrad Aiken: A Life of His Art, Harvests of Change: American Literature 1865–1914, Nathanael West: The Art of His Life, Always Merry and Bright: The Life of Henry Miller*, an autobiographical romance titled *Winter Dreams: An American in Moscow*, and several other books. He is also a Research Clinical Associate of the Southern California Psychoanalytic Institute and practices in Irvine.

BARTON LEVI ST. ARMAND is professor of English at Brown University. The author of *The Roots of Horror in the Fiction of H. P. Lovecraft*, he has published essays on Poe, Dickinson, Frost, Jewett, Hawthorne, Whitman, Thoreau, and Cooper, and is working on a book about Emily Dickinson's poetry in the context of her time.

CRUCE STARK is associate professor of English at the University of Delaware. His articles on nineteenth-century American literature and intellectual history have appeared in such journals as *American Literature, Clio*, and *New England Quarterly*.

G. R. THOMPSON, professor of English at Purdue University, is the author of *Poe's Fiction: Romantic Irony in the Gothic Tales*. The former editor of *Poe Studies* and *ESQ*, he also has edited volumes of critical essays on the Gothic, of Gothic tales from the Romantic period, of the writings of Poe, and with Virgil L. Lokke, *Ruined Eden of the Present: Hawthorne, Melville, and Poe: Critical Essays in Honor of Darrel Abel*.

CHARLES N. WATSON, JR., is professor of English at Syracuse University. He is the author of *The Novels of Jack London*, and his articles on Melville, London, and other American writers have appeared in *American Literature, New England Quarterly, ESQ, Studies in the Novel*, and *Western American Literature*.

Index

Adams, Henry, 7, 224; *The Education of Henry Adams*, 214–16; *Mont-Saint-Michel and Chartres*, 215
Alcott, Brownson, 91
Ariès, Philippe: *The Hour of Our Death*, 42–44, 48, 53–54

Baetzhold, Howard G., 182
Bangs, John Kendrick: "A Psychical Prank," 206 (n. 8)
Banta, Martha, 138, 143, 145
Barclay, Glen St. John, 41
Barham, Richard: "Henry Harris," 31
Bartell, Jan Bryant: *Spindrift: Spray from a Psychic Sea*, 171
Barthes, Roland, 63
Baudelaire, Charles, 140, 142, 143, 148 (n. 21)
Baym, Nina, 111, 113–14
Becker, Ernest: *The Denial of Death*, 46, 55, 61
Bellamy, Edward, 1, 5–6, 124, 126, 128–29; *Looking Backward, 2000–1887*, 128–29; "The Blindman's World," 129; "The Old Folks' Party," 129
Bierce, Ambrose, 1, 7, 14, 33, 212–13, 224; "The Death of Halpin Frayser," 34; "The Eyes of the Panther," 34; "The Damned Thing," 34, 212–13, 225; "One of the Missing," 225; "The Man and the Snake," 225; "An Occurrence at Owl Creek Bridge," 225
Blair, Robert: *The Grave*, 41
Briggs, Julia: *Night Visitors: The Rise and Fall of the English Ghost Story*, 14, 16–17, 35 (n. 6)
Brontë, Emily: *Wuthering Heights*, 32
Brontë sisters, 111

Brown, Charles Brockden, 17, 32, 39
Brownson, Orestes, 1, 69–96 passim; *The Spirit-Rapper: An Autobiography*, 4–5, 71–95 passim; *The Convert*, 72
Bryant, William Cullen: "Thanatopsis," 44
Buitenhuis, Peter, 146
Butler, Pierce, 88–89, 97 (n. 27)

Calef, Robert: *More Wonders of the Invisible World*, 176
Caprell, Madame, 172–73
Carpenter, William B., 125, 126
Carter, Paul A.: *The Spiritual Crisis of the Gilded Age*, 174, 177
Carus, Carl Gustav, 125
Charcot, Jean, 154, 155
Chatterton, Thomas, 51
Cheiro. *See* Hamon, Louis
Chopin, Kate: *The Awakening*, 118 (n. 4)
Church, Frederic Edwin, 112
Clemens, Henry, 182
Clemens, Olivia, 177
Clemens, Samuel L. [pseud. Mark Twain], 1, 4, 5–6, 6–7, 124, 126, 127, 129, 154, 171–89: Works: *Adventures of Huckleberry Finn*, 45, 128, 137, 176–77, 178, 179, 180, 183, 186, 202; *Extracts from Captain Stormfield's Visit to Heaven*, 127, 178; "Which Was It?" 128; "Three Thousand Years among the Microbes," 128, 176; "No. 44, The Mysterious Stranger," 128, 176, 182; "Mental Telegraphy," 128, 179, 181; "Which Was the Dream?" 128, 182; "The Enchanted Sea-Wilder-

Clemens, Samuel L. (*continued*)
ness," 128, 183–84; "The Recent Carnival of Crime in Connecticut," 128, 184; *The Innocents Abroad,* 157, 179; *A Connecticut Yankee in King Arthur's Court,* 174, 177, 185; "A Double-Barrelled Detective Story," 175; *Pudd'nhead Wilson,* 175, 180–81; "Bible Teachings and Religious Practice," 176; "The Esquimau Maiden's Romance," 176; "The Secret History of Eddypus," 176; "The Chronicle of Young Satan," 176, 182; "The Story of Mamie Grant, the Child-Missionary," 177; *The American Claimant,* 178; "Schoolhouse Hill," 178; *The Mysterious Stranger,* 178, 181; *Life on the Mississippi,* 178, 183, 184, 187; "Mental Telegraphy Again," 181; "Palm Readings," 181; "Clairvoyant," 182; "The Great Dark," 182; "A Ghost Story," 183; "The Golden Arm," 183; *A Tramp Abroad,* 184; "The Californian's Tale," 184; "Doughface," 184; "Villagers of 1840–43," 184; "Little Bessie," 185; "The Five Boons of Life," 185
Coleridge, Samuel Taylor: *The Ancient Mariner,* 52
Conrad, Joseph: "The Secret Sharer," 184
Cooper, James Fenimore, 175; *The Spy,* 2
Crookes, William, 216–17
Cusack, Mary Francis: *Three Visits to Knock,* 177

Davidson, Edward, 60
De La Mare, Walter, 13
Descartes, René, 57
Diamond, Arlyn, 103
Dickinson, Emily, 101–2, 111, 112, 115, 118 (n. 15)
Doane, T. W.: *Bible Myths,* 179
Donnelly, Ignatius, 7, 224; *Caesar's Column,* 220–21
Douglas, Ann, 44

Dreiser, Theodore: *Plays of the Natural and Supernatural,* 130

Edel, Leon, 140
Edwards, Lee, 103
Eliot, George: *Daniel Deronda,* 175
Eliot, T. S., 39; *The Waste Land,* 51
Emerson, Ralph Waldo, 33, 80, 87, 90–92, 167 (n. 13); *Nature,* 211

Fechner, G. T., 213, 222, 223
Fitzgerald, F. Scott: *Tender Is the Night,* 156
Flournoy, Theodore, 8, 10 (n. 7)
Folio, Fred (pseud.): *Lucy Boston,* 95 (nn. 2, 4)
Fowler, Samuel P.: *Salem Witchcraft,* 177
Fox sisters, 4, 69, 70, 74
Freud, Sigmund, 8, 9, 10 (nn. 7, 12), 43, 51, 130, 153, 156, 200, 204; "The Unconscious," 6, 130; and Josef Breuer (*Studies on Hysteria*), 9
Fry, Elizabeth Gurney, 87, 89–90
Funk, Isaac K., 7, 224; *The Psychic Riddle,* 178; *The Widow's Mite,* 217–20, 221
Fussell, Edwin, 79

Garland, Hamlin, 129–30; *The Mystery of the Buried Crosses,* 129; *The Tyranny of the Dark,* 129
Gautier, Théophile, 17; *Une Nuit de Cléopâtre,* 111
Gilbert, Alan D., 64 (n. 4)
Gilman, Charlotte Perkins: "The Yellow Wall-Paper," 183
Goethe, Johann Wolfgang von: *Sorrows of Young Werther,* 51

Hale, Nathan, 154–55
Hamon, Louis [pseud. Cheiro], 181
Harte, Bret, 175
Hartmann, Eduard von: *The Philosophy of the Unconscious,* 123
Hauptmann, Gerhart: *The Sunken Bell,* 130

Hawthorne, Nathaniel, 1, 2, 6, 14, 16, 17, 32, 34, 62, 69–94 passim, 116, 117 (n. 4), 135–39, 140, 143, 146; *The Blithedale Romance*, 4–5, 70–73, 79 84–85, 87, 90, 95 (n. 4), 111, 114, 136–39; "Earth's Holocaust," 69; "The Procession of Life," 69; "The Hall of Fantasy," 69, 90–91; *The House of the Seven Gables*, 104, 111, 136, 140; *The Marble Faun*, 113–14, 123; "Young Goodman Brown," 176

Hays, Lola V. *See* Hutchings, Emily Grant

Hearn, Lafcadio: "Artful Ambidexterity," 137

Hedge, Frederic Henry, 32; "Ghost-Seeing," 212

Henry, O. *See* Porter, William Sydney

Higginson, Thomas Wentworth, 101, 118 (n. 15)

Hill, Hamlin, 178

Hoffmann, E. T. A., 16–17, 39, 142, 143

Hogg, James: *Private Memoirs and Confessions of a Justified Sinner*, 32

Holmes, Oliver Wendell, 9, 124

Holt, Henry: *Cosmic Relations*, 204

Home, Daniel Dunglas, 179

Howells, Elinor, 154

Howells, W. D., 1, 4, 6, 7, 9, 33, 129, 144, 151–68, 175, 181. Works: *Shapes that Haunt the Dusk*, 1–2, 34, 152; "A Sleep and a Forgetting," 6, 152, 155–68; *Between the Dark and the Daylight*, 129, 152; *Questionable Shapes*, 129, 152; *The Undiscovered Country*, 144, 168 (n. 25), 178; *Venetian Life*, 152; *Literary Friends and Acquaintance*, 152, 167 (n. 13); *The Shadow of a Dream*, 154; "Father and Mother: A Mystery," 162–63, 165; *A Modern Instance*, 168 (n. 25)

Hutchings, Emily Grant, and Lola V. Hays: *Jap Herron: A Novel Written from the Ouija Board*, 171

Ibsen, Henrik: *Ghosts*, 130

Ingersoll, Robert G., 173–74

Irving, Washington, 1, 14, 16, 17, 18–31, 32, 34, 39, 45; "The Adventure of the German Student," 3, 9, 19, 27–29, 31, 32; "Strange Stories by a Nervous Gentleman," 9, 19, 21, 22, 24, 27, 30–31, 34, 35 (n. 9); "Dolph Heyliger," 18; "The Legend of Sleepy Hollow," 18; "The Spectre Bridegroom," 18; "Rip Van Winkle," 18–19; "The Stout Gentleman," 19; *Tales of a Traveller*, 19, 21, 35 (n. 9); *Bracebridge Hall*, 19, 23; "The Adventure of My Uncle," 19–23, 27; "The Adventure of My Aunt," 23–24, 27; "The Bold Dragoon; or, The Adventure of My Grandfather," 24–27; "The Adventure of the Mysterious Picture," 29–30; "The Adventure of the Mysterious Stranger," 30; "The Adventure of the Young Italian," 30

Jackson, Andrew, 143

Jacobs, W. W.: "The Monkey's Paw," 185

James, Henry, 1, 4, 5–6, 7, 9, 10 (n. 12), 13, 33, 115, 118 (n. 14), 118–19 (n. 16), 124, 126–27, 129, 135–48, 154. Works: *The Turn of the Screw*, 2, 13, 15, 17, 34, 127, 135, 139, 142, 146, 225; *The Bostonians*, 4, 69, 95 (n. 4), 97 (n. 26), 119 (n. 16), 136, 139, 144; "The Jolly Corner," 34, 127, 135, 184; "The Friends of the Friends," 34, 145–46; review of *The Amber Gods and Other Stories*, 112–13; review of *Azarian*, 118 (n. 14); "A Romance of Certain Old Clothes," 118 (n. 16), 135, 139, 146; "De Grey: A Romance," 118 (n. 16), 135, 139; "The Ghostly Rental," 126, 127, 135–36, 137, 139–46; "Professor Fargo," 126, 127, 135–39, 140, 145, 146; *The Aspern Papers*, 126; "The Great Good Place," 127; "Is There a Life after Death?" 127; "The Private Life," 127; *The Sense of the Past*, 127, 129, 135; "Sir Edmund Orme," 127, 135; "The Last of the Valerii," 135; *Hawthorne*, 136; *Roderick Hudson*, 144; *Daisy Miller*, 157

James, William, 4, 5, 7–8, 10 (n. 12),
126, 139, 154, 162, 212, 213–14,
221–24. Works: "Census of Hallucinations," 126; *The Principles of Psychology*, 154, 161; *The Will to
Believe*, 161, 204; *The Varieties of Religious Experience*, 204, 222; "What
Psychical Research Has Accomplished," 217–18, 221–22; *Human
Immortality*, 223
Janet, Pierre, 156
Johns, Cloudesley, 194, 196
Jones, Ernest, 8, 10 (n. 12)
Jung, Carl Gustav, 200; *Psychology of
the Unconscious*, 204

Kafka, Franz, 9
Kant, Immanuel, 32
Keats, John: "La Belle Dame Sans
Merci," 111
Kelley, Cornelia P., 140
Kemble, Fanny, 88–89, 97 (n. 27)
Kierkegaard, Sören, 51, 60
Kipling, Rudyard: "The Mark of the
Beast," 186; "They," 186; "Wireless,"
226–27 (n. 14)
Kuhlmann, Susan, 182

Leek, Sybil, 180
Le Fanu, Joseph Sheridan, 14–16, 32;
"Schalkin the Painter," 14–15, 31;
"Green Tea," 14–16, 29, 31
Lewis, "Monk," 116
Lind, Sidney P., 140–41, 143
Lippmann, Walter, 221
London, Charmian, 193, 197, 204–5
London, Jack, 1, 4, 7, 193–207. Works:
The Star Rover, 7, 201–3, 204; "A
Ghostly Chess Game," 195; "The Ma-
hatma's Little Joke," 195–96; "Plan-
chette," 197–200, 201; "The Eternity
of Forms," 200–201; *The Call of the
Wild*, 203; *Martin Eden*, 203; *The
Sea-Wolf*, 203
Lovecraft, H. P., 15, 33

Maeterlinck, Maurice, 130; "Of Immortality," 160

Malory, Sir Thomas: *Le Morte d'Arthur*,
185
Mather, Cotton: *Magnalia Christi
Americana*, 75, 78, 83, 176; *Wonders
of the Invisible World*, 176
Maupassant, Guy de: "The Horla," 17
Melville, Herman, 1, 69–97 passim,
123; *The Confidence-Man: His Masquerade*, 5, 76–92 passim: "The Apple-Tree Table," 76, 77–79, 83; *Moby-
Dick*, 77; *Pierre*, 102, 104–5, 110, 123
Mérimée, Prosper, 17; *Vénus d'Ille*, 111
Mitchell, S. Weir, 153–54, 156, 166–67
(n. 13)
Mott, Lucretia, 96 (n. 9)
Myers, Frederic W. H., 10 (n. 7), 162,
178–79, 217–18; *Human Personality
and Its Survival of Bodily Death*, 179;
and Edmund Gurney and Frank Podmore (*Phantasms of the Living*), 179

Oliphant, Margaret, 123
Owen, Robert Dale, 71, 72, 93, 143–45,
148 (n. 31)

Paine, Albert Bigelow, 172
Parsons, Coleman, 23
Pascal, Blaise, 142, 148 (n. 31)
Pater, Walter: *Studies in the History of
the Renaissance*, 116
Payne, Edward Biron, 207 (n. 25)
Pearson, Karl, 215–16
Phelps, Elizabeth Stuart, 1, 5, 126, 127,
129; *The Gates Ajar*, 5, 102, 117 (n.
4), 124–26, 127, 177; "Stories That
Stay," 102, 115; "Sealed Orders," 117
(n. 4); *Men, Women, and Ghosts*, 126
Piper, Leonora E., 4, 162
Poe, Edgar Allan, 1, 3–4, 6, 14, 15, 16,
17, 32, 34, 39–40, 43, 45–65, 102,
116, 123, 135, 140–43, 146, 148 (n.
19), 172, 184. Works: "Mesmeric Revelation," 3, 4, 58–59, 61; "Ligeia," 3,
15, 46, 54, 56–57, 108, 110; "MS.
Found in a Bottle," 3, 15, 51, 52–53,
62; "Morella," 3, 15, 54–56; "The
Masque of the Red Death," 3, 47–50,
115; "Metzengerstein," 3, 51–52, 62;

"The Facts in the Case of M. Valdemar," 4, 61–63; "The Fall of the House of Usher," 6, 15, 55, 56, 140–43, 146, 148 (n. 19); "The Tell-Tale Heart," 15, 50–51; "Berenice," 15, 54, 55, 62; "William Wilson," 15, 110, 184; *Tales of the Grotesque and Arabesque*, 40; "Marginalia," 46; "Shadow—A Parable," 47–48; "The Conqueror Worm," 48, 110; A Descent into the Maelstrom," 50; *The Narrative of Arthur Gordon Pym*, 50; "Sonnet—Silence," 50; "The Black Cat," 50–51; "The Imp of the Perverse," 50–51; "The Cask of Amontillado," 50–51, 184; "The Oval Portrait," 54, 55–56; "Eleonora," 54, 56, 57, 58; "The Premature Burial," 57; *Al Aaraaf*, 58; "Israfel," 58; "The Power of Words," 58, 59; "The Colloquy of Monos and Una," 58, 59, 103; "The Conversation of Eiros and Charmion," 58, 59, 103; *Eureka*, 60; "The City in the Sea," 60; review of Hawthorne's *Twice-Told Tales*, 102–3
Pollin, Burton R., 141
Porter, Noah: *The Human Intellect*, 123–24
Porter, William Sydney [pseud. O. Henry]: "The Furnished Room," 178
Poyen, Charles, 72
Praz, Mario: *The Romantic Agony*, 111, 112
Punter, David, 40
Putnam, James Jackson, 153
Pynchon, Thomas: *Gravity's Rainbow*, 227 (n. 22)

Quackenbos, John D.: *Hypnotic Therapeutics*, 182–83

Radcliffe, Ann, 17, 32, 39, 40
Reid, Whitelaw, 175
Ribot, Théodule-Armand: *Diseases of Personality*, 154
Rogers, Henry H., 174, 181
Roppolo, Joseph Patrick, 48
Royce, Josiah, 225

Sargent, Epes: *Planchette*, 124
Schofield, Alfred T.: *The Unconscious Mind*, 124
Scott, Sir Walter, 19, 23; "The Tapestried Chamber," 22–23
Search, Pamela: *The Supernatural in the English Short Story*, 13–14, 35 (n. 2)
Shelley, Mary: *Frankenstein*, 45, 185
Smith, Henry Nash, 157
Smith, Joseph, 74
Spacks, Patricia Meyer, 40
Spencer, Herbert, 196, 204
Spofford, Harriet Prescott, 1, 101–19; "The Amber Gods," 5, 101–19; "Circumstance," 101; "In a Cellar," 101; *Sir Rohan's Ghost*, 101; *The Fairy Changeling*, 114; *Azarian*, 118 (n. 14)
Stanley, Henry M., 174
Stannard, David, 45
Stanton, Elizabeth Cady, 96 (n. 9)
Stead, W. T., 181, 188 (n. 27)
Stevenson, Robert Louis: *Dr. Jekyll and Mr. Hyde*, 184
Stoehr, Taylor, 137
Stoker, Bram: *Dracula*, 104
"Story of an Apparition," 22–23
Stowe, Harriet Beecher, 4, 102; *The Minister's Wooing*, 112
Strindberg, August: *A Dream Play*, 130; *The Ghost Sonata*, 130
Sullivan, Jack: *Elegant Nightmares: The English Ghost Story from LeFanu to Blackwood*, 14–16, 17
Swanson, Mildred Burris: *God Bless U, Daughter*, 171
Swedenborg, Emanuel, 74; *True Christian Religion*, 125

Taylor, Bayard: *Hannah Thurston*, 95 (n. 4), 97 (n. 26)
Thoreau, Henry David, 33; *Walden*, 79, 87, 96 (n. 18)
Tieck, Ludwig, 17, 39
Todd, Mabel Loomis, 118 (n. 15)
Todorov, Tzvetan, 2, 9, 10 (n. 6), 35 (n. 2)
Tolstoi, Count Leo: "The Death of Ivan Ilych," 55

Tuckey, John S., 179
Twain, Mark. *See* Clemens, Samuel L.

Walker, Franklin, 178
Wallace, Lew: *The First Christmas,
from "Ben-Hur,"* 174
Walpole, Horace, 39
Weber, E. H., 213, 221
Wellman, Flora, 194, 197
White, Andrew D.: *A History of the
Warfare of Science with Theology in
Christendom,* 177
Whitman, Sarah Helen, 61
Whitney, Adeline: *Patience Strong's
Outings,* 123, 120
Whittier, John Greenleaf, 117 (n. 4)
Wordsworth, William: "Ode: Intima-
tions of Immortality," 158–59, 160, 165
Wright, Frances, 71, 72

Young, Edward: *Night Thoughts on
Death,* 41